Economic Decentralization and Public Management Reform

NEW HORIZONS IN PUBLIC POLICY

General Editor: Wayne Parsons
Professor of Public Policy, Queen Mary and Westfield College,
University of London, UK

This series aims to explore the major issues facing academics and
practitioners working in the field of public policy at the dawn of a new
millennium. It seeks to reflect on where public policy has been, in both
theoretical and practical terms, and to prompt debate on where it is going.
The series emphasises the need to understand public policy in the context of
international developments and global change. New Horizons in Public
Policy publishes the latest research on the study of the policy making process
and public management, and presents original and critical thinking on the
policy issues and problems facing modern and post-modern societies.
   Titles in the series include:

Innovations in Public Management
Perspectives from East and West Europe
Edited by Tony Verheijen and David Coombes

Public Policy Instruments
Evaluating the Tools of Public Administration
Edited by B. Guy Peters and Frans K.M. van Nispen

Beyond the New Public Management
Changing Ideas and Practices in Governance
Edited by Martin Minogue, Charles Polidano and David Hulme

Economic Decentralization and Public Management Reform
Edited by Maureen Mackintosh and Rathin Roy

Public Policy in the New Europe
Eurogovernance in Theory and Practice
Edited by Fergus Carr and Andrew Massey

Politics, Governance and Technology
P.H.A. Frissen

Public Policy and Political Institutions
The Role of Culture in Traffic Policy
Frank Hendriks

Economic Decentralization and Public Management Reform

Edited by

Maureen Mackintosh

Professor of Economics, Open University, UK

Rathin Roy

Deputy Director, Programme in Public Policy and Management and Lecturer in Economics, School of Oriental and African Studies, University of London, UK

NEW HORIZONS IN PUBLIC POLICY

Edward Elgar
Cheltenham, UK • Northampton, MA, USA

338.9
E1996

Published by
Edward Elgar Publishing Limited
Glensanda House
Montpellier Parade
Cheltenham
Glos GL50 1UA
UK

Edward Elgar Publishing, Inc.
136 West Street
Suite 202
Northampton
Massachusetts 01060
USA

A catalogue record for this book
is available from the British Library

Library of Congress Cataloguing in Publication Data

Economic decentralization and public management reform / edited by
    Maureen Mackintosh, Rathin Roy.
        (New horizons in public policy)
    Includes bibliographical references.
    1. Economic policy. 2. Public administration. I. Roy, Rathin,
    1966– . II. Mackintosh, Maureen. III. Series.
    HD87.E249 1999
    338.9—dc21   99–21718
                                                                       CIP

ISBN 1 85898 995 7

Printed and bound in Great Britain by Bookcraft (Bath) Ltd.

JK

Contents

v

Figures

Tables

List of contributors

Dr Jane Harrigan is Senior Lecturer in the School of Economic Studies, Manchester University. She is co-author of *Aid and Power: the World Bank and Policy Based Lending* (Routledge 1995).

Trevor Hopper is KPMG Professor of Management Accounting at the School of Accounting and Finance at the University of Manchester. He is co-editor of the *British Accounting Review*.

Maureen Mackintosh is Professor of Economics at the Open University. She is at present collaborating with Dr Paula Tibandebage on a DFID-funded study of health care regulation in Tanzania.

Dr D. Narayana is Associate Professor at the Centre for Development Studies, Trivandrum, India. He is at present working on the political economy of Indian economic reforms with special reference to infrastructure, irrigation and the social sectors.

Dr A. Premchand has recently retired from the Fiscal Affairs Division of the International Monetary Fund, Washington, DC. He has written and edited several books on public financial management.

Dr Rathin Roy is Deputy Director, Programme in Public Policy and Management, Department of Economics, the School of Oriental and African Studies at the University of London. He specializes in the political economy of fiscal management, governance, and decentralization.

Richard Schofield lectures in law at Bolton Business School and Manchester University. Prior to this, he worked for a number of large law firms where he was involved in the privatization of the water industry.

Dr Jean Shaoul is Lecturer in the School of Accounting and Finance, Manchester University. She specializes in the use of financial analysis to evaluate public policy.

Dr Paula Tibandebage is Research Fellow at the Economic and Social Research Foundation, Dar es Salaam, Tanzania. She is a political economist specializing in social sector service provision and policy.

Dr Shahzad Uddin is Lecturer in Accounting and Finance at the School of Management, Queen's University, Belfast, with a Ph.D. from the University of Manchester, and has published on accounting theory, privatization and public financial management.

Marc Wuyts is Professor of Applied Quantitative Economics at the Institute of Social Studies, The Hague, The Netherlands.

1. Introduction: economic decentralization, issues of theory and policy

Maureen Mackintosh and Rathin Roy

1. ECONOMIC REFORM AND ECONOMIC DECENTRALIZATION

Economic reform programmes across the world in the 1980s and 1990s – in industrialized countries, transitional economies, and many poor and industrializing countries – have been constructed around two core elements. The first is fiscal restraint, whether designed by conservative macroeconomic policy makers, imposed by structural adjustment or economic transition programmes, or reluctantly accepted as the implication of increasingly global financial markets. The second is economic decentralization. Since this latter element is a central theme of this collection of papers, we will start by defining this concept carefully.

By *economic* decentralization, we mean the decentralization of economic decision making within national economies. Economic decentralization is thus distinct from, but, as this collection of papers is concerned to explore, closely interlinked with, decentralization of political power and decision making. In recent multilateral policy documents the arguments for political and for economic decentralization have become inextricably entangled. Thus the World Bank justifies 'formal, political' decentralization on economic efficiency grounds: 'public goods and services should be provided by the lowest level of government that can fully capture the costs and benefits'. The Bank goes on to argue that this rationale is 'similar' to the rationale for 'liberalization, privatization and other market reforms' (World Bank, 1997, pp. 120, 121). This elision of the distinction between economic incentives and the exercise of political power obscures the important debate about the links between politics and economic decentralization. The papers by Roy, Harrigan and Narayana (Chapters 2, 4 and 5) in this book consider explicitly the relationship between political processes and the extent of economic centralization or decentralization.

The concept of economic decentralization as used in this book is much broader than its use in the economic literature of the 1960s and 1970s (for a survey see Oates, 1998). From the point of view of policy design, six distinct types of economic decentralization are referred to in the papers in the book: they range from the traditional emphasis on the proper assignment of fiscal and expenditure functions between higher and lower levels of government, to the shift from public provision to decentralized market decision making as a result of privatization.

The first type of economic decentralization, which might be labelled fiscal decentralization, is the subject of a large literature on the assignment of fiscal and expenditure functions between lower and higher levels of government. This literature, addressed in the paper by Roy, has recently grown rapidly under the impetus of political concerns with supranational federalism in Europe.[1] As the next section explains, the intellectual history of decentralization theory falls within the Keynesian tradition in economics, distilled by Richard and Peggy Musgrave in their path-breaking text on public finance (Musgrave and Musgrave, 1976). This is the intellectual tradition to which the World Bank refers in the above quotation, although, as noted below, this tradition sits uneasily with the 'new political economy' theories underlying other Bank analyses of decentralization. The Bank's two categories of 'fiscal decentralization' and 'devolution' (World Bank, 1997, p. 120) fall within this general type of economic decentralization, and both need to be associated in practice with the creation or strengthening of local government structures. The paper by Premchand (Chapter 3) discusses the grant-making processes associated with this type of decentralization.

The second type of economic decentralization addressed in this book, quite distinct from the first, is decentralization of public *management* decision making. This is not necessarily associated with any devolving of economic decision making to local *government*; indeed in the UK quite the opposite has been the case (Walsh, 1995; Clarke and Newman, 1997). Decentralization of the management of public funds for the delivery of publicly funded services is a core element of the so-called 'new public management' (Dunleavy and Hood, 1994). A common structural approach is the creation of public sector 'executive agencies' to which is devolved the management of given budgets in pursuit of specified performance criteria. Contractual or semi-contractual relationships are established between the central government funding body and agency, and forms of competition are introduced such as 'market testing': the comparison of agency proposals with alternative public and private tenders. The core element of this form of economic decentralization is increased managerial discretion over the use of a given budget for agreed ends. The paper by Premchand considers the new managerialism, while Mackintosh (Chapter 7) examines the public sector regulatory problem facing central ministries in such a framework.

The third type of economic decentralization, often emerging as a corollary of the second but quite distinct in its economic implications, is the proliferation of service-providing institutions supported by mixed public/private funding. This has been driven by a mixture of fiscal pressure and incentives for 'entrepreneurial' behaviour by project and agency managers (Mackintosh, 1992). The mixed sources of funding may include among others, in addition to national and local public sector resources: individual payments by users of services, charitable support and overseas aid donor funding on a direct project basis, the sale of services to other organizations, and private loans and investments. Mixed funding of this type creates a distinct economic logic in the decision making at project and agency level, quite different from that generally assumed to emerge from public sector decentralization, since the organization's strategy needs to be directed at satisfying private and non-governmental funders and clients. The papers by Harrigan, Narayana and Premchand all consider some of the perverse effects of mixed public/private project funding.

The fourth type of economic decentralization is another element within the 'new public management' framework: the contracting out of publicly funded service provision to private commercial or non-profit firms. Governments have long had tendering procedures for the supply of goods and services to the public sector; the 1980s saw an explosion of tendering for the supply of publicly funded services to the public. Some of this shift to private contractors arose from market testing to drive down costs, but some simply reflected a political preference for private over public supply. Premchand examines some of the problems arising from these contracting processes.

The fifth type of economic decentralization concerns the introduction of market mechanisms into decision making about the *allocation* of public funds, including aid funding from donors. An example of this process with substantial implications for economic allocation in aid-dependent economies is the distribution of aid funds for balance of payments support through auctioning of open general licences to import. Private economic actors are thus bidding for aid funding to support commercial activity; the allocation of aid funding is being decided through decentralized decision making in a market mechanism.

The implications of this form of decentralization are discussed in the paper by Wuyts (Chapter 6).

Finally, privatization of public sector economic activity, and the liberalization of sectors monopolized by government, create new decentralized economic decision making within markets, replacing public sector institutions with private firms as decision makers. In areas where public interest concerns remain strong – for example in social sectors and utilities where access and externalities, including environmental effects, are of major public concern – marketizing provision replaces a public allocative role with a public regulatory role. The regulatory role in this context is likely to go well beyond competition policy and basic health and safety regulation, towards more interventionist regulation. The papers by Schofield and Shaoul (Chapter 9) and by Uddin and Hopper (Chapter 10) discuss the behaviour of privatized firms and the implications for government regulation. Where some public sector provision remains within a market-driven system, public policy for public provision needs to be rethought, a problem addressed by Tibandebage (Chapter 8).

In classifying economic decentralization in this way, we are *not* suggesting – *pace* the World Bank – that public management decentralization on the one hand, and marketization and privatization on the other, form a continuum of 'similar' reforms, much less that there is a logic to reform that necessarily carries forward from public sector decentralization to privatization. Rather, we are interested in the ways in which each type of decentralization carries with it its own problems of entanglement of public interest and private interest concerns.

The classification of economic decentralization just outlined is a classification of structural or institutional change, and later sections of this introduction consider some of the theoretical justifications put forward for these structural changes. Each type of decentralization creates new patterns of institutional incentives and behaviour. The first three types all involve the restructuring of public sector economic activity that was at least formally organized in a hierarchical control mode into more decentralized modes of operation. The last three all centre on a transfer of property rights to the private sector. Many of the papers in this collection analyse how these more decentralized institutions behave and why. A theme that runs through the papers is that the answer to this question is strongly context- and culture-dependent. We cannot predict behaviour from economic structure and incentives alone.

The book is thus concerned with what is sometimes called 'meso'-level economic analysis: neither the analysis of the national economy, treated as a set of economy aggregates, nor the analysis of individualised decision making within markets, but the awkward intermediate terrain of institutional behaviour within and across the boundaries of the state. This field of economic analysis is still underdeveloped; it is essential to an understanding of the consequences of transition from formally hierarchical to more decentralized mixed patterns of economic organization and incentive structures. Two themes which run through these papers particularly merit future research. Premchand and Harrigan both examine the conflicts that emerge from the mix of macroeconomic constraint and administrative and organizational reform typical of economic reform programmes, noting in particular the problems for public expenditure control these programmes generate. And a number of papers, including Harrigan, Premchand, Mackintosh, Wuyts, and Schofield and Shaoul, note the unintended microeconomic and social consequences arising from reform programmes.

Decentralized economic institutions emerge from pre-existing political and economic accommodations, and their legitimacy is only established – if at all – over time. Political and social pressures produce informal behaviour, including informal patterns of economic decentralization, that are different from planned effects. Narayana and Harrigan analyse such informal behaviour, in terms of processes of accountability and political process. Tibandebage, Premchand, Mackintosh, and Schofield and Shaoul discuss implications for access and equity.

In more formal terms, the relation between institutional economic change and political and social pressures can by analysed using the concept of a political or social 'settlement'. As the term is used by Roy in this book, a political settlement is defined as a balance of political power that in turn defines a structure of rights: politically defended claims over resources. Such a political settlement enables and constrains the achievement of particular public policy objectives. Particular policy outcomes from particular forms of economic decentralization can only be achieved within compatible political settlements; some objectives require new settlements.

The 'social settlement' concept, related to but distinct from this idea, has emerged in the social policy literature (Williams, 1992; Lewis, 1996; Mackintosh, 1999). In this perspective, the publicly supported and regulated services are understood both as a set of institutions and as a political terrain. The institutions reflect within their organization the inequalities and imbalances of power in the wider society but they *also* offer an arena for political struggle over inequality and exclusion. The more the public services are framed within universalist concepts, the greater is the extent to which excluded groups can (and do) invoke such concepts to claim inclusion. A 'social settlement' is thus a particular balance between inequality and inclusion that, in a given period, is widely regarded as legitimate or at least liveable; such settlements can and do disintegrate in times of economic and political crisis.

These concerns with political and social legitimacy imply that the theoretical terrain of the book is that of political economy. None of the papers takes for granted the individualist, rational choice framework of neo-classical and neo-institutional economics. Some papers, including those by Roy and Mackintosh, explicitly criticize and propose alternatives to that framework of thought. All of the papers are concerned to understand the interaction between changing economic incentives, narrowly understood, and policy processes.

2.   ECONOMIC ARGUMENTS FOR DECENTRALIZATION

This section considers the evolution of the orthodoxy within economics concerning the economic theory of multilevel government. It then introduces the critiques in this book both of this orthodoxy as applied to decentralization within government, and of the broader extension of these narrowly economic arguments to justify contracting-out, privatization and marketization processes.

In the earlier Musgravian approach (see above) to the state and to the proper balance of activities between different levels of government, the public sector exists to perform the primarily Keynesian function of generating and maintaining high levels of output and employment, and of fulfilling any equity-enhancing mandate that it may have. These functions resolve into the three primary economic problems of public finance. These are: the attainment of what society considers a fair distribution of income; the maintenance of a stable economy; and the pursuit of an efficient allocation of resources. The analysis of decentralization, in this framework, begins by posing the question: what level of government is best equipped to resolve these three problems?

Some of these problems, Musgravians argued, were best resolved by *centralized* government. Thus certain stabilization functions are best carried out at national level: a nation state must have only one agency that controls money supply, that sets the institutional conditions for international trade, and performs other such core functions. Local government, Musgravians argued, was inhibited in using fiscal policy efficiently for allocative purposes by the existence of 'spill over effects'. For example, the second round economic effects (the so-called 'multiplier effects') of a fiscally induced increment in local spending may be transmitted outside the local community. This spill-over problem applies equally to the provision of pure public goods: goods which, once produced, are consumed by all within their reach. This high degree of 'non-excludability' of those who may not have paid for the public goods applies to such goods and services as defence systems, foreign relations activities, water purification schemes and floodworks. Such public goods, it was argued, should be provided by national governments if their economic benefits are national.

Another argument for centralization of economic activities of government is that different communities hold different levels of debt. When a government borrows abroad, again, there is need for a centralized agency to negotiate and guarantee such loans and their amortization. Of course, local governments may also borrow abroad if constitutionally permitted. However, all such borrowing is guaranteed by the apex level of government, becoming then a contingent liability of the central government and, transitively, of the country as a whole (Hansen and Perloff, 1944). Hence it is argued that final decisions regarding the level of the aggregate public debt must be centralized.

There is also a problem if different regions follow different distributive policies among their citizens. The result can be that people with similar incomes and preferences will tend to move into the same community, causing some communities to be enriched and some to be impoverished. This phenomenon is called the 'Tiebout effect' (Tiebout, 1956) and will reinforce national inequality. Hence Musgrave saw the implementation of policies to make the income distribution more equal as a core function of central government.

Against these arguments for centralization, the older orthodoxy set a number of arguments for decentralizing some functions. Local communities vary in terms of the preferences of their citizens, and central governments, it was argued, could not adequately take local preferences into account. Local governments are better able to address the preferences of local communities, thereby improving resource allocation. This is to argue that the 'Tiebout effect' may cut both ways: people may choose local communities which share their preferences. Centralized provision of a set of goods and services that ignores local preferences yields fewer benefits for citizens than decentralized provision adapted to local wishes.

Furthermore, if public goods with a strong local impact are provided centrally, economists have argued that people do not perceive the real resource costs of expenditure decisions. Local beneficiaries can 'free-ride' on the benefits of expenditures partially financed elsewhere. These 'externalities' are reduced if public goods with mainly local impact are provided by local government. The local taxpayers have to decide whether to finance the local benefits they enjoy, and 'free-riding' declines (Olson, 1971).

In essence these arguments stem from two propositions in economic theory. The first is that state intervention to resolve externalities and to address other reasons why the market fails to allocate resources efficiently requires a unitary governmental framework. It follows that the fewer externalities there are of public good provisioning – that is, the more the costs and benefits are contained at local level – the smaller the economic incentive for centralization. The second proposition is that lower levels of government are more sensitive to individual preferences for public goods provision than are higher levels of government. This assumption is really a version of the much more general orthodox or neo-classical economic assumption that individuals are the best judge of their own preferences, as Oates (1972), the most influential theorist of decentralization, makes clear in his 'decentralization theorem'.[2] In essence the decentralization theorem argues that variances in preferences in a local area are always lower than variances in national preferences. For example the inhabitants of the same city would differ less about the extent of police provisioning that they feel necessary than would the inhabitants of a country as a whole. Thus, if (a) it costs no more for all local governments to provide a public good than it does for the central government to provide it, and (b) there are no 'spill-overs' (in the sense discussed above), then it follows that it is better for that good to be provided locally.

This theorem can be expected from the intellectual tradition of main-stream economics. In this tradition everything works best when all economic actors are able to engage in economic activity in a manner that enables them to best match their individual preferences. In market activities this is automatic. Everyone produces and sells goods and services in line with their own preferences. In the case of publicly provided goods, however, it is necessary to deduce the outcome that best accords with individual preferences. This is what Oates's theorem sets out to do in the context of the decentralization problem. Note that in the final instance Oates's theorem would lead us to conclude that if an individual can provide a public good as efficiently as a collective, then it is preferable that the individual do so, as long as there are no spill-overs.

In early work on decentralization, local governments were modelled as having preferences that were homogeneous (Williams, 1966; Wilde, 1968). This approach was criticized (Atkinson and Stilglitz 1987) for ignoring the question of the mechanism of collective decision making. But older decentralization theorists (Bradford and Oates, 1971; Oates, 1972) argued that the assumption was reasonable, on the grounds that standard models of voting in political science generate the proposition that the 'median voter' – the voter with the most middle-of-the-road views in the local political spectrum – tends to determine communities' consumption choices for public goods, as long as local government powers are modelled as unconstrained and administratively costless. So individual local governments can sensibly be treated as reflecting a set of individual preferences.

This Musgravian framework of argument fell within the Keynesian–neo-classical consensus in economics that broke down from the 1970s onward. It was replaced by a much more individualist, market-based analysis of the state that came to be called neo-classical political economy (Glyn et al., 1995). The result was that a sharply different approach to decentralization emerged within neo-classical economics.[3] The crux of the modified approach lay in the departure from the assumption of the benevolent state that underlay the Musgrave approach: the assumption that the state sought to act in the public interest. In contrast the new political economy viewed the state as being run by bureaucrats and politicians who sought to expand their sphere of operation to the maximum extent possible. The bigger the state, the greater the power of politicians and bureaucrats who were in charge of state activity. Hence the state contains within it an automatic tendency to expansion. In a fiscal sense this means a 'tax and spend' government, and the empirical proof offered for this is contained in the observation that governments have tended to expand their share both of revenue and of expenditure (as a percentage of gross domestic product) over the last hundred years.

With the new political economy, the departure from the Musgravian approach in the economics of decentralization was contained in two new propositions. The first concerned the Oates theorem – that local government choices are closer to individual choice than choices made by central government, subject to the political decision-making rule. It was mooted by the doyen of public choice theory, James Buchanan and his colleague Geoffrey Brennan (Brennan and Buchanan, 1977; 1978; 1980), following on from their work on the over-expanded 'Leviathan' state. The argument is simple. When local government jurisdictions compete for business and residency, then political authorities will be constrained by citizens' 'exit' possibilities in their attempts to maximize the public sector GDP share in their jurisdiction. Hence, the more local are fiscal decisions, the lower the tax burden on the community per unit of public good produced. Thus 'Leviathan' is constrained.

The second political–economic proposition is that decentralized decision making works best work if preferences are homogeneous – that is, they work like 'clubs' (Pauly, 1967). A 'club' here is defined as an institution which supplies public goods to all its members. To become a member of a club, credentials are required. Thus, to enjoy the benefits of, say, a sports facility in region X, the credential required may be residency in a particular geographical location. When the credential is residency in a local area, people would move geographical location to find the 'club' that best suits their preferences. With no or limited mobility, clubs could trade to achieve desired outcomes (Cornes and Sandler, 1986; Helm and Smith, 1987). For example, imagine two areas: Matureville, populated by old people who require specialist medical resources but have little need for spending on schools, and Youngville, which is populated largely by people with young children who require less expensive health care provision but do require good educational facilities. In both areas there would be some untypical people who would require the services of the other area. In such a situation it would pay for the two local authorities to 'trade', with Matureville using Youngville's schooling facilities in exchange for allowing Youngville residents to use Matureville's health facilities.

When coordination costs are high, gains from trade limited, or spill-overs occur, clubs could pay into a 'super club' – the central government. However, the theory envisages this circumstance arising only in the case of a limited number of functions.

These two propositions have influenced much of the recent neo-classical literature on decentralization, particularly after the intellectual merger of the Harvard and Chicago schools of neo-classical political economy, represented by the new political economics of Romer (1990) and Alesina (1988).[4] The major postulate of the new political economy that derives from the above two propositions is therefore this: in general, goods are best provided through the market mechanism. When and only when there are cost savings in providing goods from *outside* the market mechanism, Leviathan tendencies are minimized when the provision of public goods happens through the use of credentials – through a network of 'clubs'. The *politico-philosophical* framework is therefore based on the idea that the optimal society is one where self-governing individuals exchange goods and services in the marketplace. The 'cost' of public provisioning – by all government – is the loss in consumer welfare that accrues as a consequence of citizens not being able to achieve exactly their desired preferences (for consumption), as they would in a market economy. Thus, 'in the limiting case, that of a purely private good, it is clearly better to allow each individual to select the level of consumption that suits his taste' (Oates, 1972, p. 42), implying that in all other cases the loss in choice that occurs is a cost that must be measured against other benefits of collective provision. In Musgravian theory these benefits are measured in terms of the stabilization, allocation and distribution functions of a government. When these functions are equally well performed by decentralized units, then it is desirable that these units be endowed with these functions – *because* they are closer to individual preferences than centralized units of government. With the new political economy the discussion also takes on board the postulate that government left to itself will expand automatically, to the detriment of the individual. Hence it is better to decentralize government, as the individual is then better able to exercise control over such expansionist tendencies. Further, the institution of local government works, according to the theory of clubs, through the supply of credentials. The smaller a club, the more homogeneous it is, and the less is lost by way of distortion of consumer preferences.

The unity in the mainstream economic approach to decentralization thus comes from universally applied propositions in the new political economy. Clearly in the new political economy it is then analytically irrelevant whether decentralization occurs from the public to the private or from the central to the local. These decisions are taken *purely* by looking at the benefits of public provision – at either the central or the local level. As a consequence, the study of decentralization *within* the state now occupies the same analytical terrain as the study of privatization and, generally, the private provision of public goods and services. Whether it is the new public management that is the focus of decentralization or, as discussed in Wuyts's paper, the decentralization of aid resources to support private sector development, the message of the new political economy is the same: decentralization initiatives occupy a wider domain than purely that of intergovernmental devolution of powers. However, this broadening of domain does not involve a more eclectic or issue-specific approach to the question. Rather, a general set of tools of economic analysis can be applied to look at different types of decentralization. In Roy's paper the application of such a monoeconomic set of analytical tools is critiqued for failing to take account of the broader political terrain in which decentralization is embedded. Once cognizance is taken of this political terrain, the 'answers' provided by the standard toolbox appear simplistic.

Roy's point echoes in many of the empirical papers in this book. In Jane Harrigan's paper, pressure to meet IMF expenditure targets led to a collapse in accountability as a consequence of the decentralization of fiscal responsibilities away from Treasury and towards parastatal agencies, through a weakening of the Treasury control function of the Ministry of Finance. Uddin and Hopper similarly reveal how privatization initiatives in the name of more effective decentralized management decision making often proved to be counterproductive. Premchand, too, argues that the effectiveness of public–private partnerships needs to be judged on the basis of the precise theatre in which the public and private sectors act. These theatres can be diverse, and political mediation often changes the predicted results.

The application of a monoeconomic set of principles to analyse the optimal level of decentralization, where 'economic decentralization' is defined to include privatization, is not confined to academic literature. This is reflected in the 1997 World Bank *World Development Report* on 'the State in a Changing World'. Roy's paper discusses and puts forward a critique of the linking of economic decentralization with the broader and older theme of devolution of state power to the private sector in that report. The three postulates used to argue for greater decentralization – taken in the report (World Bank, 1997, p. 120) to mean *simultaneously* the process of devolution to lower levels of government *and* the privatization of government functions (including their replacement by non-governmental non-commercial organizations' activity) – are:

- the minimum size of self-sufficient government has declined;
- decentralization can enhance efficiency and better meet diverse preferences;
- decentralization improves accountability through increased participation.

Many of the papers in this volume take on these generic propositions and seek to examine their veracity. In his paper, Narayana persuasively argues that creeping privatization in infrastructure investment and health care provisioning was neither efficient nor preference-sensitive, as do Uddin and Hopper in the case of a Bangladeshi privatization. Premchand argues that the very concept of public–private 'partnership' needs to be unpacked, and the different dimensions in which the state interacts with the private sector examined in their own terms. The three postulates listed above may be true or not, depending on the dimension of state involvement. Thus a fall in accountability may trigger a demand for a larger role for government, and not downsizing of that particular function. This recognition of the different roles of interaction between the public and the private has profound implications for decentralization, and is a theme that recurs in the papers by Roy, Mackintosh and Wuyts, in very different contexts.

3. CONTRADICTIONS OF DECENTRALIZATION IN PUBLIC MANAGEMENT REFORM PROGRAMMES

Given the problems these authors raise with the monoeconomic framework, it is important to distinguish between the theoretical underpinnings of fiscal decentralization and *managerial* economic decentralization. As noted above, public management reform programmes – our second and third categories of economic decentralization – do not necessarily imply fiscal decentralization. Indeed, many of the problems public managers and government ministers have experienced in practice with running these programmes stem from their inherent tension between political centralization and 'management' decentralization.

The tension stems in part from the political origins of the 'new public management'. The UK was one of the pioneers of public management reform, and the programme in the UK in the 1980s and through to the mid-1990s was explicitly driven by Conservative governments' political objectives of controlling social sector public spending and reducing the leverage over the public services of both trades unions and local government. The UK version of the new public management thus included the following now familiar elements (Walsh, 1995; Helm, 1994; Stoker, 1999):

- capped budgets for social provision allocated to decentralized agencies by the central government, with repeated enforced 'efficiency gains' in the form of percentage cuts in budgets;
- contractual or semi-contractual relationships between central government and executive agencies or local government departments that were increasingly treated by central government as service delivery agencies instead of governmental bodies in their own right; contracts included quantitative performance targets;
- a range of forms of competitive bidding to provide services, with an emphasis on using competition to drive down costs;
- privatization of utilities and service delivery agencies, and contracting out to private providers on the basis of competitive tender;

- the encouragement, through incentives and matching funding, for the levering in of private funding and private investment in public services; explicit encouragement of public–private partnerships;
- new regulatory bodies 'offshore' from the political process, the regulators themselves given contractually specified targets and their activity construed as establishing implicit contracts with those regulated.

All of these policies are now being promoted for suitable contexts in developing countries. In aid-dependent countries, a further economic factor has reinforced pressure for economic decentralization of the management of public funds. There has been strong pressure from aid donors, both bilateral and multilateral and including non-governmental international donors, to allocate and employ aid funding within an organizational framework of autonomous and semi-autonomous projects. This pressure required local aid recipients to organize services on a project basis, separate from central or local government budgetary processes, including passing over local tax funding to such project budgets.

This process of disaggregation of public service systems in developing countries into a set of poorly integrated projects has sometimes been defended along new public management lines as replacing inefficient hierarchical services with responsive local provision. The problems of fragmentation and waste generated by this approach have now been recognized in a shift towards programme aid, but donors' preferences for local projects that can be labelled with their name still provide one political motivation behind new public management-style decentralization of management.

Before analysing the tensions within this mix of policies that has been emerging over time, it is worth noting some aspects of the 'new public management' package as it is currently being promoted internationally that were *not* found in the UK. The new public management in the UK was not promoted in general as an equalizing initiative. A good deal was claimed for it in terms of improving productive and allocative efficiency, by cutting costs and instituting local allocative and regulatory mechanisms that better addressed resources to local needs. But as a package, the reforms are best understood as an attempt to rework the social settlement framing these services in a *less* egalitarian form: to increase social acceptance of inequality. The economic decentralization mechanisms allowed increased inequality to be politically attributed to the working of local or 'quasi-market' mechanisms, distancing it from central government political decision making. Resistance to this reworking of the political and social settlements – and to central government hand-washing – is an important part of the story about the conflicts that the reforms have engendered.

In the multilateral policy documents, by contrast, the new public management reforms are presented as a coherent and integrated package of changes to the organization of the public sector. There is now a welcome recognition of the technical demands made by the reforms in terms of specifying and managing contracts: the World Bank (1997 p. 151) notes that they require 'an institutional capability that many developing countries lack'. New public management is characterized as the reform of the 'institutions for delivery' of services (World Bank, 1997 p. 86), a formula that implicitly accepts the distinction between policy and management that lies at the heart of the reforms. However, as the 'social settlement' framework suggests, policy and politics are not so easily separated from management ('delivery'). There are a number of political and technical contradictions at the heart of the new public management reforms that come home to roost with the managers – and politicians – who have to try to make them work.

Managers of decentralized agencies note that they face a set of contradictory and partially perverse incentives concerning the use of public funds. The performance measures by which they are judged normally mix evidence of cost-cutting ('efficiency') with measured increases in throughput (output). Both types of measure have their strengths in terms of reducing organizational 'slack', but they contain significant elements of moral hazard. 'Efficiency' measures based on costs create incentives for initial cost-padding, and penalize those who were already efficient. Units costs are hard to measure in services with high proportions of overhead costs and a large number of joint products; hence there are strong incentives to manipulate cost calculations to support 'strategic' pricing of bids, transferring costs into areas where competitors are few or collusive conditions prevail. Throughput measures are highly manipulable – and manipulated (Mackintosh and Smith, 1996). The ghost at the feast is quality of service: hard to measure, therefore never central to quantitative performance measures, it is almost inevitably reduced when cost pressures bite. In the worst case, rising cynicism among managers about perverse contractual incentives can drive rising costs, perverse behaviour and declining service standards (Mackintosh, Chapter 7, this volume).

Furthermore, one-year contract funding and competitive bidding can worsen the tendency to short-termism usually endemic among politicians. Contractors and franchisees with short contracts will be unwilling to invest; managers on short-term contracts or with short-term performance goals will leave the future to be 'worried about later'.[5] There are ways of resolving this problem, such as longer contracts and less specific, more consensual performance measures, but they undermine the pressures for cost-cutting that were initially at the heart of the reforms, and indeed reduce the extent of decentralization.

There are also contradictions in the notion of accountability within the new public management. The contractual structure of relations between central government and agencies focuses on accountability 'upwards'. Decentralization of management is, however, promoted in part as a way of ensuring greater responsiveness of services, and this is also part of aid donors' justification for project-based organization. These two forms of accountability can, quite evidently, conflict. Where they do, the outcome will depend on the strength of local lobbying and the political orientation of managers: either local needs will be overridden or the system will be manipulated to undermine central objectives (Harrigan, Chapter 4, this volume).

Finally, where devolved management is associated with mixed public/ private/donor or voluntary sector funding, a series of other unforeseen consequences can emerge. Managers running such projects and agencies have to respond to multiplying forms of accountability. Low on this list are likely to be the consequences of project or agency decisions for central government budgetary programming. Thus even agencies committed in principle to programme budgeting often make decisions within large projects that bid away funds and personnel from centrally agreed programmes (Wuyts, 1995). Where mixed funding increases pressures to sustain projects or activities beyond their planned date, or where private matching funding is available only for certain projects in conditions of a fiscal squeeze, the effect can be radically to divert the use of associated public funds from planned ends, as Narayana explains in Chapter 5.

An implication of the contradictions at the heart of these reforms is that fiscal decentralization and the strengthening of local government's role in managing and delivering services may not be compatible with the two main types of economic decentralization central to the new public management reforms: decentralization to public agency managers and to managers of mixed public/private projects. Both, furthermore, may conflict with effective central fiscal programming (Premchand, Chapter 3, this volume). The elision of differences between types of economic decentralization and the resultant obscuring of the problems of conflicting accountabilities are not helpful to coherent policy making.

4.   ISSUES OF POLICY AND REGULATION

One effect of the complex mix of types of economic decentralization
being promoted for services where there are strong public concerns
with quality and equity of access is that the concept of 'regulation'
requires some rethinking. Governments have had to face the fact that
if they decentralize government or public management, then the public
sector itself needs to establish internal regulatory mechanisms to
monitor and shape the behaviour of devolved units. Similarly, new areas
of contracting out require good monitoring to avoid the problems of
corruption and cost escalation endemic to sectors such as defence and
construction where contracting was already extensive. Finally, while it
is widely accepted that wholesale privatization requires new regulatory
bodies, the form of those bodies and their ability to achieve their
objectives are still open to question.

The approach to policy and regulation in this book derives from the
theoretical considerations already outlined. Much of the conventional
wisdom on policy and regulation stems from the monoeconomic and
individualist framework of thought that, as just suggested, underpins
the mainstream arguments for economic decentralization. Many of the
chapters in this book argue for the need for a broader approach to
policy analysis and regulatory design. The key issues addressed are the
following.

First: the nature of the state. If regulation is a problem *within* the
state, as well as across its boundaries, this poses a challenge to current
conceptualizations of the state. The state is being disaggregated, as
governments further devolve provisioning responsibilities to public
managers, to different levels of government, and to parastatals. In the
new public management the state is an actor involved in a contractual
relationship with a provider, which may also be part of the public sector.
The regulatory role is sometimes, as with UK utility regulation, hived
off to an independent regulator, but the central state must still set the
objectives and monitor regulatory behaviour. The central state is thus
being asked to play two distinct roles, as contractor and as regulator.
In both, it is expected in some sense to act as the repository of the
public interest.

How then is the public interest to be defined and secured? This is an
old question, of course, but the new patterns of decentralization, and
the institutional behaviour they generate, pose the question in new
forms. The new political economy, faced with this question, simply stops.
It sees legislators and central civil servants – as it sees all those who
work for the public sector – as self-interested. While this narrow frame-

work may have been a useful corrective to a naive public interest view implicit in the Musgravian framework, it is patently incomplete and indeed inaccurate as a behavioural assumption. It has nothing to say about how the commitment of the regulatory and contracting authorities to the public interest can be enhanced.

An alternative framework might have several elements. The first is formal and constitutional. It is that the public interest, *pace* the new political economy, is shaped by constitutional warrant that lists the state's powers to intervene in private activity, to revoke to the public sector activities that are judged to be best carried out by the public sector in the public interest, and to regulate the various arms of the state in accordance with constitutionally specified provisions. This is a set of powers and of terms for the state's behaviour; it carries no guarantees of behaviour. It does, though, provide one framework of accountability against which the state is judged, through reporting to a constitutionally sanctioned body (parliament, the president, and so on) which in a democracy is ultimately responsible to the body politic or the electorate. And it defines a regulatory role: where activities are wholly in the private sector, the state is an independent public interest regulator above the fray of the marketplace.

The second element concerns the mandates of particular governments. In democracies, governments are elected not only to carry out particular specific commitments, and to serve the interests of their core supporters, but also to govern on a day-to-day basis following their understanding of the public interest. Much of that understanding at any time is taken for granted: it arises from the existing social settlement and hence is shared with a good many of the electorate as working assumptions. The 'public interest' as understood within day-to-day government is thus shaped by existing social institutions; it is not some set of ideas independent of context.

The third element concerns the behaviour of the state: to what extent do legislators and government officials in fact pursue the public interest as opposed to sectional or private concerns? As recent debates on governance have emphasized anew, the answer to this question varies across countries. There has been some approving commentary on the increasing willingness of the World Bank to take seriously issues such as accountability, consultation, judicial independence and merit-based recruitment of civil servants, rather than concentrating too narrowly on material incentives and technocratic solutions (Cornia, 1998). But, as Martinussen (1998) notes, there is little acceptance of the social embeddedness of particular states, and hence little reflection on how to improve governance within specific contexts.

A number of chapters in this book also focus on this problem of institutional design in context. Changing property rights, incentive structures and organizational forms are not technical exercises; how institutions and people respond depends on political and social context. The chapter by Mackintosh argues that institutional design, in this case of regulatory structures, needs to be compatible with and sustained by at least some of the existing culturally specific expectations and principles. There are no institutional 'blank sheets', though sharp changes are possible. Effective institutional design requires attention to *both* material incentives and cultural expectations about responses to such incentives.

Many authors focus on a related issue: the problematic effects of too close an attention to material incentives, and too little attention to sustaining and developing public interest behaviour within the state. Schofield and Shaoul (Chapter 9) examine the pressures on regulators of the privatized water industry in the UK. They analyse the dilemma of a water regulator caught between two explicit objectives: to ensure the financial viability of an industry with a huge appetite for capital investment and demanding shareholders, and a duty to sustain service standards and protect the interests of consumers. They explain the pressures that have led the regulator in the UK to give priority to shareholders' interests. Harrigan (Chapter 4) discusses the perverse public expenditure effects of governmental responses to institutional changes that are not 'owned' by those who have to implement them.

As the structure of the state changes, the regulatory and expenditure management functions of the state may need to grow. Premchand (Chapter 3) emphasizes the need to 'customize' support and monitoring arrangements according to the diverse history and culture of the non-governmental organizations supplying publicly supported services. He spells out the implications for the management of public expenditure when it is the case that the state has several dimensions in which it interacts: both internally in terms of its vertical and horizontal constituents, and externally in interactive provider–purchaser relationships with the private sector. A public–private partnership can require more, rather than less, of an information-provisioning and regulatory role for the apex of government even as the implementing role reduces as a consequence of decentralization. This issue has been obscured in the traditional literature. Decentralization has been equated with the 'downsizing' of government. Many of the papers in this book argue that this need not, and often cannot, be the case.

The tendency in the mainstream literature to regard decentralization as a management exercise has blocked off clear thinking about regulation as an essential counterpart to different forms of decentralization. The World Bank's 1997 report, for all its recognition of the importance of responsiveness and accountability, still tends strongly to thè technocratic specification of manuals for reform, because of its commitment to the particular economic approach discussed above. This has been delightful for economists, since it fits neatly with the decline in social science literacy that the discipline has suffered in its attempt to portray economics as a narrowly specified, individualist science. However, many of the authors in this book depart from the new public management prescriptions in their emphasis on a concept that is at best inconvenient, and at worst anathema, to the economist and the technical creators of manuals alike: the political dimension. The public interest is subject to expression in the political arena in a variety of ways, and relationships between the public and private sector are inescapably political. While the World Bank's mandate constrains it from explicitly political considerations, its attempt to specify the nature and role of a developmental state, in the 1997 report, undermines the separation between economic and political considerations that it propounds. It is a core theme of this book that political processes are central to governmental reform, to policy making and to regulatory design. Relationships between the public and private sector, and between central and local government, are inescapably political. This is often recognized in the applied and policy literature, but the thrust of policy research has been to *minimize* the space for political action in institutional design or, at best, to take political variables as parametric constraints in designing an optimal decentralized relationship. An important aim of this book is to do precisely the opposite: to make explicit the political element in economic decentralization.

As Thatcherism fades into unfashionable obscurity and the multilateral institutions see their best-laid plans collapse across Asia, Africa and the transitional economies, it is no longer possible to make one's policy case purely as a technocratic apolitical 'expert'. Policy economists and management experts in government aid agencies and multilateral institutions are now forced to confront the issues we raise in this book. However, with technocratic manuals off-stage and politics centre-stage, the intellectual inadequacies of the economists and 'management specialists' become particularly apparent, leaving a black hole in mainstream approaches to the problem of decentralization and public management. In this book we attempt to address this inadequacy in the only way possible – through the infusion of a variety of fresh and always interdisciplinary perspectives, addressing both theory and the applied policy context.

NOTES

1. This decentralization literature also examines the reassignment of an economic function to a supranational unit and then the direct negotiation of that unit with a subnational public sector unit or a private sector unit for delivery of public goods and services at a subnational level. This is not a theme that is covered in this volume.
2. Formally the decentralization theorem is as follows:

    For a public good, the costs of providing which are identical for central and local government in any jurisdiction, it will always be at least as, or more, efficient for the local government to provide the good in respective jurisdictions than for the central government to provide any of the good across specific jurisdictions. This is because the Pareto-efficient levels of provision differ for each individual and hence addressing local preferences minimizes distortions in individual preferences – simply because the variances across subsections of the population are always lower (or the same) as the variance across the overall population.

    Variations in preferences across subsections of the population – such as citizens in one local government area – are assumed to be always lower than (or the same as) national variations in preferences. Hence, if local government responds to those preferences effectively, and if – a crucial assumption – it costs no more to produce the public good in each local jurisdiction than it does to produce it centrally, then the public goods should be produced locally. Local production will match preferences more closely than national provision. This is the argument one would expect from within a framework – neo-classical economics – where the optimal method of producing and distributing goods is market production to individual buyers' preferences.
3. For a survey of this approach, variously called 'the new political economy', the 'economic theory of politics', 'public choice political economy', 'neo-classical political economy', see Cullis and Jones (1992).
4. The Harvard branch of the new political economy was focused on free-riding problems arising out of the collective action isssue (Olson, 1971). It sought also to deploy a 'rational choice' approach to economics, where political problems were analysed using tools of economic analysis. The Chicago branch of the new political economy, led by Becker (1985), sought to apply the tools of economic analysis to the study of pressure-group politics. The merger of these two separate schools of new political economy is represented by a new approach to the problem of growth, often called 'endogenous growth theory' or 'new growth theory'. This approach seeks to broaden the horizon of growth theory. In doing so it also researches questions such as the influence of decentralization on growth and the way in which political variables affect the growth optimization problem.
5. The phrase is from a public sector chief executive: drawn from some recent interviewing by Maureen Mackintosh of public sector managers in the UK.

REFERENCES

Alesina, A. (1988), 'Macroeconomics and politics', *NBER Macroeconomics Annual*, **3**.

Atkinson, A.B. and Stiglitz, J.E. (1987), *Lectures in Public Economics*, London and New York: McGraw-Hill.

Becker, G.S. (1985), 'Public policies, pressure groups and dead-weight costs', *Journal of Public Economics*, **28**.

Bradford, D.F. and Oates, Wallace (1971), 'The analysis of revenue sharing in a new approach to collective fiscal decisions', *Quarterly Journal of Economics*, **85**.

Brennan. G. and Buchanan, J.M. (1977), 'Towards a tax constitution for Leviathan', *Journal of Public Economics*, **8**.

Brennan, G. and Buchanan, J.M. (1978), 'Tax instruments as constraints on the disposition of revenues', *Journal of Public Economics*, **9**.

Brennan, G. and Buchanan, J.M. (1980), *The Power to Tax: Analytical Foundations of a Fiscal Constitution*, Cambridge: Cambridge University Press.

Clarke, J. and Newman, J. (1997), *The Managerial State*, London, UK and Thousand Oaks, CA: Sage.

Cornes, R. and Sandler, T. (1986), *The Theory of Externalities, Club Goods and Public Goods*, Cambridge: Cambridge University Press.

Cornia, G.A. (1998), 'Convergence on governance issues, dissent on economic policies', *IDS Bulletin*, **29** (2), 32–8.

Cullis, J. and Jones, P. (1992), *Public Finance and Public Choice*, Maidenhead: McGraw-Hill.

Dunleavy, P. and Hood, C. (1994), 'From the old public administration to the new public management', *Public Money and Management*, July–September, 9–16.

Glyn, A., Hughes, A., Lipietz, A. and Singh, A. (1995), 'The rise and fall of the Golden Age', in Chang, H.J. and Rowthorn, R. (eds), *The Role of the State in Economic Change*, Oxford: Clarendon Press.

Hansen, A. and Perloff, H. (1944), *State and Local Finance in the National Economy*, New York: W.W. Norton.

Helm, D. (1994), 'British utility regulation: theory, practice and reform', *Oxford Review of Economic Policy*, **10** (3).

Helm, D. and Smith, Stephen (1987), 'The assessment: decentralisation and the economics of local government', *Oxford Review of Economic Policy*, **3**.

Lewis, G. (1996), 'Welfare settlements and racialising practices', *Soundings*, **4**.

Mackintosh, M. (1992), 'Partnership: issues of policy and negotiation', *Local Economy*, **7** (3), 210–24.

Mackintosh, M. (1999), 'Public management for social inclusion' in Polidano, C., Minogue, M. and Hulme, D. (eds), *Beyond the New Public Management: Changing Ideas and Practices in Governance*, Cheltenham, UK and Lyme, US: Edward Elgar.

Mackintosh, M. and Smith, P. (1996), 'Perverse incentives: an NHS notebook', *Soundings*, **4**.

Martinussen, J. (1998), 'The limitations of the World Bank's conception of the state and the implications for institutional development strategies', *IDS Bulletin*, **29** (2), 67–74.

Musgrave, R. and Musgrave, P. (1996), *Public Finance in Theory and Practice*, New York: McGraw-Hill.

Oates, Wallace (1972), *Fiscal Federalism*, New York: Harcourt Brace Johanovich.

Oates, Wallace (ed.) (1998), *The Economics of Fiscal Federalism*, Cheltenham, UK and Lyme, US: Edward Elgar.

Olson, M. (1971), *The Logic of Collective Action*, Cambridge, MA: Harvard University Press.

Pauly, M.V. (1967), 'Clubs, commodities and the core', *Economica*, **34**.

Romer, P.M. (1990), 'Endogenous technical change', *Journal of Political Economy*, **98**.

Stoker, G. (ed.) (1999), *The New Management of British Local Governance*, Basingstoke: Macmillan.

Tiebout, C. (1956), 'A pure theory of public expenditures', *Journal of Political Economy*, **64**.

Walsh, K. (1995), *Public Services and Market Mechanisms: Competition, Contracting and the New Public Management*, Basingstoke: Macmillan.

Wilde, J.A. (1968), 'The expenditure effects of Grant-in-aid Programs', *National Tax Journal*, **21**.

Williams, A. (1966), 'The optimal provision of public goods in a system of local government', *Journal of Political Economy*, **74**.

Williams, F. (1992), 'Somewhere over the rainbow: diversity and universality in social policy', *Social Policy Review*, **4**.

World Bank (1997), *World Development Report 1997: The State in a Changing World*, Washington: The World Bank.

Wuyts, M. (1995), 'Foreign aid, structural adjustment and public management: the World Bank experience', ISS *Working Paper Series* 206, The Hague.

PART I

Decentralization: Public Management Issues

2. Economic theories of decentralization: towards an alternative political economy approach[1]

Rathin Roy

1. INTRODUCTION

The argument in this chapter is that the notion of decentralization used in mainstream economics is based on inadequate foundations in political theory. As a consequence, the case for decentralization that emerges from analyses in mainstream economics is weak. An alternative, political economy approach to the analysis of decentralization is outlined with a discussion of some policy applications.

The structure of the chapter is as follows. Section 1 takes the discussion on decentralization in Chapter 1 further, looking at some analytical treatments of the decentralization question in mainstream economics, including neo-classical political economy. In Section 2, the mainstream position is critiqued. Section 3 outlines a political economy framework for the study and analysis of the decentralization question. Section 4 presents some applications of this approach.

2. NEO-CLASSICAL THEORIES OF ECONOMIC DECENTRALIZATION

As explained in the Introduction (Chapter 1), the move from 'Musgravian' approaches to decentralization to those that derive from the new political economy enabled economists to make a profound claim – that economic models were now able to address political considerations. In the 1990s, many mainstream economists have sought to examine the question of decentralization using the tools of neo-classical economic theory and public choice. In this section we will examine three prominent examples of such mainstream theorizing in the context of the decentralization question.

A recent paper by Gilles and Scotchmer (1998) provides an example of the application of the theory of 'clubs' to the question of decentraliz-ation. In this paper, the authors seek to extend club theory by arguing that there exist complementarities between the public goods provided by a 'club' and the private goods that members of a 'club' may seek to consume. This paper is a good example of the elision of decentralization theory with theories of the public and the private. Thus, for example, the type of school that is provided by a local government may influ-ence the demands for private goods like learning materials, sports goods and so on. In such a circumstance, the authors argue, the optimum level or type of decentralization also depends on how the existence of a 'club' affects the prices of private goods. The thrust of the argument is that unless there exists a set of 'conjectural' prices for the public good, an efficient economic equilibrium with decentralized 'clubs' providing public goods is difficult to achieve. These 'conjectural prices' are the prices that club members 'expect' private goods (that are complemen-tary to public goods) to have. If these conjectural prices exist, then – and only then – is any decentralization efficient.

The second paper of interest is by Seabright (1996), who attempts to explore and formalize the general idea that decentralization may be the best way to create incentives for politicians to differentiate adequately between the needs of different groups of citizens. Citizens seek to maximize their own welfare. Politicians, in the public choice tradition of Brennan and Buchanan (1977), are self-interested creatures who frame policies purely to maximize their chances of re-election. Sea-bright's key political proposition is that the politician and the citizen have a contract which is incomplete, as the actions of governments cannot be observed; only outcomes can. Hence the mapping between individual welfare and political action cannot be perfectly written into the political contract. As a consequence, contracts may be rewritten (through re-election of politicians by citizens) if infringed, but not enforced over the contract lifetime. Decentralization implies only that two sets of contracts are written. The first set of contracts is between all citizens with the central government. The second set of contracts is between different subgroups of electors with the local governments under whose jurisdiction they fall. In this framework, in Seabright's words, 'the difference between centralisation and decentralisation is then a matter of which groups of electors are collectively given the power to decide a government's re-election' (p. 65).

In Seabright's model, governments trade-off their preference for 'indolence and empire building' (p. 69) against the threat of not being re-elected. The difference between central and local government in this context is that the central government is influenced by the direct and spill-over impacts of policy on different localities and the political clout of different localities. Local governments are purely influenced by the welfare of their own locality. Both types of government are influenced by *alpha* – the 'value of being in government' – which amounts to their ability to reap the spoils of office. The higher the value of the spoils of office, the stronger the case for centralization.

In terms of our discussion in Chapter 1, Seabright's conclusions are not novel, even if rigorously and systematically presented. The trade-off between central and local government is based on the assumption that central government is less accountable than local government and less capable of representing community preferences. Only when *alpha* is high for central government does it become an optimal policy executor, as it is only in that case that the accountability trade-off is weighted in its favour. The value of this crucial *alpha* is not a concern. For Seabright, this is 'an empirical matter, . . . and may depend a great deal on the culture of the country concerned' (p. 76). Thus the very heart of the puzzle – represented by *alpha* – is assumed away!

Two other conclusions from Seabright's paper bear mentioning. First is the fact that decentralization may harm some and help others within a local government area, while centralization permits special-interest coalitions across regional boundaries. If, and only if, centralization allows special-interest groups so to coalesce, is it the case that a central-ized state is less pernicious than a decentralized state. Second, the less mobile a factor of production is, the smaller the Tiebout effect, and hence the lower the incentive for a government to curb its predatory tendencies. The focus of the paper is thus: *Given* that governments exhibit predatory tendencies, and *given* that these tendencies are smaller the greater the level of decentralization, under what circumstances *may* centralized governments be less predatory than decentralized ones? Both these conclusions seek to make 'special cases'. That the state is 'predatory' is accepted without further comment or political theorizing.

Another refinement and exploration of the predatory state with potential implications for the neo-classical political economy of decen-tralization can be found in a paper by Alesina and Rosenthal (1996). The authors attempt to explain why split-ticket voting (distinct party preferences for senators and the presidential candidate) occurs in the USA. As such it can be used to explain the incidence of split preferences in central and local government as well. In this model, policies matter to politicians, who are partisan and moderate their policies to get

elected. Voters in the middle of the policy spectrum choose governments
with different policy preferences to balance the final policy vector. This
result is speculatively extended to the decentralization question. Thus,
when there exist significant policy-making powers in the hands of local
government units, 'It would be possible to balance, at least partially, a,
say right-wing national government with a left wing local government'
(pp. 1335–6).

This paper applies the predatory state concept in an electoral domain:
voters prefer moderate policies; politicians are extreme. This behavioural divergence leads to voters enforcing incomplete contracts by
choosing politicians with divergent policy preferences at different levels
of government as the best strategy to ensure policy moderation.

3. DECENTRALIZATION: A CRITIQUE OF MAINSTREAM THEORIZING

The mainstream economic arguments for and against decentralization
focus on the following proposition: public goods are best provided to
self-governing individuals unless there are cost savings in joint provision.
These, and only these, are to be traded off against the loss in consumer
surplus that occurs as a result of collective provision. 'In the limiting
case, that of a purely private good, it is clearly better to allow each
individual to select the level of consumption that suits his taste' (Oates,
1972, p. 42). As argued in Chapter 1, this is a natural outcome of the
microeconomic approach to politics that is the hallmark of the new
political economy.

The argument for decentralization in both the versions of mainstream
economic theory discussed in Chapter 1 work with this proposition. In
the Musgravian approach, the state has three objectives. Stabilization
is best undertaken centrally, while allocation is best decentralized.[2] The
rationale for this is that allocation functions affect private economic
choices at the microeconomic level whereas stabilization is more of a
macroeconomic venture. The political quality or capability of the local
or central state is not an issue in this approach since all levels of
government exhibit the same level of benevolence. The problem is
therefore one of minimizing consumer distortions. The state works best
when it does not distort consumer preferences and the ideal level of
decentralization is therefore one that causes minimum distortion in
these preferences. In the quotation from Oates in Chapter 1, it is thus
apparent that the ideal level of decentralization is the self-governing
individual! Only where public good provisioning is required – whether

in the form of stabilization policy or in the form of allocations for non-rival non-excludable public goods – does government enter the picture. The level of government best equipped to provide the public good is then the one that distorts individual preferences least, subject to the cost constraint.

In the public choice approach, the issue is one of controlling Leviathan. Leviathan can be controlled through decentralization, as decentralization affords scope for competition. This is a powerful argument when Leviathan is an accepted political truth but it is really the only argument that is provided. This is made explicit in applications of the Leviathan hypothesis, as, for instance, in Seabright's model. Equally, club theory seeks to address the 'complication' introduced by the revelation that public and private goods may be complementary (as in the paper by Gilles and Scotchmer, 1998, outlined above) purely through an attempt to deliver a 'conjectural' price mechanism whose evolution and basis are left unspecified.

The recipients of public goods are modelled equally simply. 'Citizens' are in contract with a state, with democracy providing the opportunity to rewrite contracts. When preferences are homogeneous, 'clubs' provide public goods, with the size of the club being determined by the benefits of public provision versus the costs, implicit in free-riding. 'Citizens' use the political process to moderate government action (Alesina and Rosenthal, 1996) and to minimize government 'indolence' (Seabright, 1996). The optimum level of decentralization is thus a problem in constrained optimization.

Both mainstream economic approaches thus deploy extremely rudimentary notions of state intervention and state–citizen interaction. This is clearly a limited base on which to construct a theory of decentralization. The poverty of political theorizing within mainstream economic theory makes it an extremely unsatisfactory advocate of the decentralization case, despite the fact that this is the case which is, in general, made. It is possible to argue that this is so in two ways.

The first critique is internal. There is no reason why individually decentralized governments may not all seek to maximize revenues by raising taxes and increasing provisioning, when the number of decentralized governments does not approach infinity. With homogeneous citizen preferences, and identical electoral cycles, the political 'game' is monopolistic. Decentralized governments would seek to raise revenues that would add to, rather than substitute for, the central tax burden. If this happens, then citizens cannot 'choose' between the two levels of government; they would have to live with both.[3] In this circumstance decentralized provision is costlier than centralized provision. This happens because there is no competition between central and local governments for consumer revenues or votes; the electoral process separates the local and central domains of state activity and hence they may well be additive.

The Tiebout (1956) hypothesis (see Chapter 1) should prevent this, with citizens moving out of local areas that present them with unacceptably high tax burdens into areas that compete for their residency by offering lower tax burdens. But pushed to its logical conclusion, this hypothesis says that *all* citizens should move to the most efficient local area (assuming no congestion, as all these models do), since that area would provide the most efficient and/or non-distortionary tax/output ratio. In this limiting case, the most efficient 'decentralized' government becomes unique and, therefore, unitary!

In effect, the very framework of the model collapses once it is recognized that with identical production functions, heterogeneity is irrelevant. Either all local governments are equally efficient or the one that is the most efficient attracts all citizens. In the first case, a single inefficient central government is preferred. In the second case, only the most efficient central government survives. If all governments act as Leviathan, then the case for decentralized provisioning is extremely weak.

This internal critique leads on to the second, epistemic, critique of mainstream economic approaches to decentralization. The homogeneous and rather unsophisticated definition of the objective function of the government in the model is what makes the attempt to define the case for decentralization rather weak. Musgravian approaches embody little explicit political theory. The political theory on which public choice – and public-choice-influenced – theorizing on decentralization is based is that of the new political economy (NPE).[4] In NPE theory the state is by definition predatory. In neo-classical economics the state is superfluous except as a security device and as a corrector of market failure. This, with the assumption of politically homogeneous citizenry, severely limits the extent to which interesting things can be said about the appropriate level of decentralization. The NPE seeks to overcome this limitation by providing a theory of politics.

But is the NPE a satisfactory theoretical basis for specifying the objective function of the state? In political analysis state objectives can only be satisfactorily analysed where one has a theory of political obligation (Pateman, 1985) that specifies the rights vested in the state and the recipients of state policy. This involves a less homogeneous approach to the role of the state. A good starting point in such a venture would be to examine the nature of conflict between state objectives and citizen response. This can be modelled in a variety of ways. For example, in the Indian context (Roy, 1994; 1997a) there was complete agreement that there was a fiscal crisis in India in the post-1979 period. Pluralist theory attributed this to the inability of the state to fulfil its conflict management function. Marxists viewed the crisis as a consequence of the inability of the state to maintain an accumulation for public-invest-ment-led growth strategy, resulting in excessive demands on the state from proprietary groups and a squeeze on the consumption of the poor. The new political economy (NPE) attributed the crisis to excessive state spending. These separate diagnoses arose from separate theories about the role of the state (that is, its objective function) and about the way in which citizens were viewed (homogeneously, by class, or by plural-interest group).

More generally, in any economy, interest-group conflict can have a local–central focus. Often these struggles are captured in sectoral (for example, the agrarian question) or regional debates about whether to focus on maximizing development in forward areas or to go for balanced growth (Post and Wright, 1989). For example, when planning is used as an instrument of economic policy the question of decentralization has tended to focus on the distribution of property rights *between* the public and private sector rather than between various levels of government; as a consequence it may be argued that planning has almost invariably increased centralization. The analysis of this proposition would need to look at the distribution of property rights *within* the public sector and not *between* the public and private sector. Here NPE fails us, for there is no theory of how this can be done in that paradigm.

Once this point is recognized, the mainstream approach to the issue of decentralization is open to a number of derivative criticisms. The theory of implicit contracts, used in Seabright's paper, looks weak. There are now three separate sets of agencies with implicit contracts: central government, local government and 'citizens'. The contract between the first two levels of government is contingent on their roles, which may be separate or overlapping. These contracts may in turn affect different types of citizens differently. This is implicitly acknowl-edged by Seabright when he argues (see Section 1 above) that centralization permits special-interest groups to cross boundaries, limit-ing the Leviathan hypothesis. However, once special-interest groups are acknowledged, then there is no reason why the power of these groups may not affect local governments as well; the specific nature of the relationship would depend, *inter alia*, on the nature of interest groups and on the objectives of the different levels of government. A system of optimal checks and balances becomes a limiting case, with interest-group capture of the state being the other limit. The optimal level of decentralization would depend on the accuracy of one's political theory regarding state objectives and interest-group organization in specific cases. Further, spill-over relationships between local and central governments may make effort levels interdependent. Both these effects are parametric in Seabright's model, captured in the crucial but parametric variable *alpha*, the value of holding office, dependent on the culture of the country concerned. These questions cannot be reconciled *unless* one assumes that government is a revenue maximizer solely concerned with the benefits of those in office and not subject to unequal influences from different societal groups. In political terms little can be derived from a political theory of homogeneous citizenry that assumes that the state is without political obligation or a set of defined rights.

The Alesina model is subject to similar criticisms. Split-ticket voting assumes that the majority of citizens are bi-partisan about policy outcomes; it also assumes an equal assignment of rights to make policy, at all levels of government, for all elements of the policy vector. It is a combination of these two model-specific assumptions that passes for political theory and provides the outcomes speculated on.

Club-theoretic approaches perhaps look the weakest of all. With the existence or possibility of 'conjectural' prices left unspecified, the implicit conclusion is that political failure is synonymous with market failure. Without a set of prices that permits a satisfactory optimization by consumers, no public-good provisioning is possible, or compatible with general economic equilibrium. In a sense, all this theory requires governments to do is to undertake the technically unspecified task of 'finding' the set of conjectural prices that would allow 'clubs' to provide public goods without distorting equilibrium in private goods markets! What, then, are these 'conjectural prices'? On what do they depend? How are they formed? Would they differ by income, community or political choice? Club theory does not answer these questions.

4. AN ALTERNATIVE FRAMEWORK

Some Definitions

An alternative way to view the role of state economic activity would be to see it as one of allocating rights over resources to achieve a chosen set of objectives subject to political and economic constraints. To explicate further this rather general definition we need to define the state, its objectives and the constraints.[5] Martinussen (1992), in an exhaustive review of the notion of the state and its applicability in an LDC context, distinguishes over twenty definitions of the term in the social sciences. To avoid getting bogged down in this embarrassment of riches, we confine ourselves to a relatively narrow definition:

D1   The *state* is the set of institutions vested with the supreme coercive power to protect and legitimate rights, with the purpose of attaining stated public policy objectives. The state defines and redefines the matrix of legislated rights including the mechanism for enforcing, maintaining and changing these rights which are used to decide which parts of the state and the private sector gain and lose from public policy decisions and who is entitled to undertake certain activities.

D2   *Rights* are politically defended claims over assets and resource flows.

D3   The state has two levels. The *centre* is the level which has a veto over assignments of rights to other levels. All other levels are called *local* or *non-central*. It follows from this definition that the centre has supreme coercive power over the non-centre.[6] Even when residual rights rest with the local level, the centre always has the coercive power to resume these rights.

D4   *Public policy objectives* are a set of objectives, the achievement of which is the principal responsibility of the state.

What of constraints? We define constraints in terms of the 'political settlement' first defined by Khan (1989) and used in various forms by several different scholars (Roy, 1994; Sayeed, 1996).

D5   The *political settlement* is a collective balance of power arrangement that enables the definition of a structure of rights which, in turn, allows for the pursuance, by the state, of a set of public policy objectives without further reference to the ontology of the rights definition and articulation process.

The political settlement sets the initial conditions for, and specifies the constraints over, the achievement of a given set of public policy objectives. For example, the objective of growth maximization is chosen on the assumption that there exists a political settlement which permits it to happen; it is thus a problem in constrained maximization in that it is subject to the maintenance of a compatible political settlement. It is the political settlement that defines state autonomy, and the feasibility with which, as well as the extent to which, a defined public policy objective can be achieved.

The Argument for Decentralization

Typically the focus of work in this rights-based approach has been the political settlement in terms of public and private property rights (Khan, 1989; Roy, 1994; 1996; Sayeed, 1996), partly in response to the normative literature on the subject emanating from the NPE and the new institutional economics (North, 1990). Little attention has been paid to the question of the impact of the political settlement on the articulation of various levels of government.

When the political settlement is defined, then so is the role of the state. The decentralization problem can be addressed by posing one of the following questions:

1. How can the political settlement be maintained to achieve a given set of public policy objectives?

or

2. How can the political settlement be changed to achieve a given set of public policy objectives?

To a large extent, addressing these questions depends on the 'given set of public policy objectives'.[7] The assignment of rights to the state and between different levels of the state has to be such that the political settlement is maintained, so as to make the achievement of these objectives feasible. The precise assignment of rights that makes the achievement of a given set of public policy objectives possible depends on the concrete–historical framework of state–society interaction, and on the precise nature of political organization. For example, in countries where class interest unites special-interest groups (like capitalists) at the central level, the political settlement is defined centrally, as it is only at that level that political claims can be defended and hence, *qua* the definition, rights are well defined. Equally, if changing the political settlement involves incorporating hitherto excluded groups, which are kept out of power by the centralized articulation of the political settlement, then decentralization can serve as a powerful tool to reduce political contestation by diversifying it.

The second element that enters the picture is the relationship between the state and the citizen, or groups of citizens. Conventional economic models assume that the state–citizen interaction takes place on the basis of a well-defined set of rights. However, rights may be weakly defined or absent. Typically there are continuous challenges to rights from interest groups contesting the existing allocation (Khan, 1989). The extent to which public policy objectives are achieved then depends on having – or acquiring – an appropriate political settlement that allows the state to achieve its public policy objectives without an unacceptably high level of political contestation. What this means (Khan, 1996) is that the transfer and creation of appropriate rights will depend not just on the economic or electoral bargaining between interest groups and the state, but also on the relative political power of interest groups *vis-à-vis* the state. In this context it is worth noting that most neo-classical (whether Musgravian or public choice) modelling uses, in Hirschman's terms (Hirschman, 1970), the notion of 'exit' to define the state–citizen contract. In our analysis the more important concept is that of 'voice'.[8] The political settlement is often constructed taking into account only those with 'voice' in an extant balance of power; often the objectives of the state encompass those without voice, involving decisions that are rejected if the present political settlement is to be maintained. Thus the viability of a political settlement may be threatened when an economic or political crisis affects the sustainability of a chosen economic strategy; one option in such a case is to change the coalitions that are parties to a political settlement or to change the terms of reference of these parties. It is here that decentralization can play an extremely powerful role.

First, decentralization can alter the set of possible outcomes by allowing for a wider political settlement. This can happen in circumstances where the political settlement is defined by a set of élites whose ability to exercise power, either consociationally[9] or as an oligarchy, requires centralization to (a) exclude those not in the political settlement from the public policy process, and (b) be used as a method for creating a bargaining platform where other cross-cutting cleavages may be subsumed to meet the larger interest. For example, suppose a country has a dominant regional élite whose will prevails over that of other regions. At the same time there is a capitalist élite which comes from all regions. This capitalist élite seeks to use the state to further its class interest, subject to the maintenance of a political settlement. With a centralized state, the political settlement could be achieved without costly replication of bargaining on the regional issue, but at the same time, there could be public policy outcomes that would not be feasible if the regional élites had to also acquiesce in the political settlement. Thus the development of a backward region might be the interests of capitalists, but this would not be a feasible outcome as it would make the political settlement unacceptable to élites from the dominant region. Decentralization in this case would enable regional capitalists to collaborate with other élites, who, at the central level, were excluded from the public policy decision making process. In this sense, decentralization can provide 'voice' to interest groups who can then alter the existing political settlement to permit the achievement of a wider set of public policy outcomes.

The reverse case can also be made. Decentralization may inhibit the achievement of a public policy objective by generating an incompatible (plural) political settlement. For instance, take the case where the provision of a public good like drinking water is a desired public policy objective in a country where a population minority of powerful élites in every locality have access to potable water but the rest do not. Foreign aid is available to provide water supply. The political settlement in each region is such that resources are unavailable for the provision of universal drinking water and aid assigned for the purpose is diverted. The right to bargain for aid, and to spend or devolve it, is, however, centralized. In such a situation it is best if the right to bargain for aid is used jointly with the right to decide its distribution to provide drinking water; the latter right must then be vested with the centre.

The second argument for decentralization in this context has to do with the fact that local and central governments are in a hierarchical relationship. This hierarchical relationship (*qua* D3 and note 6) determines the minimum assignment of rights to the centre. The question of assignment of rights within this hierarchy is subject to the considerations elucidated in the previous paragraph. However, within this hierarchy, there is no reason for rights to be centralized. Collective action does not require a unitary assignment of rights *unless a case can be made for doing so*. The success of the case then depends on the desired public policy objective and the compatibility of the political settlement. Thus the centre typically has the rights of the night-watchman state, while all other rights can be devolved, in principle. This is because the right to use the supreme coercive power rests in the final instance with the centre. Other units of the state have no equivalent sanction over the centre in the hierarchy. This is a seemingly obvious point, but is completely omitted in mainstream economic theorizing. This is because (a) such theorizing ignores the fact that the various units of government exist in a hierarchy, this in turn being ignored because the theory of the state that informs the analysis does not permit this question to be addressed, and (b) the proposition requires a theory of original rights, again absent in economic theory except in the case of the individual.

This obvious point has an important implication. The case for centralization of devolvable rights needs to be made rather than the other way round. This is a political and not an economic argument; it is thus more powerful than any of the mainstream arguments for decentralization

which treat the assignment of rights between the central and decentralized units of the state as neutral.

5.   POLICY APPLICATIONS

Spill-overs

Consider a situation where lump-sum taxes are raised by a provincial
government to reduce aggregate deficits, thereby altering the income–
consumption preferences of all taxpayers. This can differentially and
separately affect the incidence, buoyancy and elasticity of tax and
spending patterns of different local governments due to spill-overs in
private expenditure response. A single lump-sum tax does not have this
impact. This is used as an argument for centralization. With the rights-
based structure in place, however, the fallacy of this argument becomes
clear. Spill-overs are caused by differential taxation, not by the right to
tax being decentralized. If all provincial governments were to undertake
similar taxation policies, then the problem would be resolved. This is
clearly bound to happen once the fiscal hierarchy is recognized. Provincial government bankruptcy is not an outcome which a central
government can allow. Deficits raised by provincial government are, by
this assignment of rights, underwritten by the central government. If
deficits need to be amortized, then central taxation is inevitable to
'make up' the difference. The appropriate right to vest in the centre is
therefore the right to run a deficit and not the denial of the right to tax
to the provincial units. With deficits 'capped', states will have combin-
ations of taxes and expenditures which yield identical levels of welfare
to consumers with identical preferences (and with identical production
functions). Hence net spill-overs would be zero in a typical, neo-
classical, instantaneous adjustment model! Again, a simple result but
one whose derivation is contingent on the understanding of the place
of the centre in the hierarchy of the state.

Fiscal Policy

We begin by defining *fiscal surplus*. The fiscal surplus is the sum of
income flows and wealth stocks to which the state has access through
its tax and borrowing instruments, given the institutional arrangements
in a society.

  What are the elements of fiscal surplus? Institutional arrangements,
in the above definition, pertain to the structure of rights extant in a

given society plus the political settlement that legitimates these rights.
Typically, the rights generating government revenues are the rights to
tax, to borrow, to run a deficit and, in an open-economy context,
to bargain internationally for securing credit and aid. In a mixed
economy, we can add to this the state's ability to impose restrictions on
the activities of other agents. Thus the state's ability to impose restrictions on the activity of potentially competitive agents can earn its
revenues from productive activity and from direct investment of the
resources it accumulates.

The rights generating government expenditures are more complex.
Clearly, the very nature and scope of the political settlement itself
generates state expenditures. The precise magnitudes and pattern of
state expenditures are dependent on the concrete–historical nature
of the political settlement. In general, the fact that the state is vested
with coercive power generates security expenditure. Further, some
expenditures flow from the very rights that generate revenues. In industrial democracies, the existence of a welfare state, in which state–society
relations are embedded, generates a tax and transfers ensemble,
involving rights generating revenues as well as expenditures. In
command economies and in many mixed economies, the rights to
impose restrictions upon the activity of agents generates expenditures
for the state in terms of contingent productive activities that the state
itself must undertake. In India, for example, the right to exclude private
ownership of banks directly obliges the state to provide banking
services. Thus, while 'general services' in the functional classification
derive fairly unambiguously from the minimal functions of the state,
'social' and 'economic' services involve a more complex set of expenditures.

In a situation where institutional arrangements do not constrain the
incidence of the government's fiscal rights, the entire resources of
the economy would be the basis for fiscal incidence and there would
then be a one-to-one relationship between the size of the GDP, the
growth rate and the fiscal surplus. However, wherever institutional
arrangements are imperfect and rights are weakly defined, there arises
a disjuncture not recognized in mainstream economic theorizing.

We capture this distinction by defining the *disposable fiscal surplus*.
This differs from the fiscal surplus to the extent that revenue, debt and
public expenditure are affected by the need to maintain the political
settlement. We call these expenditures *stability payments* which are
payments made to maintain the political settlement in situations where
stability is a continuous political issue because the rights to certain
key assets are continuously contested. Stability payments have two

components. When the contest centres around well-defined rights, then the process of contest can be viewed as a constraint on the maximization of net present value of social product. Rent-seeking is a term from the new political economy literature that seeks to describe these contingent pay-offs (Krueger, 1974; Bhagwati, 1982). However, there are other pay-offs that are possible. When rights are weakly defined, then pay-offs accrue not through some constrained maximization of net present social product but to prevent threats to disrupt the ability of those in charge of the state to discharge their functions. These pay-offs are separate from those generated by 'rent-seeking' activity as they occur when rights are *not* well defined.

In a dynamic context, the revenue and spending aspects of the fiscal surplus can be closely related. Weakly defined rights clearly affect the disposable fiscal surplus negatively and increase the magnitude of resources outside the incidence of the resource mobilization mechanism, representing, if significant, a major source of variance between the fiscal surplus and the disposable fiscal surplus. In Figure 2.1, the 'political–fiscal statement' (for want of a better phrase) of government activity

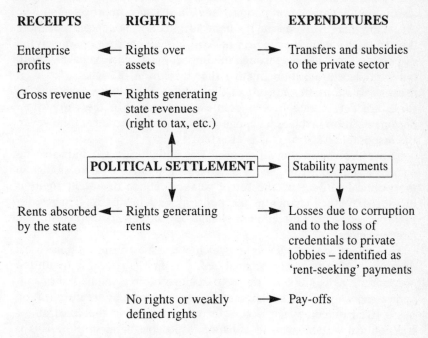

Figure 2.1   A political–fiscal statement

indicates, at a highly simplified level, the separate effects of weakly defined rights and rent-seeking on fiscal policy.

The rent-seeking literature does not capture this distinction. Rents are generated by scarcity and by the restricted legality of certain types of economic activity where some right-holders obtain economic power and credentials which entitle them, in theory, to capture the difference between scarcity and free-market prices. This difference is generated by the fact that the ability to supply a particular commodity is restricted by credentials (licences, membership of clubs, parties, lobbies, and so on). Rent seeking also generates stability payments which are the result of contestation over 'well-defined' rights to access rent. The weaker the state's (well defined) rights to rents, the higher the stability payments made on this score. They need to be made to maintain the political settlement, just as in the case where rights are absent or weakly defined. When rights are weakly defined, however, pay-offs do not originate from the restriction of supply as a consequence of rights over credentials but, rather, from the ability of a coalition to generate an increase in its resource flows through its ability to organize pressure against existing right-holders.

Decentralization affects the above picture in two ways. First, fiscal devolution *with a given political settlement* may improve economic efficiency, thereby increasing the fiscal surplus. Second, decentralization, through a *change in the political settlement*, may improve or worsen the disposable fiscal surplus through the impact on stability payments. Both types of decentralization involve the devolution of rights. However, fiscal devolution does not affect the volume of stability payments, as these are determined by the political settlement. In the case where decentralization involves a change in the political settlement, however, the disposable fiscal surplus is affected.

Figure 2.2 shows the difference. The equals sign (=) indicates no change while the arrow sign (→) indicates a change. With no change in the political settlement, the set of weakly defined or absent rights is unaltered. With a change in the political settlement this changes, for better or worse. The direction of change depends on concrete–historical circumstances.

Thus there are two levels at which the issue of appropriate fiscal decentralization needs to be analysed. The first is concerned with the appropriate assignation of rights to achieve desired public policy outcomes *given* a political settlement. The second form of decentralization has a fiscal outcome that occurs through changes in the constraint – the political settlement – to enhance disposable fiscal surplus. This is unidentifiable in mainstream theorizing. In this decision framework, it

Decentralization given a political settlement

CENTRE	Decentralization	LOCAL

```
┌─────────────────────┐                    ┌─────────────────────┐
│ 'Well-defined' rights│    ═══════►        │ 'Well-defined' rights│
│                      │                    │      devolved        │
└─────────────────────┘                    └─────────────────────┘
          ▲                                            
┌─────────────────────┐         ═══        ┌─────────────────────┐
│ Political settlement │                    │ Political settlement │
└─────────────────────┘                    └─────────────────────┘
          ▼                                            
┌─────────────────────┐         ───        ┌─────────────────────┐
│ Weakly defined rights│         ───        │ Weakly defined rights or│
│    or no rights      │                    │ no rights (no devolution)│
└─────────────────────┘                    └─────────────────────┘
```

Decentralization with a changed political settlement

CENTRE	Decentralization	LOCAL

```
┌─────────────────────┐                    ┌─────────────────────┐
│ 'Well-defined' rights│    ═══════►        │Less/more of well-defined│
│                      │                    │        rights        │
└─────────────────────┘                    └─────────────────────┘
          ▲                                            ▲
┌─────────────────────┐                    ┌─────────────────────┐
│ Political settlement │                    │ New political settlement│
└─────────────────────┘                    └─────────────────────┘
          ▼                                            ▼
┌─────────────────────┐                    ┌─────────────────────┐
│ Weakly defined rights│                    │  Less/more of weakly │
│    or no rights      │                    │ defined and/or no rights│
└─────────────────────┘                    └─────────────────────┘
```

Figure 2.2   Fiscal decentralization and the political settlement

is the nature of the change in the political settlement that determines the optimal distribution of rights between the centre and the local units. One straightforward implication is that the first type of decentralization – which we call devolution – has no impact on the weakly defined rights problem. If that is the identified problem, then it is the second type of decentralization that needs to be addressed.

Macroeconomics and Political Economy

One construction of a political settlement is that based on the coincidence between the place of a group in the income distribution hierarchy and the type of control over property rights. Thus if we can specify a distribution of income where the top decile earns income from property and shares Kaldorian consumption patterns (Kaldor, 1956), then it can be shown (Taylor and Bacha, 1976) that the macroeconomic growth process can be sustained even with increased inequality. In such a scenario, there develops a self-reinforcing unequalizing spiral, with a tendency for the production structure to shift toward luxury goods and for trickle-down to be absent. Such an economy has been termed

'Belindia'. In Roy (1997b) it was shown that 'discontent' with the under-lying political settlement affects the investment-maximizing accumulation strategy of capitalists in Belindia. Dealing with this conflict is possible if capitalists act to minimize conflict by accepting a slower rate of growth of capital stock and a lower rate of return on capital stock. Thus centralization, in the form of a conflict-minimizing macroeconomic strategy, can maintain an unequal model. Decentralization of macroeconomic powers would require a replication of the conflict-minimization exercise to maintain the political settlement. This raises the costs of maintaining the political settlement.

Now in this model, discontent is contained, and if this is the intention, then centralization is efficient. However, if the public policy objective is to alter the unequalizing spiral, then the existing political settlement inhibits the dismantling of Belindia. In such a circumstance, what is to be done?

The political settlement may be threatened when there is an economic crisis which affects expected distributive shares; in such a situation an economic crisis generates constituencies which have the incentive to mobilize against the political settlement. In the limit this involves a revolutionary political challenge which overthrows the existing state. As a special case, if the crisis is a result of the existing property rights structure being inappropriate to the current or emergent relations of production, then we have the classical Marxist scenario of revolution. Normally, declining viability of one regime as a consequence of such mobilizations is capable of being accommodated by altering rather than replacing the existing institutional apparatus.

In this context decentralization assumes significance as a tool that enables improved conflict management by, paradoxically, making the theatres of plural conflict more explicit. This is not merely a case of contracts being better specified; decentralization in response to those excluded from a political settlement allows contracts to be rewritten in a manner that is more explicit (even if not more inclusive); this in itself constitutes an expansion of a political settlement but not a replacement of it (corresponding to the case described in the upper half of Figure 2.2). The introduction of proportional representation may increase 'voice' options in a country dissatisfied with a Westminster electoral system without necessarily bringing more of the community into the decision-making process; what happens here is that the 'voice' option is promoted to avoid the exit option becoming a reality. In the same way, a devolution of powers can widen the terms of public policy debate without altering them. Thus decentralization can reduce costs of containing discontent by widening the political settlement, for a given objective function. In the Belindia model, decentralizing power allows the choice of an alternative growth path where growth rates are the same as in Belindia but distribution is more equal.

Decentralization may also be cheaper for the capitalists in Belindia. One possible trajectory where this may be an option is when 'discontent' emerges in one part of Belindia, but the transmission effects of this discontent are large enough to make the current strategy infeasible throughout Belindia. Here capitalists may not be willing to 'socialize the costs of discontent' by sharing the costs of local discontent nationally. Thus decentralizing the costs of local discontent allows the political settlement to be maintained.

6. CONCLUSION

Mainstream economics is either unwilling or unable to address the decentralization issue satisfactorily, with the result that policy recommendations are often vague or incorrect. They are, nevertheless, influential. For example, the recent *World Development Report* (World Bank, 1997) enthusiastically advocates decentralization. The reason is interesting:

> The rising demand for decentralization has come as part of the broader process of liberalization, privatization and other market reforms in many countries. These reforms are distinct from one another but their underlying rationale is similar to that for decentralization: that power over the production and delivery of goods and services should be rendered to the lowest unit capable of capturing the associated costs and benefits. (p. 120)

While the report admits that the arguments for decentralization must be country-specific, the rationale is not. As a consequence the analysis then proceeds to generalize about what ought and ought not to be decentralized; however, the guidelines for successful decentralization are contingent on an 'assessment of institutional capability' (p. 128) and on 'Bridging the gap between State and citizen' (p. 129). The acceptance of NPE reasoning renders the political framework for recommendations inadequate, and as argued above, weakens the case for decentralization.

The rights-based approach attempts to remedy this shortfall by emphasizing the essentially political nature of economic decentralization; with the notion of political settlement in place the success or failure of decentralization applications of the approach can thus place the analysis of decentralization on a sounder, political-economy footing.

NOTES

1. I would like to thank Maureen Mackintosh for detailed and illuminating comments and advice. The usual disclaimer applies.
2. The third function – distribution – is more controversial. Musgrave and Musgrave (1976) themselves call for a more centralized approach to this function.
3. In technical terms, taxation may exhibit downward rigidities when public good providers are additively separable and monopolistic.
4. For examples of NPE theorizing see Srinivasan (1985) and Lal (1988).
5. A detailed exposition of what follows can be found in Roy (1994).
6. Even when residual rights rest with the local level, the centre always has the coercive power to resume these rights.
7. The word 'given' is used to mean the public policy objectives that exist at a concrete–historical moment. The very choice of these objectives is, of course, political. But it is not possible to generalize further about such objectives without reference to a specific concrete–historical context.
8. Hirschman's third concept of 'loyalty' is of course highly relevant here. Its interpretation in our context would have to be in terms of legitimation. See, in particular, Habermas's (1984) discussion of a legitimation–motivation crisis wherein there arises a crisis as a discrepancy develops between the state's announced motives (which could be interpreted as its announced public policy objectives, in the terminology used here) and the political settlement. The issue of legitimation of the political settlement can also be discussed – as Habermas does – in contexts other than that of an economic crisis. Equally, legitimation issues arise when there are politico-economic problems in the maintenance of a political settlement. These issues are insufficiently discussed in the framework presented here. I am indebted to Subir Sinha for raising this point.
9. In the sense used by Lijphart (1974).

REFERENCES

Alesina, A. and Rosenthal, H. (1996), 'A theory of divided government', *Econometrica*, **64**.
Bhagwati, J. (1982), 'Directly unproductive profit-seeking activities', *Journal of Political Economy*, **90**.
Brennan, G. and Buchanan, J.M. (1977), 'Towards a tax constitution for Leviathan', *Journal of Public Economics*, **8**.
Gilles, R. and Scotchmer, S. (1998), 'Decentralization in club economies: how multiple private goods matter', in Pines, D., Sadka, E. and Zilcha, I. (eds), *Topics in Public Economics*, Cambridge: Cambridge University Press.
Habermas, J. (1984), 'What does a legitimation crisis mean today? Legitimation problems in late capitalism', in Connolly, W. (ed.), *Legitimacy and the State*, Oxford: Basil Blackwell.
Hirschman, A.O. (1970), *Exit, Voice and Loyalty*, Cambridge, MA: Harvard University Press.
Kaldor, N. (1956), 'Alternative theories of distribution', *Review of Economic Studies*, **23**.
Khan, M. (1989), *Clientelism, Corruption and Capitalist Development*, Ph.D. dissertation, University of Cambridge.

Khan, M. (1996), 'A typology of corrupt transactions in developing countries', *IDS Bulletin*, **27**, April.

Krueger, A. (1974), 'The political economy of the rent-seeking society', *American Economic Review*, **64**.

Lal, D. (1988), *Hindu Equilibrium*, Vol. I, Oxford: Clarendon Press.

Lijphart, A. (1974), 'Consociational democracy', in McRae, K. (ed.), *Consociational Democracy: Political Accommodation in Segmented Societies*, Toronto: McClelland and Stewart.

Martinussen, J. (ed.) (1992), *Development Theory and the Role of the State in Third World Countries*, Roskilde: International Development Centre, Roskilde University.

Musgrave, R.A. and Musgrave, P.B. (1976), *Public Finance in Theory and Practice*, New York: McGraw-Hill.

North, D. (1990), *Institutions, Institutional Change and Economic Performance*, Cambridge: Cambridge University Press.

Oates, Wallace (1972), *Fiscal Federalism*, New York: Harcourt Brace Johanovich.

Pateman, C. (1985), *The Problem of Political Obligation*, Cambridge: Polity Press.

Post, K. and Wright, P. (1989), *Socialism and Underdevelopment*, London: Routledge.

Roy, Rathin (1994), *The Politics of Fiscal Policy*, Ph.D. dissertation, University of Cambridge.

Roy, Rathin (1996), 'State failure in India: political–fiscal implications of the black economy', *IDS Bulletin*, **27**, April.

Roy, Rathin (1997a), 'Riches amid sterility: debates on Indian fiscal policy', in Byres T.J. (ed.), *Debates on the Indian Economy*, New Delhi: Oxford University Press.

Roy, Rathin (1997b), 'On discontent in Belindia: a theoretical note', paper presented at the International Studies Association Conference, 18–22 March, Toronto.

Sayeed, Asad (1996), *Political Alignment, the State and Industrial Policy in Pakistan*, Ph.D. dissertation, University of Cambridge and forthcoming, Karachi: Oxford University Press.

Seabright, P. (1996), 'Accountability and decentralisation in government: an incomplete contracts model', *European Economic Review*, **40**.

Srinivasan, T.N. (1985), 'Neoclassical political economy, the state and economic development', *Asian Development Review*, **64**.

Taylor, L. and Bacha, E. (1976), 'The unequalising spiral: a first growth model for Belindia', *Quarterly Journal of Economics*, **90**.

Tiebout, C. (1956), 'A pure theory of public expenditures', *Journal of Political Economy*, **64**.

World Bank (1997), *World Development Report*, Washington, DC: Oxford University Press.

3. Public–private partnerships: implications for public expenditure management

A. Premchand[1]

1. INTRODUCTION

Major changes have been taking place during the last two decades in the interrelationships between society, the state and the economy. These changes, in turn, have had a substantial impact on the approaches to and processes of expenditure management in public bodies. Although the perennial concern has been with the growth in government expenditures and the need to restrain them, the way in which this concern has been addressed has differed over the years. During the 1960s, the emphasis was more on the collection and analysis of data, particularly the quantification of costs and benefits, so that objective decisions could be taken after a careful assessment of the alternatives. This emphasis, however, did not have a significant impact on the growth of expenditure, although the approach represented a radical departure from the previous practice of budgeting and expenditure control. While factors such as wars and related political phenomena have had their impact on the growth of expenditures, advances made during this period did not fully address the other major issues raised. Can governments deliver services efficiently? How can they be made more responsive to the changing needs of society? Can some of the public services be supplied by other forms of organization? These issues and related analysis pushed public choice theory to the forefront and have dominated the discussion since the late 1970s. This theory suggested, among other things, that bureaux in government tend to expand, not in response to growing public demand, but as an extension of their normal endeavour to augment the individual utilities of the employees. Inevitably, then, bureaux would be less concerned with either efficiency in the services provided or in meeting the needs of the community. The theory also implied that for this reason government organizations would always have considerable slack and that the agencies could be reduced in size without any discernible impact on the quantity and quality of services provided. The debate about the relevance of this theory came to receive additional impetus with the growing size of fiscal deficits and their persistence during this period. The fiscal realities made governments search for and mobilize all available means that might reduce the fiscal deficits.

2. RECENT TRENDS

The search revealed three approaches relevant to the discussion here. First, in order for governments to be more responsive to citizens and to be more effective, they needed to be structured to focus more on service management and coordination, while the actual delivery of services would be in the realm of private profit and non-profit organizations. This approach emphasized that governments stand for the most part to benefit from the extended application of commercial practices. The acceptance of this approach has contributed, among other things, to growing partnerships between the government and the private sector. The approach had a natural appeal to those who perceived this joint partnership as providing much-needed relief to the fiscal pressures on the public bodies.

Second, it was recognized that the provision of civic services cannot be left entirely to market forces or to the imperatives of the state, and that participation of voluntary associations and political organizations was vital for the successful functioning of modern society. This participation implied a major reorientation of the welfare state that so far dominated the philosophy of governments. The belief hitherto was that the public sector would continue to be the major, perhaps the only, sector responsible for the funding and provision of social welfare. There was little or no role for voluntary non-profit organizations. Now, however, this belief is seriously questioned and many share the view of 'voluntary associations, self-help groups, social movements and other intermediary organizations as important alternatives to state social provision that can provide a crucial empowering role for citizens'.[2] This approach has its own limitations. The critics suggest that citizen participation in policy making, as well as in the different phases of implementation, could contribute to too much democracy, with inevitable legislative gridlocks and associated policy paralysis. They argue that community organizations are inherently incapable of sustaining political participation and that excessive decentralization could have the effect of empowering the wrong people. While experience is not conclusive in this regard and there are as yet many unresolved areas, it has to be recognized that during recent years community participation has proved extremely useful in several developing countries in reaching sections of the community that earlier did not benefit from government services. The role of community organizations went far beyond the creation of an awareness about the availability of government services to the modification of the design of the services to meet the needs of specific sections of the community and to ensuring that those services did indeed reach the public for whom they were intended in the first place. The experience of development planning shows that five-year plans had a better chance of being successful when public participation and support were available. Indeed, the partnership proved to be vital in some areas. It should be added that during recent years many donors have been insisting that as a part of the participation of the community, non-governmental organizations should be assigned a prominent role in the provision of services.

That said, it should be noted that much is dependent on the form of public–private collaboration, the functional area selected for collaboration, and the care taken in delineation of the specific links between tasks, responsibilities and financial power. No single organizational form has been acceptable to all or has been free from bureaucratic tension or conflict. Each country had to find its own level of smooth functioning, depending on the traditions of administrative culture as well as the levels of perception of trust between the public and private sectors to specify the location of managerial authority and responsibility for programme implementation.

Third, there has also been a significant change in the approaches of government financial management reflecting the new fiscal realities. Years of continued growth in public expenditures and deficits have demonstrated the leakages in the control system and the futility of centralized controls. Experience has shown that the ministries of finance were too absorbed in creating multiple levels of procedural control that had a greater impact on restraining the initiatives of the civil servants than on expenditures and that, in general, the tactical approaches to expenditure reductions proved to be ineffective. It would appear that in most cases the measures taken as a part of cutback management were so superficial that they drew no more than a perfunctory and equally superficial response from the spending agencies. The other side of the picture was that the persistent underfunding of services did not bring about, as expected, a reduction in the demand for public services. Rather, the approaches toward containment only contributed to large sections of the community remaining outside the ambit of services provided by government. The recognition of these aspects brought about changes in the patterns of expenditure management. These changes, however, cover a wide area and it is not possible, within the scope of this chapter, to capture them comprehensively. Major features of these changes are summarized in Table 3.1. As shown therein, the traditional incrementalist approach has yielded place to a new managerialism and to new strategic approaches involving major shifts in technical and organizational aspects. The new approaches recognize that decentralization is not merely inevitable but essential. Decentralization does not necessarily mean a loss in the capacity for supervision on the part of central agencies. The two major questions to be answered in this context were: How could the rate of growth in expenditures be moderated? How should finance ministries equip themselves to function in an effective way in a decentralized context? The answer to the first question was that public expenditure management needs to be far more diversified in its approaches than before. Hence the importance of global limits, application of market tests, break-up of internal monopolies and emphasis on cost recovery. The main cornerstones of this managerialism are to be found in the creation of small agencies (with public participation where appropriate), specifications of tasks, insistence on performance standards and greater accountability for the results. Providing an answer to the second question became easy in the context of greater application of information technology. These aspects collectively suggest the pursuit of performance budgeting in a more organized form than in the past.

The above-mentioned three factors have had a significant impact on public–private collaboration, and more significantly on the expenditure management machinery, its approaches and techniques of control, in public bodies. To facilitate a more detailed coordination of these aspects, the chapter considers first the structure of government transactions and the role played by the private or, more appropriately, non-governmental sector. This is followed by a consideration of five distinct roles of public authorities and an analytical framework is delineated indicating the implications of each role for budget formulation and implementation in governments. Finally, the issues that arise in the management of the complex pattern of relationships between the public and private sectors are considered in some detail.

Table 3.1 Containing expenditure growth: elements of various approaches

Incrementalist approach		Managerialism		Strategic approaches	
Technical	Organizational	Technical	Organizational	Technical	Organizational
• Percentage cuts • Budget pruning at fringes • Postponement of expenditures • Postponement of payments	• Frequent intervention by central agencies • Centralization of financial controls • Centralization of payments	• Specification of costs • Specification of quality and quantity of services • Specification of accountability standards • Indication of global limits on categories of expenditure	• Identification of organizational weaknesses in regard to procurement and contracting out and addressing them • Creation of agencies with specified tasks, resources and services to be delivered	• Restructuring of government goals • Revised priorities through abandonment or scaling down of selected activities • Identification of major leakage centers (subsidies, entitlements, medical sectors, etc.) and formulation of	• Appointment of high-level commissions to enquire and make recommendations so as to secure a wider consensus • Organizational improvements secured in the previous stages pave the way for a smoother implementation

- Emphasis on greater cost recovery
- Application of market tests
- Break-up of internal monopolies

- Establishment of evaluation units to ascertain the lessons of experience
- Greater application of information technology
- More emphasis on decentralization

- cost reduction strategies
- Emphasis on contracting out provision of services to private organizations
- Exploration of partnerships and other forms of cooperation with the private sector so that pressures on public resources could be contained

- of the strategic shift
- Application of private sector creativity and management experience to governments

3.   STRUCTURE OF PUBLIC TRANSACTIONS

From time immemorial, governments have been buying goods and services from the public. Although the means of production, such as agriculture, were largely in the hands of the crown, governments relied on the services, in addition to those directly employed by them, provided by the private sector. The primary distinction between the public and the private sector was drawn with reference to the ownership pattern. It was assumed that private actions were guided by the profit motive, while it was expected that the public authorities were more guided by the service motive. The purchases of governments often tended to be substantial during periods of war, and when the resources available to government were relatively limited, kings incurred formal and informal debts to the private sector.

The range of services and goods bought by governments from other than internal sources grew steadily over the years as their role expanded and many tasks and functions had come to be assumed by them.[3] Now governments procure their requirements either through competitive tendering processes or through direct orders, from a variety of domestic and foreign sources including individuals, government-owned agencies as well as private corporate bodies. The financing of these purchases at the lower levels of government may be managed from the federal/ central transfers. In developing countries, the resources provided by the donors are similarly utilized for purchases of goods and services from the non-governmental sector. These aspects are illustrated in Figure 3.1.

During recent years, the way in which these services and goods are acquired has contributed to a new pattern of relationships between governments and the private sector. There has been a phenomenal increase in the quantity of goods and services bought. With emphasis on efficiency and demands for higher levels of service, governments have divested their in-house operations and are relying more on the private sector for meeting their needs.[4] In turn, this has meant that the share of government expenditures on directly provided services has been rapidly declining. Thus, for example, in the USA, expenditure on directly delivered services by the federal government in 1994 was only 4 per cent of the total. (The rest is accounted for by payments to individuals (58 per cent), interest on national debt (15 per cent), contracts with private companies (13 per cent), armed forces (5 per cent), and grants to state and local governments (5 per cent). Although comparable data are not available for other countries, it is not unreasonable to assume that the experience of the USA is by no means unique. This declining trend in outlays on directly provided services also reflects in

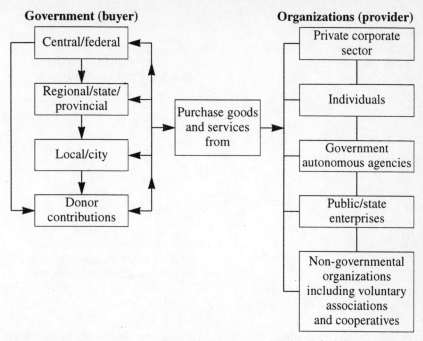

Figure 3.1 Structure of government transactions

part the growth of third-party transactions. As part of entitlement and related benefits programmes, many services such as child care, medical care and others are now being directly provided by individuals and organizations that are not a part of governments. In these cases, neither the provider nor the client providing the service comes into contact with government, although it is the funding agency. The relationships in this regard are illustrated in Figure 3.2. In some cases, the services may be provided, not by individuals, but by voluntary or other non-governmental organizations.

There are several operations where government is the only consumer of the services produced by the private sector. In the USA, many of the products of the defence industrial base are supplied only to government. From the research and development of new weaponry to their final delivery, the operations, although conducted by private sector companies, are for the benefit of a monopoly consumer, that is, government. Similarly, in some developing countries, fertilizer, whether produced in the government sector or by corporate bodies, is sold only to government, which then arranges its subsidized sale. Electricity produced by the private sector is sold into the grid owned by public

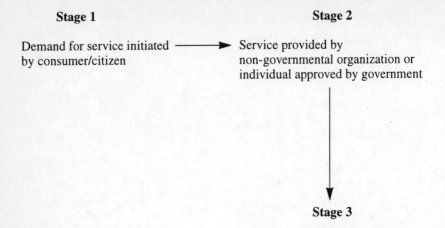

Figure 3.2　Third-party transactions

sector bodies. In these cases, the distinction between public and private sector becomes nebulous. The conventional dichotomy of government and non-government, based on ownership, is of limited utility in illustrating the complex buyer–seller relationships that exist at other levels.[5] These sectors, which have only government as consumer, should be more appropriately considered as appendages of the public sector with a personality that may be less corporate that is usually presumed. Indeed, it is often suggested that companies and non-governmental organizations become, in several major and minor aspects, clones of the one and only consumer. These relationships are likely to be more complex as the amount of contracts for services and goods issued by governments increases. (The Department of Defense in the USA issues more than 52 000 contracts each day: Gansler, 1989, p. 4.)

There are other activities undertaken on behalf of government or paid for by it but undertaken outside its direct control. A traditional approach of financing in this regard has been for the governments to provide grants-in-aid to organizations that may be within the fold of a broader government, or outside.[6] Such grants are given to bodies that are registered, have their own articles of agreement governing their operations, and are generally engaged in activities that complement the policies or objectives of government. In many cases, such bodies may be organized by the government itself but endowed with a degree of functional and financial autonomy so that they could be outside the bureaucratic control systems. In other cases, they may be organized by individuals or voluntary associations.

The primary difference between a purchase and a grant-in-aid is that the former is a market exchange with an explicit contractual obligation between a buyer and a provider. The grant-in-aid, which is more informal, implies an arm's-length relationship between the recipient and the grant-giving agency, although the grant *per se* is included in the budget and is, therefore, appropriated by the legislature. Many grant-receiving bodies, however, have very few resources of their own and are dependent for their financial survival on government transfers. This is the case with many non-governmental organizations in developing countries. Their dependence on government is so overwhelming that to all intents and purposes, other than legal, they are indistinguishable from government. Here again, the blurring of financial responsibilities raises many issues about the validity of government–non-government dichotomy.

4.   FIVE ROLES OF GOVERNMENT

Government activities where collaboration is envisaged with the private sector, as noted above, cover a large area. Such collaboration could be contractual in that the government may be buying services for its own use, or funding selectively some activities aimed to provide services to the community. The government could be providing grants-in-aid to organizations engaged in provision of public services. Or it could be working as a coordinator, specifying various forms in which participation by private bodies would be welcomed. In addition, the state would be providing services, although on a declining scale in some countries, on its own to the public. Finally, it has the role of a regulator, seeking to promote competition in the economy. Thus a government can function as a provider, as a buyer, as a funding agency, as a coordinator and, finally, as a regulator.

Each of the above roles and the activities undertaken by governments as a part of the government financial management cycle are illustrated in Table 3.2. From the point of view of financial management, the role of the public authority as a regulator is less important, notwithstanding the enormous impact on the overall quality of public life itself. The purposes of regulation are, in addition to promoting competition, to ensure transparency in transactions, compliance with established codes of behaviour and related standards, and to ensure that in undertaking

Table 3.2 Public–private partnerships: financial management cycle

Activity	Public as a provider	Public as a buyer of services	Public as a funding agency	Public as a coordinator	Public as a regulator
1. Advance planning, including determination of objectives, cost, estimates, and related details	As a full provider of services, this is an internal activity of the public agency	When the public is engaged in the purchase of services for internal use, it is also responsible for advance planning. Advance planning is undertaken by the public entity	In this case, services are funded by the government but are provided by private entities to the community	Here again, the initiative lies with the government in indicating the areas where private participation is welcomed – its form, content, and implications	In some cases, where environment or other societal and ethical concerns are paramount, advance approvals of private sectors' plans may be needed. But this has to be tempered by the need to limit regulations
2. Formulation of annual or multi-year budgets	Internal exercise whose parameters are determined by laws, traditions and institutions	Internal exercise	Although budgets would be formulated by the private entity, they may need prior approvals by the funding agency. For example, hospitals that provide services funded by governments are required to submit their budgets to governments in some industrial countries	Budgets would be the internal activity of private entities. Where partnership is envisaged, usually a corporate form is given to that activity. The corporation will have directors drawn from both sectors. In these cases, an arms length is maintained with the government	No government approval may be needed except in cases of bankruptcy or financial restructuring

3. Determination of the areas for contracting out and their financial implications	Internal exercise particularly when the services are provided by in-house facilities	Internal exercise. Contracts have to specify the performance standards, costs and warranty implications	Contracts will need to be drawn up in greater detail specifying the respective responsibilities of the public and the private. These include incentives and penalties. The framework of monitoring will depend on the detail of contracts	Contracts will be the responsibility of the corporation	Generally, no involvement except to ensure that there is adequate competition and scrupulous adherence to specified ethical standards. Monitoring, which will be selective, is needed to ensure the transparency of bids and related decision making
4. Budget implementation					
(a) Release of funds	Internal exercise	Internal exercise	The public entity has to ensure that funds are available on a regular basis to the service provider. There should be monitoring to ensure that there is no build-up of funds with the receiver	Self-financing for the corporations. Release-of-funds procedures are applicable only for the public entity's share or budget support	Not applicable

Table 3.2 Continued

Activity	Public as a provider	Public as a buyer of services	Public as a funding agency	Public as a coordinator	Public as a regulator
(b) Specification of costs	Internal exercise but the full specification of costs is rarely done	Costs are specified for the purchase of equipment. Major projects reveal, however, significant shortcomings in the financial management processes of governments in this regard	Significant improvements have been made in this area, particularly in the health sector. In industrial countries costs cannot be exceeded. Regular monitoring of costs by the funding agency is needed only to be aware of the trends and for future adjustments	Responsibility of the corporation	Not applicable
(c) Performance indicators including quality of service	Although these are intended to provide internal efficiency, they are not undertaken regularly	Specified as part of a contract	The experience of several industrial countries shows that these are utilized on a growing scale. The monitoring framework is focusing on these aspects. These need to be developed to ensure compliance in the provision of	As an independent entity, it is expected to publish periodic information about the progress made as well as on the financial aspects	The regulating agency has to indicate accounting and performance standards and ensure their compliance

			service and to anticipate any disruption in services arising from contractual failures		
(d) Borrowing powers and issue of debt instruments	Internal exercise of governments	Internal exercise	Internal exercise of the funding agency. Contracts cannot create additional liabilities for the government	Safeguards are needed to ensure that there are no contingent liabilities for the government. Prior approval from government may be indicated where a guarantee is provided	Standards need to be established for borrowing from the public and the information needed to be made available in that context
5. Year-end evaluation	Although inherent in the responsibilities, it is not undertaken	Contract performance is evaluated	Evaluation is now being undertaken by the sponsoring entities. In some areas (e.g. UK) citizens are also appointed to evaluation committees. For the most part, however, what remains to be done is far more than what has been achieved so far	Evaluation in this respect is at a very incipient stage	Standards need to be set up for the purpose to safeguard the interests of the citizens. Progress is painfully slow

these activities, the overall cost of regulation is not disproportionately high relative to benefits. As a regulator, the government would be interested in specifying certain minimum standards, such as internal controls, accounting practices to be in conformity with internationally accepted principles, and credit ratings where the organizations are engaged in raising resources from the public. These standards would be applicable to corporate bodies as well as non-governmental organizations.

From the point of view of financial management, however, the other four roles of government are more important because of their immediate relevance. The government is a major buyer of materials produced by the private sector for its own use. This function is by no means new but will continue to be a major factor with significant impact on the economy. In several cases, private sector activity is initiated in the light of expenditure proposals included in the new budget. Purchases by governments are preceded by contracts specifying the quality, quantity and price aspects, as well as penalties for defaults. Monitoring in their case is intended to serve a dual purpose – a regular tracking of the various phases of budget implementation, and a judgement on how well the supplies are linked to the needs of government, which may vary depending on the function and the season.

The public authorities are also engaged in the provision of services. These are funded, managed and delivered by the public authorities from their in-house facilities. Such services include, in many countries, education and health. These are conducted as a part of the publicly approved budgets and to that extent the normal procedures of financial management are applicable. As an integral part of this effort, monitoring systems have also been traditional in function. Divestment of some of these functions implies that they would hereafter be funded by the public authorities but provided by private organizations, or may involve joint financing. These two roles represent a major departure from the traditions of public financial management and to that extent may need a new start in adapting the expenditure management machinery to the issues that arise in this regard.

Private sector organizations engaged in the provision of public services come in different forms with varying tangible and intangible capabilities. Some of them may be specifically organized for the purpose and may have no tradition in the provision of public services. Others may be politically inspired or supported, with little or no organizational identity or culture of their own. Each of these, in turn, influences the initial scrutiny of bids for the provision of services and the design of the expenditure controls. Organizations with no history may need more intensive monitoring, while those with an established track record and published results may require a different treatment. Although the relationships between the public and the private would largely continue to be on the basis of arm's-length principle and therefore different from the traditional bureaucratic exercise, the actual content and focus of expenditure control would depend, in part, on the nature and organizational form of the private entity.

The purposes of expenditure management in a context of the public as a buyer and as a provider are different in some ways and yet have a good deal of common ground with traditional approaches. The common factors relate to the budget implementation compulsions and the need to avoid excess expenditures, while ensuring that the quality and quantity of services are being maintained. The differences primarily arise in regard to three areas. First, excessive dependence on a contractor to provide services could also lead to unexpected interruption in the provision, in that the contractor may not have the requisite financial backing or may be the victim of labour strife or may have some other consideration, not excluding negotiation for a higher price at the threat of an interruption. This factor requires that the base of expenditure control should be rather broad, transcending the traditional areas covered as a part of budget implementation. Second, experience shows that there is often a problem of moral hazard in the context of third-party transactions funded from the government budget. Payments for medicaid and medicare or related provision of health services may often be higher because the provider has a major interest and potential for benefiting from the transaction. Thus more tests may be ordered and needless but expensive procedures may be resorted to. While some of these practices raise issues of ethical standards, it may be noted that the incidence of these expensive procedures is fairly high. The fact that the financing agency is remote may contribute to a situation where the provider can afford to be less than financially responsible. The expenditure control machinery should take this into account in its design. And, third, where a separate agency is established to foster public–private partnerships or to provide services, and is endowed with financial autonomy, there is a distinct possibility that guarantees may be provided by the government for the borrowing undertaken by that entity. Such guarantees contribute to the emergence of contingent liabilities, which tend to rise in direct proportion to the number of agencies and the market borrowing undertaken by them. From the point of view of monetary policy, there may be a need to coordinate the borrowing so that the market is not flooded with issues at the same time, contributing in turn to higher costs. From the point of view of financial management, those guarantees need to be monitored so that contingent liabilities can be anticipated and appropriate arrangements made for funding.

These purposes emphasize the need for a broad-based expenditure management while illustrating the points of departure from the conventional approaches.

5. BUDGETARY INSTRUMENTS

The issues that arise in the day-to-day management of finances are dependent on the nature of the budgetary instruments. The range of instruments is fairly large, and following from the above approach may be subdivided into two broad groups – grants-in-aid and contractual payments. The instruments under each group, together with an indication of the nature and applicability, are illustrated in Table 3.3. The impact of each of these instruments tends to vary with the organizational form of the recipient. Broadly, however, grants are applicable to nongovernmental organizations, while contractual payments are applicable to corporate bodies as well as other organizations engaged in a buyer–provider relationship with government.

From the government's point of view, the provision of grants raises issues about matching contributions and the actual provision of a service. In many cases, mobilization of resources by non-governmental organizations tends to be difficult, as they are dependent on private contributions. When these funds are not available to meet the levels specified by the grantors, the latter may have to forego the grant. This in turn could endanger the services provided by that organization, not to mention its financial health. Most organizations are so fragile financially that they do not enjoy any credit facilities from established financial institutions. As for service, the performance standards specified by governments may introduce additional outlays on infrastructure facilities, and hiring of professional staff that entails additional outlays. These very requirements, which may be considered as legitimate from the government's point of view, may be seen as onerous by the recipient organizations. From the point of view of the receiving organization, it is often contended (supported by a good deal of empirical evidence) that it is not so much the design of the grant as the actual implementation process which tends to be problematic. The grant money is often not released in time, thus weakening what is already a fragile financial structure of the organization. Such releases, it is suggested, are contingent on the liquidity of government rather than the needs of the recipient.[7]

Cost

The most important anchor for expenditure management is the cost of a project, programme or an activity. Once the total and variable costs are estimated, the controlling agency should have an adequate understanding of the factors contributing to cost movements, and how they may be controlled through the deployment of the various techniques available to it. In reality, however, this also constitutes an Achilles' heel in public expenditure management. Most governments do not have consistent, up-to-date data on costs, nor are most of them equipped with the accounting systems that are capable of producing meaningful data on costs. In general, governments continue to operate cash-based accounting systems that are found to have serious limitations in providing needed policy inputs. Indeed, in some industrial countries cost estimates have been formulated (for example health services) to serve as a basis for reimbursement. These are constantly updated in order to be relevant; but this is a practice that is in need of extension to other levels of governments and to other countries. In the absence of these data, governments tend to be vulnerable, and the familiar charge that governments have a good deal of catching up to do turns out to be accurate.

Fraud

The experience of many countries shows that fraud tends to be ubiquitous wherever there is a large-scale contracting out of services and procurement. Cases of advance payments, overpayments and fraudulent billing are quite common to defence, construction, health and social service sectors. The magnitude of transactions in all these areas has tended to grow during recent years, and substantial strengthening of officialdom has yet to prove effective in preventing fraudulent transactions. Even as new restrictions are being envisaged and sanctions formulated, available computer software for medical practitioners providing services to the public enables them to 'unbundle' the package and conduct remunerative clinical tests on a scale not justified by medical considerations. Some countries, such as the USA, have introduced quality control systems aimed at 'correcting faults in program administration that contribute to erroneous payments and reducing the extent of misspent dollars'. As a part of this effort, target error rates for error

Table 3.3 Public–private partnerships: role of budgetary instruments

Budgetary instruments	Remarks
Grants-in-aid	
Budgetary support grants	The term refers to the broad range of transfers from one level of government to another, and to non-government organizations. Governments make transfers for the sole purpose of compensating budget deficits of the receiving organizations and governments
Conditional/specific/ targeted grants	Specific conditions are stipulated for the use of government funds. Releases during the fiscal year are subject to observance of conditions. Some governments have evolved, during recent years, performance agreements that also specify quality standards to be observed in the process of utilizing these transfers
Unconditional/general block grants	These transfers have the broad purpose of improving the financial condition of recipient organizations
Matching grants	Funds are made available by governments on condition that they are matched by specified contributions from others or by the recipient organizations
Institutional support	These transfers are in the nature of general grants. In some countries, governments have reverted to this type of financial assistance after recognizing that compliance with specific grants may, while reducing the functional autonomy of the recipient organization, be adding to overall administrative costs
Capital grants	Governments may also provide grants for the specific purpose of acquiring different types of assets. In some developing countries, these grants continue to be operational, while their incidence is less in advanced economies
Contractual payments	The main distinction between grants-in-aid and related budgetary instruments on the one hand, and contractual payments on the other, is that the former are at the discretion of government, while the latter are more in the nature of an obligatory transaction after a firm commitment has been made to enter into a contract. A contract legitimizes a market or exchange transaction between a buyer and a provider
Advance payments	Contracts generally provide for advance payments so as to alleviate the problems associated with the arrangements for working capital required by the contractor. In some cases, this instrument is also used as an integral part of industrial policy to encourage newcomers into the market

66

Progress payments	Contracts relating to construction or for supply of items that need fabrication also provide for progress payments by governments. From an accrual accounting point of view, there may be no delivery of services or products. As such, the concept of constructive delivery or the assumption that the part of the goods so financed are deemed to be delivered to governments is used
Full/final payments	In general, contracts provide that a part of the payment will be made after all conditions have been met and only after the warranty period has elapsed. Meanwhile, quality lapses and other contractual failures are evaluated and recourse may also be made to arbitration proceedings
Reimbursements	Services may be provided on behalf of governments, by individuals, e.g. physicians. Here a scale of remuneration is laid down for different services, and the provider is reimbursed the compensation due for the service provided. These services may also be provided by non-governmental organizations
Payment for capital-related costs	In some cases, a rate of return on equity or capital is assumed by government and reimbursement made to provide the return. The range of activities covered by this category include pure commercial transactions such as newspaper publication, fertilizer production, generation of electricity, and the provision of medical care. In addition, governments may also reimburse part or whole of interest costs on the borrowing to finance construction of hospitals, depreciation for plant and equipment, and property taxes
Lending operations	Governments may lend directly from their budgetary resources, or cause to lend by financial institutions owned by them, or act as a conduit to lending by international/regional financial institutions or donors. Loans may be extended to contractors/corporate bodies/non-governmental organizations. The determination of the terms as well as collection of amounts due are subjects of discretionary decision making during the annual process of budget formulation
Guarantees	Governments may also offer guarantees to contractors and organizations when they receive loans from independent financial institutions. Liabilities in the event of default are determined as a part of this agreement. In some cases, guarantee fees may be payable by the recipient organizations
Tax expenditures	In addition to direct payments and reimbursements, governments also provide indirect payments to individuals and organizations. These include special tax exemptions, deductions, exclusions and credits. Some of these benefits are extended by a law that specifies eligibility criteria, and some are determined on a case-by-case basis by governments.

tolerance levels are established and sanctions are imposed when these
levels are exceeded. But the effort is way behind the incidence of fraud.
Kautilya's remark, made more than two millennia ago, seems to be an
apt description of the current situation (see Kautilya, 1987, p. 281). He
stated: 'just as it is impossible to know when a fish moving in water is
drinking it, so it is impossible to find out when government servants in
charge of undertakings misappropriate money'. It is now applicable to
government servants as well as those in the non-government sector,
providing services on behalf of public authorities.

Risk Sharing

The scope of public–private partnerships is expanding progressively and
is linked in many ways to the growing size of the public budget deficit.
As more pressures are felt to provide expanded services, governments
are looking for the private sector to join in investments and operations.
This approach would appear to have received additional impetus from
the recognition that many of the problems experienced in the arm's-
length relationships could be avoided by making these relationships
partnerships. This could also prove helpful, it is suggested, in reducing
the transaction costs that are inherent in any process of detailed specification of outputs and outcomes. The critics, on the other hand, argue
that under these arrangements the private sector is exploiting the opportunity while leaving the risks, particularly where there is a guaranteed
return, to governments. More significantly, the locus of expenditure
management shifts, in these cases, from government to the private
sector. The former is now viewed, for most intents, as a hobbled giant.
This whole area is one where there are few balanced judgements. Expenditure management is now required to evaluate the risks and their
potential impact on what the public authorities intend to do, and on
their budgetary operations. This is a task that in the past has often
received *ad hoc* responses from the ministries of finance; evidently,
more organized responses are indicated.

Internal Controls

The success in contracting out, whether to the corporate or non-profit
sector, is dependent, for the most part, on the way in which internal
controls are utilized in the receiving organization. In this regard, it is
noted that while the corporate sector is governed by internationally
accepted principles and standards, there are no similar specifications
for the non-governmental organizations. As these organizations become

important vehicles for the delivery of services on behalf of governments, it becomes necessary to ensure that they are equipped with adequate machinery to comply with requirements of disclosure, analysis, dissemination, standards and sanctions.[8] Meanwhile, however, despite repeated demands for audit and accountability, very little is known about the accounting practices of many of these organizations. As Herzlinger (1996 p. 75) noted, 'unlike publicly traded corporations, the performance of non-profit organisations and governments is shrouded behind a veil of secrecy that is lifted only when blatant disasters occur'. If this is the case with one of the most developed countries, the situation in the developing world and in the former centrally planned economies can be better imagined than described. This represents an area where a beginning remains to be made (1996, p. 98).

Cost of Control

Whenever there is a recognition that the public expenditure management machinery is ill equipped to manage effectively the new tasks that are imposed on it, there is invariably a demand for the establishment of additional points of control, more staff, more powers of monitoring, and greater application of technology. These additional demands are frequently made at a time when governments are faced with the more urgent task of reducing their own size, operations and outlays. But the new tasks are such that they call for a radical reorientation in the approaches and techniques of control employed by the expenditure management machinery. The traditional systems have been largely designed for situations when a major part of the service delivery was performed by government agencies themselves. With the separation of funding from delivery, a new orientation is indicated for the expenditure management machinery. Now, more skills in contracting are needed. Similarly, accounting systems must develop cost measurement and related monitoring systems. These necessarily entail more expenses and, consequently, the cost of control is likely to go up. But these costs need to be capped. In turn, this implies that each demand for an additional point of control must be evaluated in terms of its effectiveness. So far, however, the cost of control has not been explicitly recognized as an issue. The emerging public–private partnerships demand that it be taken into account in rationalizing the expenditure management machinery.

6. MONITORING

All the above tasks imply an expanded monitoring process within governments. The emphasis on a broad-based framework should not, however, be considered as an open invitation to design over-elaborate and over-specific monitoring formats and procedures. The application of the arm's-length principle implies that the other agency should be given management authority and responsibility and the public body should be more trusting and less intrusive in its approaches. Experience, however, shows that the systems are often too elaborate and more information is required to be produced at short intervals, entailing an enormous amount of work at the generating end. Moreover, the monitoring frameworks tend to be too general, seeking a universal application, while the actual need is for a customized reporting system that reflects the working realities of the reporting organization. These organizations also tend to hold the view that the enthusiasm shown in the design of the system is never matched by the effort in the actual monitoring. This generates the cynical belief that those responsible for the design of the system have very little understanding of the needs of the policy maker or the perceptions of those responsible for the submission of reports. The former expects capsule information that provides a quick survey of the benchmarks and the actual progress made. The latter, it should be noted, is the first level of management where the leakages and slippages need to be addressed, and that level would have little interest in generating data that are not directly related to its own immediate needs.

Experience also shows that the monitoring system may often emphasize the financial aspects, ignoring the linkages between physical and financial aspects. In most cases, the reports are mere chronicles of events, with no benchmarks. Reports are generally late, thus reducing their utility. Some of these aspects may be more illustrative of the organizational failures than of the limitations of monitoring design. They also show convincingly that the monitoring design should be rooted firmly in the organizational realities.

The monitoring framework should pay attention to two issues. First, there is the issue of access to information when services are provided by a separate entity, regardless of the form of ownership. Such access is usually determined in law and frequently, if experience is any guide, governments or public bodies and their audit agencies may not have the right to demand information. In the USA, however, both by tradition and by law, the General Accounting Office has legal access to the accounting records of the contractors. Such an access was only natural given that the entire funding for the services came from the government budget. Elsewhere, however, the position is less certain and it may be necessary to provide specifically for such access. As an extension of this, it should be noted that agencies engaged in the provision of services should come under some sort of scrutiny by the public. Thus either regulatory agencies may have to be empowered to undertake reviews of the working of the privately provided services or, alternatively, some standards of behaviour that go beyond the accounting area must be specified for compliance by the private agencies. As more experience was gained with the introduction of on-line systems, there would be demands for their installation in non-governmental organizations and provision of simultaneous access to the funding agencies. Such on-line systems would prove a boon from the point of view of governments. The down-side of this is that the non-governmental organizations would stand to lose their independent status in a context where technology would unwittingly pave the way for vertical integration between the buyer and provider. Experience shows that the monitoring of privately provided services is far too important to be left to the government alone. Such monitoring should seek to provide information to the public. In turn, the content of that information as well as its periodicity need to be specified so that the public would have ready access to it.

Second, the above aspect also shows that the monitoring framework should not be viewed as a limited bilateral transaction between the financing and service-providing agencies. Rather it should be seen as a tripartite relationship between the public, the government and the private agencies. This recognition implies that two aspects merit more detailed attention:

1. The specification and promotion of standards regarding the business activities of the private agency are essential steps, and should not be regarded as substitutes for effective financial and management systems in the agencies. The public and the government must have opportunities to assure themselves that those systems are adequate. The need for such an assurance is an inevitable part of the emerging new framework in which the 'production' function would mostly be in the sphere of the private sector and the 'distribution and stabilization' functions in the realm of the government. Its capacity to perform the latter two roles would be adversely affected if the former were not equipped with dependable management structures and laws.

2. The reporting framework needs to recognize explicitly the diverse

requirements of the different segments of the public, that is, media, security dealers, public, legislature and other groups. Experience shows that while these groups have some common core elements on which information is sought, there are also different requirements. These need to be taken into account and efforts made to ensure that the monitoring framework is not so elaborate as to discourage the primary generator of data from being an active participant in the process. The effectiveness of the much-needed dialogue between the three parties depends on the attention paid to these aspects. Moreover, the same type of service may be provided by more than one level of government. In such cases, the public would like to have a monitoring framework that enables them to assess the relative capabilities of each level of government.

7. EVALUATION

It is generally recognized that although evaluation has been in the fiscal management landscape for more than three decades, its application has been, by and large, limited, with the result that it is still considered to be in a formative or incipient stage. Evaluation has, however, become even more important in a context where publicly funded services are increasingly provided by the private agencies. Despite this importance, it has not received much attention in the literature. Therefore it is appropriate that the discussion of this aspect is undertaken in a somewhat normative tone. The two essential questions that need to be answered are: what are the specific purposes of evaluation in this context? And what are the issues that need to be addressed?

Purposes of Evaluation

Evaluation, as is generally recognized, is different from monitoring in that the latter is concerned with the ongoing operation of projects and programmes while the former is concerned with their impact and results.[9] The purpose of evaluation is to ascertain whether the underlying objectives of programmes have been achieved and whether more could have been done with the allotted resources. In the context of public–private partnership, however, there are additional criteria that need to be addressed by the evaluation system, such as the following:

- An implicit proof must be provided. This proof is that the private provision is indeed a better alternative to the direct provision of services by the state.

- Evaluation should demonstrate that there is no unethical behaviour in the selection and management of projects and that these projects and programmes have not become surrogates for government as domains of patronage created at public expense but maintained outside the realm of institutional scrutiny.
- The public is getting value for money.
- The lessons of evaluation can be harnessed for designing improved delivery systems of services.

These criteria reflect a broad-based concern and to that extent impose additional tasks on evaluation. In addressing them, however, experience suggests that more attention needs to be paid to the following issues.

A vexatious issue that remains to be resolved relates to the location of evaluation responsibility. When evaluation is undertaken by the agency concerned, it tends to be, human nature being what it is, very subjective and self-serving. On the other hand, an external agency organized specifically for the purpose can become a bastion or a cult of perpetual criticism, often contributing to an adversarial atmosphere that in turn may reduce the effectiveness of evaluation. Each approach has its advantages and abuses, but in making the final choice, it has to be ensured that, in either event, there is openness in decision making and that the public has access to the agency's records.

Another major issue relates to the design of evaluation itself. Experience of industrial countries clearly shows that this is often a contentious issue in that it tends to reflect the bias of those designing the survey. In part this is inevitable, as the links between process and outputs are not always precise expressions of causal relationships. An increase in the number of teachers may not always contribute to higher educational standards, which are the results of a large multitude of tangible and intangible factors. The difficulties of evaluation have to be explicitly noted if it is to become a viable instrument of management and if it is to be accepted by the public.

8. CONCLUSIONS

The preceding discussion, which is summarized in Table 3.4, shows that expenditure management machinery has to be updated in order to meet the new demands. In undertaking the various tasks, it is to be remembered, as Darwin noted, that 'it is not the strongest of the species

Table 3.4 Public–private partnerships: impact on public expenditure management

Area	Impact
Resource allocation	Impact is different depending on the type of arrangements with the private sector. Where the role of the private sector is viewed as a supplier of services/goods in response to a bid, governments would be expected, as a minimum, to have full completed cost estimates of the proposed contract. Where the private sector is viewed as a partner, governments would need to be assured of risk implications as well as the continued maintenance outlays on completed projects
Specification of responsibilities	The responsibilities of each party need to be spelled out in detail
Budgetary decision making	Specification of the role of the private sector as a partner would continue to be undertaken as a part of central policies of governments. The sectors as well as the projects to be handed over to the private sector would be specified as a part of the national plans or similar macroeconomic framework.

In regard to individual contracts, the concerned agencies in government would be dependent on internal information systems and on reports furnished by contractors to determine the next year's outlay. Formulation of annual budget estimates for demand-driven entitlement tends to be difficult and even a small error in this regard can add to the fragility of budget balance. The most important considerations in the award of contracts are cost and financial implications of risk. Where it is difficult to gain information on these aspects, the agency awarding the contract would be dependent on the contractor and the latter would have many opportunities to manipulate the contract, despite all legal specifications, and in some cases, because of them, in their favour.

Further, where the government provides a guarantee on a net rate of return for the contractor, there would be little incentive for him to economize on costs

Budget implementation	Specification of advance payments, as is the case in most contracts, contributes to liquidity strains for the government. Regular monitoring is needed within government to oversee the progress in the provision of the service and the quality of the service. Frequently, contractors try to accelerate the progress of projects so that they can shift their capital to other operations. This may add to the liquidity strains of government and where the magnitude of payments is high, such accelerated completion of projects may have a short-term adverse impact on the size of the budget deficit.
	Performance monitoring is a vital ingredient of this phase of public expenditure management. As an integral part of this effort, quality control systems are essential in major areas such as administration of benefit or entitlement programmes
Resource utilization and evaluation	Evaluation of the services provided is important not merely to ascertain the fulfilment of contractual obligations but, more significant, to explore ways in which the delivery could be made in a more cost-effective manner
Resource use accounting	A system of recording limited to cash flows – from government to contractors – has obvious shortcomings. Therefore the accounting system should also have accrual-based recording to register the assets and liabilities and to monitor the cost drivers

that survives, not the most intelligent: it is the one that is most adaptable
to change'. The challenge for public authorities is to adapt their
machinery, their approaches to decision making, and their day-to-day
work, to the changing patterns and realities.

NOTES

1. Views expressed are personal and do not in any way represent those of the Inter-
    national Monetary Fund.
2. See Ingram and Smith (1993, p. 3). It may be noted in passing that the American
    experience in this regard reveals an irony. Salamon states that social institutions
    aimed at providing private solutions to public problems have experienced the most
    dramatic growth during precisely the period of most rapid expansion of the state. To
    a large extent, the growth in this social institution was fuelled by the extension of
    the American welfare state. See Salamon (1995, p. 1).
3. The term 'purchases' as used in the paper includes leasing arrangements. For a
    discussion of leasing arrangements, see Bodsma (1995).
4. For an illustration of what business can do for governments, see Goldsmith (1997)
    who reflects on his experience as Mayor of Indianapolis, Indiana, USA.
5. Mintzberg (1996) also argues that the dichotomy of public and private sectors does
    not fully reflect the reality. His concern relates to the exclusion of cooperatively
    owned organizations from consideration.
6. For a detailed discussion of grants-in-aid, see Grove (1952) and Premchand (1963).
7. This phenomenon is not limited to developing countries. Smith and Lipsky (1993)
    have provided ample evidence to show that it is also a common problem in the USA,
    particularly at the level of state governments.
8. See Herzlinger (1996) and the extensive correspondence that her article evoked from
    prominent politicians and management gurus including Peter Drucker. See *Harvard
    Business Review* (May–June 1996, pp. 164–71).
9. A more detailed discussion of these and related aspects is provided in Premchand
    (1993, pp. 204–5).

REFERENCES

Bodsma, Peter B. (1995), 'Leasing in the public sector with special reference to
    the Netherlands', *Public Finance*, **50** (2), 182–200.
Domberger, Simon and Hall, Christine (1996), 'Contracting for public services: a
    review of Antipodean experience', *Public Administration*, **14**, Spring, 129–47.
Edwards, Michael and Hulme, David (eds) (1995), *Non-Government Organiza-
    tions – Performance and Accountability*, London: Earthscan Publications.
Gansler, Jacques S. (1989), *Affording Defense*, Cambridge, MA: The MIT Press.
Goldsmith, Stephen (1997), 'Can business really do business with government?',
    Harvard Business Review, May–June, 110–21.
Herzlinger, Regina E. (1996), 'Can public trust in nonprofits and governments
    be restored?', *Harvard Business Review*, May–June, pp. 75–83.
Ingram, Helen and Smith, Steven Rathgeb (eds) (1993), *Public Policy for
    Democracy*, Washington, DC: The Brookings Institution.
Kautilya (1987), *The Arthashastra*, New Delhi: Penguin Books India.

Mintzberg, Henry (1996), 'Musings on Management', *Harvard Business Review*, July–August, 61.

Premchand, A. (1963), *Control of Public Expenditure in India*, New Delhi: Allied Publishers.

Premchand, A. (1993), *Public Expenditure Management*, Washington, DC: International Monetary Fund.

Salamon, Lester M. (1995), *Partners in Public Service*, Baltimore, MD: Johns Hopkins University Press.

Smith, Steven Rathgeb and Lipsky, Michael (1993), *Non Profits for Hire*, Cambridge, MA: Harvard University Press.

4. The multilateral institutions and budget accountability in Jamaica[1]

Jane Harrigan

1. INTRODUCTION

Since the early 1990s international aid agencies have become increasingly concerned with the issue of good governance in aid recipients. The concept of good governance encompasses such issues as: respect for human rights; encouragement of political pluralism, particularly in the form of multi-party democracy; and promotion of transparent and accountable government. Multilateral and bilateral donors have promoted good governance in two ways: by withholding aid funds from countries which refuse to move towards good governance; and by providing finance to support projects which improve the quality of governance.

It is widely agreed that accountability is a fundamental tenet of good governance (Hyden and Bratton, 1992, p. 14; World Bank, 1992; Healey and Tordoff, 1995). Accountable governance means holding those in public office who manage political affairs and public resources responsible for their actions and performance. This concept of accountability encompasses both political accountability, by which political leaders are held accountable to their people, and administrative accountability, by which the public administration or bureaucracy is held accountable to the political leadership and the people.

This chapter analyses one particular aspect of accountability, namely the positive and negative effects of IMF stabilization programmes and World Bank structural adjustment programmes on the accountability of public expenditure management in Jamaica. The chapter focuses particularly on the accountability implications of the meso-level reforms that formed part of these stabilization and adjustment programmes, and includes a detailed consideration of these effects within the health sector. It covers the period 1980–92 when the multilateral institutions were particularly heavily involved in the Jamaican economy and before the 1993 re-election of the People's National Party (PNP) government under its new leader P.J. Patterson, who was committed to improving accountability.

Since 1978 Jamaica has been under a series of IMF- and World Bank-guided economic reform programmes. The objective was to restore macroeconomic balance by controlling the budget deficit and adjusting the exchange rate (guided by the IMF loan conditions) whilst promoting diversified private sector export-led growth (guided by the World Bank loan conditions). A policy framework was devised aimed at reducing the government's direct and regulatory involvement in the economy through removal of import restrictions, divestment of state enterprises, and reduction of price and exchange rate controls. Incentives to attract private investment, particularly foreign investment in new export sectors, were also established (Harrigan, 1991). Jamaican policy makers, however, have been able to get away with a fair amount of slippage on implementing these reform programmes, partly because large inflows of American aid, aimed at stopping the spread of Castro's communism in the Caribbean basin, have reduced the government's dependence on IMF and World Bank Finance (ibid.). It is a central contention of this chapter that the Jamaican government exhibited slippage on the IMF budget deficit reduction targets by introducing countervailing actions that had negative accountability implications.

The involvement of the IMF, the World Bank and other donors in the Jamaican economy affected public expenditure in three distinct ways: influencing the allocation of resources within the budget; advocating and supporting reforms to improve general financial management in the public sector; and setting macroeconomic targets under stabilization and structural adjustment programmes which affected the nature and outcome of the state budgetary process. As this chapter will show, tensions and conflicts existed between these three types of influence.

The analysis of public expenditure accountability in Jamaica used the following criteria of accountability: the representation of societal interests and political responsiveness to interest groups; the degree of openness and transparency in public expenditure decision making; the opportunity for debate and dialogue; the government's monitoring and evaluation of its own performance, including the extent to which expenditure outcomes reflected intentions; the effectiveness of checks on public expenditure, including that of the legislature in approving and scrutinizing expenditure and that of investigative audit and follow-up sanctions; and the neutrality and accountability of the bureaucracy in posing options to the political executive.

A broader study on budget accountability found several fundamental accountability weaknesses in Jamaica's public expenditure management (Harrigan, 1995). These included: lack of public understanding of, and participation in, the budgetary process; lack of consultation outside government; an ineffective parliamentary estimates committee; budgetary timetables and procedures which lacked credibility due to a disorderly and uncoordinated budgetary process which was fragmented amongst many agencies; recourse to special and often concealed expenditures which fell outside the budgetary process; an emasculated ministry of finance which no longer played a coordinating role; weak and unreliable initial expenditure guidelines leading to a mark-up budget mentality; a political executive which intervened late and arbitrarily in the budget process such that line ministries did not feel they 'owned' the final budget; frequent and large supplementary budgets which were retrospectively approved; crisis management budget slashing which undermined transparency; and resource allocation influenced by political clientelism.

Some facets of IMF and World Bank involvement in the Jamaican economy helped to improve the accountability of public expenditure management whilst other aspects had a strong negative impact. Particular attention is given to the negative accountability effects of IMF budget deficit reduction targets imposed on a government uncommitted to meeting such targets. Many of the arguments presented in this chapter relate to expenditure accountability problems more generally and it cannot be proved that IMF conditionality was the sole cause of these problems, although it contributed. This argument is based on a large number of semi-structured interviews conducted in 1993 with Jamaican bureaucrats, politicians, donors, academics and private sector representatives and on analysis of the existing literature and data.

The conclusion reached is that donor-guided reform programmes have complex and often conflicting impacts on the accountability of the government's budgetary practices. This finding is important for three reasons. First, it shows that there is no simple positive correlation between economic stabilization and liberalization programmes, such as those promoted by IMF conditionality, and accountability, despite such a belief being implicit in much of the donor rhetoric on good governance (Wapenhans, 1994). Second, donors often try to use conditionality to promote accountability in countries undertaking IMF programmes even though such programmes can undermine accountability in the important sphere of public expenditure management. Third, donor conditionality generates accountability to external agencies sometimes at the cost of deteriorating internal accountability to the electorate.

Section 2 of this chapter looks at positive accountability effects caused by macro-level reforms. Section 3 analyses meso-level reforms affecting accountability and Section 4 assesses externally guided reforms which have negatively affected the accountability of the budgetary process. Section 5 takes a detailed look at the negative effects of IMF programmes on public expenditure accountability in the health sector; Section 6 concludes. Section 7 is a postscript which describes more recent reforms affecting budgetary accountability in the 1990s.

2. POSITIVE EFFECTS CAUSED BY MACRO-LEVEL REFORMS

The IMF's economic stabilization programme in Jamaica had several direct and indirect effects which helped to improve public expenditure accountability. A key component of the Fund's programme in the early 1990s was liberalization of the foreign exchange market designed to correct an overvalued currency. This reform has helped to make fiscal policy more transparent and hence more accountable in an unexpected manner. The previous fixed exchange rate regime enabled the government to spread the macroeconomic costs of fiscal deficits over time by using loss-making Bank of Jamaica operations to defend the value of the currency. Liberalization of the exchange rate means that the government is no longer able to mask and postpone the macroeconomic effects of fiscal deficits through annual Bank of Jamaica losses. Instead, fiscal indiscipline rapidly manifests itself in the form of exchange rate depreciation and inflation. Since 1991 rapid currency depreciation and inflation have helped to focus media, public, external agency and hence government attention on off-budget expenditures, fiscal accounting inconsistencies, and the true scale of the overall government deficit. The new market-driven transparency of fiscal outcomes has given the private sector a much stronger urge to participate in the public expenditure decision-making process so as to avoid excessive budget deficits (Private Sector Organisation of Jamaica, 1992). This is because the high levels of inflation and large exchange rate depreciations to which fiscal deficits now give rise create business uncertainty, increase the need for working capital, and increase the price of imported inputs:

> Following the removal of exchange controls the private sector now has a much greater reason to be concerned with fiscal policy. What is needed is better management by Government of its finances in a way that doesn't debauch the currency. (Personal interview, Private Sector Organisation of Jamaica representative)

The general macroeconomic stability which is the aim of an IMF stabilization programme also helps to avoid the practice of resorting to supplementary budgets. In Jamaica supplementary budgets reduce public expenditure accountability in that such budgets, which are retro-spectively approved by parliament, are not subject to the normal scrutiny of the budgetary process. An unstable macroeconomic environment increases the use of supplementary budgets, since unpredictable inflation and exchange rate depreciation often lead to budget under-estimates which must be made good through supplementary budgets. This relationship was particularly marked in the early 1990s when macro-instability re-emerged. For example, in 1991, when inflation peaked at 51 per cent and the exchange rate depreciated by 69 per cent (Table 4.1) the supplementary budget stood at a massive 21.4 per cent of the initial budget estimates (Table 4.2). Interviews with budgetary staff in the Jamaican Ministry of Health support this view. Five out of eight staff interviewed, when asked what three factors most influenced the use of supplementary budgets, pointed to uncertainties in the form of inflation and/or movements in the exchange rate.

On a broader level, IMF and World Bank programmes in Jamaica have helped to shift the general focus of politics towards issues of accountability. Since 1980 the dictates of IMF macroeconomic stabiliz-ation and World Bank structural adjustment programmes in Jamaica have left little scope for ideological debates on the merits of the mixed economy versus the market economy or on state-led versus private sector-led growth paths. As a result the country's two main political parties, the People's National Party (PNP) and the Jamaican Labour Party (JLP), have converged in terms of both ideology and policy actions. This has enabled the focus of Jamaican politics to shift away

Table 4.1   Macroeconomic indicators

| | Year | | | | | | | | | | | |
	1981	1982	1983	1984	1985	1986	1987	1988	1989	1990	1991	1992
Exchange rate:												
J$ per US$	1.78	1.78	3.28	4.93	5.48	5.48	5.49	5.49	6.48	8.04	21.49	22.96
Inflation:												
CPI %	12.9	6.5	11.1	27.8	25.6	15.1	7.0	10.0	14.4	22.6	51.1	77.2
Overall deficit:												
% of GDP	20.3	17.5	17.1	5.9	8.3	9.4	3.6	14.0	5.1	6.2	6.1	N/A

Source: IMF, *Financial Statistics Yearbook*, various years; Government of Jamaica, *Economic and Social Survey*, various years.

Table 4.2 Initial and supplementary budgets, 1980/81–1991/92 (J$ mn)

	Year											
	1980/81	1981/82	1982/83	1983/84	1984/85	1985/86	1986/87	1987/88	1988/89	1989/90	1990/91	1991/92
Total budget, initial estimates	2076	2632	2771	3227	3905	4732	5832	6966	8058	9052	11 145	14 773
Total budget, revised estimates	2466	2681	2920	3468	3754	4704	5733	6580	9164	9867	11 461	17 939
Total supplementary budget as % of initial budget[a]	18.8	1.9	5.4	7.5	–3.9	–0.6	–1.7	–5.5	13.7	9.0	2.8	21.4

[a] The difference between the initial estimates and the revised estimates gives the size of the supplementary budget.

from the content of economic policy towards issues concerning the implementation of policy, encompassing participation, consensus, transparency and other accountability dimensions of public policy, including management of public expenditure (Harrigan, 1995; Nettleford, 1992).

> The lack of ideological difference between the parties means that the opposition can concentrate more on Government performance and accountability than on policies. The 1993 election, for example, was one of style not substance, characterised by the lack of ideological divide and by absence of polarising issues in the campaign. (Personal interview, Jamaican academic)

3. MESO-LEVEL REFORMS AFFECTING ACCOUNTABILITY

Whilst reforms guided by the IMF impacted on macro-policy in ways which helped to improve accountability, meso-level reforms supported by other multi- and bilateral donors, particularly the World Bank, also had positive effects on the accountability of public expenditure management. One important avenue through which this occurred was Jamaica's Administrative Reform Programme (ARP). Launched in 1983, this programme, supported by the World Bank, had two main objectives: to improve productivity in the delivery of goods and services to the public; and to improve accountability (Mills and Slyfield, 1987). Reforms focused on restructuring the line agencies to improve their performance in service delivery. This was supported by reforms to strengthen the central core institutions, such as the Ministry of Public Service and Ministry of Finance, so as to increase the effectiveness of their policy leadership and their regulatory, facilitative and monitoring roles. This included establishment of a Budget Reform Cell and a Fiscal Policy Management Unit in the Ministry of Finance.

The ARP introduced annual rolling corporate plans for each ministry which were designed to make ministries more responsive to client needs and which required a clear statement of policy targets within the context of a medium-term strategic plan for each ministry. Such planning provides a potential avenue for interest-group input to public expenditure strategies and may well help to improve policy transparency by providing a clear statement of intentions by which to judge actual outcomes.

Another important reform under the ARP has been computerization of all government accounting and finance systems. This has helped to improve the efficacy of the Accountant General's (AG) work, which serves as an important check and control on the accountability of public expenditure. Computerization helped overcome problems caused by staff shortages in the AG's department, which meant that in the past much of the department's work consisted of ticking figures and tracking accounting errors rather than more investigative-type work which is fundamental to the accountability process.

The introduction of programme budgets under the ARP has helped to make ministry budgets easier to evaluate by presenting a functional classification of expenditure. The new functional structure is able to reflect government and ministry priorities which are specified in both national plans and in ministries' corporate plans. By linking financial inputs with targeted physical outputs, programme budgeting also makes the implications of expenditure cuts/increases more transparent in terms of end results and outcomes. This has helped to reduce the opacity and politicization of budget formulation.

World Bank and IMF involvement in the Jamaican economy since the early 1980s has also helped to strengthen the use of rolling Public Sector Investment Programmes (PSIPs) which establish medium-term expenditure priorities. Before this there was little in the way of coherent and meaningful public investment strategies, particularly as political parties seldom produced timely election manifestos. This made it difficult for groups outside government to play an effective role in inputting to, and scrutinizing, public investment decisions, despite the fact that interest groups are articulate and well organized in Jamaica.

Although the use of a PSIP provides an avenue for interest-group and line-ministry inputs to investment decisions, the influence of donors in shaping the PSIP has, however, had some countervailing accountability effects. Line ministries, for example, frequently complain that they are not adequately consulted by the Planning Institute and Ministry of Finance regarding the components of the PSIP – a common complaint in aid-dependent economies where much of the PSIP is donor-funded. In Jamaica's case the Planning Institute is given a dominant role, along with the Ministry of Finance, in the formation of the PSIP by virtue of the fact that they are the main points of contact with external donors, and are particularly keen to pull in foreign exchange through donor projects. This foreign exchange pressure, particularly when combined with the absence of a guiding national plan built up from line-ministry inputs, tends to result in reduced line-ministry contributions to the formulation of the PSIP.

As a result, the PSIP has been determined more by contact with donors, including the World Bank, than with line ministries and Jamaican society. One manifestation of this was the introduction in the early 1990s of 20 externally funded 'fast-track' investment projects which were regarded as being at the heart of the budget, the motivation being to protect these projects from cuts in government counterpart funding and to speed up implementation by ensuring timely release of expenditure warrants. The 20 'fast-track' projects were chosen by the Ministry of Finance and Planning Institute in consultation with donors in a non-transparent manner and with little input from the ministries or society at large. The overall effect has been to reduce participation in budget formulation as the 20 projects have been taken out of the normal budget negotiation.

Economic liberalization has been an important facet of World Bank and IMF policy-based lending in Jamaica. One manifestation of this has been the liberalization of the ownership of the electronic media in the early 1990s. The semi-state monopoly over the electronic media ended when liberalization led to the formation of a second independent television station, CMTV, and a proliferation of new radio stations, both national and local. This new pluralism in the electronic media has vastly increased the amount of political commentary and analysis, particularly on issues concerning economic policy, public sector management and accountability, and has helped to promote popular involvement in the decision-making process. Of the 45 interviewees in Jamaica who were asked what five factors had most influenced government accountability, 18 pointed to recent changes in the media as having a positive effect:

> Radio is the main form of mass media reaching the majority of people. The new pluralism in the electronic media is a major development which has vastly increased the amount of political commentary and analysis. This has focused particularly on economic issues, on public sector ethics and management and on the need for more popular involvement in decision-making. This has had a strong consciousness-raising effect. (Personal interview, Jamaican political commentator).

In summary, IMF and World Bank involvement in the Jamaican economy has led to numerous macro- and meso-level reforms which have affected positively the accountability of public sector expenditure and other aspects of public policy management. This, however, has been counterbalanced by a wide range of negative effects which are analysed below.

4.   EXTERNALLY GUIDED REFORMS INIMICAL TO ACCOUNTABILITY

Jamaica has had to implement externally guided economic reform programmes and austerity measures in a difficult socioeconomic environment characterized by: a strong welfare state mentality; aspirations by most of the population to living standards far beyond the economy's slender resource base; a tradition of trade union affiliations on the part of both political parties, with the associated expectation that governments should protect real wages in the formal economy; and strong private sector interest groups. In order to carry through harsh IMF and World Bank economic adjustment programmes in such an environment, governments resorted to a centralized, non-participatory, non-consensual and less accountable style of government. This was particularly true of the JLP government led by Edward Seaga in power for much of the 1980s (Harrigan, 1991). Private sector interest groups such as the Chamber of Commerce and the Private Sector Organisation of Jamaica (PSOJ – an umbrella group acting for a large number of private sector groups such as the Manufacturers' Association, the Exporters' Association, and various professional bodies) all found their ability to influence policy making significantly reduced during the 1980s as a result of Seaga's non-consensual leadership style, his suspicion of the indigenous private sector and his desire to cater to foreign investors:

> Although a number of policy committees representing private sector interests were set up to enable an active private sector role in policy formulation, there was a constant echo in private sector circles that the Seaga Government was not consulting them enough and that they were constantly faced by new policy announcements through the mass media. (Stone, 1989, p. 29)

This criticism was shared by the public at large, who felt that there should be more private sector participation in national policy making (ibid., Table 4.6). The PSOJ has felt all the more frustrated because it has clear, consistent and well articulated views on fiscal policy issues, which have been presented in occasional position papers (PSOJ, 1992), arguing for a balanced budget, separation of monetary and fiscal responsibilities, increased social welfare expenditures and improved accountability for parastatal expenditures. Although these papers were presented to the Prime Minister, the Minister of Finance and the media, the lack of an effective collaborative working arrangement meant that they made little direct impact on policy outcomes.

The move to non-participatory government in the 1980s occurred at the same time as IMF and World Bank programmes shifted the focus of Jamaican politics away from ideological issues towards issues concerning policy implementation, including accountability dimensions. Taken together, these two conflicting trends help to explain the deep-seated feeling of political alienation and cynicism which pervaded Jamaican society by the early 1990s and which, in its own right, has serious implications for future accountability (Nettleford, 1992).

One of the most important aspects of IMF programmes in Jamaica during the 1980s and the early 1990s was the setting of budgetary targets in order to reduce a large public sector deficit. Interviews with Jamaican civil servants and politicians involved in budgetary processes suggest that imposition of such externally imposed targets has had numerous negative accountability effects.[2] Eleven out of the 19 interviewees in this category responded positively when asked whether IMF budget targets had had negative effects on domestic accountability of government. Discussions on this issue suggested that, first and foremost, fiscal responsibility has been seen to depend on external pressure. Accountability to the multilateral institutions has been a more important goal for the political leadership than accountability to parliament and the public. Hence the process of budgetary debate has tended to be taken out of national institutions.

More generally, the use of IMF targets has inhibited the development of a set of norms and procedures geared to creating and sustaining appropriate and accountable fiscal behaviour. Instead, the use of IMF targets has: promoted a 'meet the target at any cost' mentality; shortened the time-horizon for budgeting; led to a focus on avoiding IMF programme disruption rather than on creating long-term fiscal balance; tended to lead to across-the-board expenditure cut-backs in the context of crisis management; and has encouraged an inefficient 'on-again', 'off-again' warrant release expenditure pattern throughout the year (USAID, 1992). Hence political accountability in the form of democratic participation in a transparent public expenditure process has been sacrificed to a narrower concept of target-based accountability to an external agency. In the words of USAID, an important donor in the Jamaican economy:

> Budgetary targets are not self-implementing and, by themselves, do not necessarily lead to improved procedures and the establishment of effective norms. Performance targets have a built-in tendency to sacrifice the long-term interests of the country to short-term imperatives. Externally-imposed targets can be no substitute for long-term political commitment to financial responsibility and the domestic technical capacity to transform that commitment into an effective and sustainable process. (USAID, 1992, p. 6)

Clearly the IMF budget targets have encouraged a budget management mentality which conflicts with the other type of external agency role, namely, the sponsoring of reforms such as the ARP, designed to improve the quality of budget management.

The crisis management approach to budgeting, whereby budgets are slashed by politicians at the last minute in order to meet stringent quarterly IMF expenditure targets, has been particularly inimical to accountability. The practice has reduced transparency, participation and consensus and has led to a feeling that public expenditure decisions are unduly politicized and then rubber-stamped by the legislature. It has also encouraged staff to submit inflated historic mark-up budget esti-mates and has left down-stream staff feeling that they do not own the final budgets they were expected to work with. As shown in Section 5 of this chapter, these tendencies were particularly marked in the Min-istry of Health.

Other aspects of the government's response to the IMF budget deficit reduction targets have also helped to undermine public expenditure transparency and accountability. The public expenditure pressures on government created by the electorate's dependency attitudes towards the state within the context of a parliamentary democracy have meant that neither JLP nor PNP governments have been politically committed to achieving the IMF targets. Hence, in the words of one private sector observer:

> Successive governments have viewed the IMF as a necessary evil and have sought to circumvent rather than comply with various conditionalities. In the 1980s governments developed expertise in masking the fiscal position and used a plethora of entities to keep funds from IMF scrutiny. The Bank of Jamaica has been drawn into this process. (Personal interview, PSOJ representative)

This reduced transparency of fiscal accounts was the combined result of competing pressures, namely: pressure from external organizations and the private sector to reduce the budget deficit; government depen-dence on financial flows from external organizations; and weak government commitment to fiscal austerity due to the desire to fulfil populist election pledges.

The trend towards lack of transparency in fiscal accounts intensified from the mid-1980s onwards. Between 1986 and 1989 the JLP govern-ment, facing declining popularity due to the social welfare effects of past budgetary austerity, sought to boost expenditures whilst remaining within the deficit targets set by the IMF. Likewise the post-1989 new PNP administration struggled with the competing pressures of fulfilling its election mandate to 'put people first' whilst simultaneously attempting to live down its image as the party of financial indiscipline, inherited from the late 1970s by appearing to adhere to tight IMF targets. These governments resorted to a variety of measures to conceal the true magnitude of the budget deficit from the IMF. The problem with such practices, however, is that they also resulted in concealment from the Jamaican public to whom both politicians and bureaucrats should have been held responsible. Interviews conducted with Jamaican civil servants from numerous ministries, including the Ministry of Finance, staff from the Bank of Jamaica, private sector observers and Jamaican academics all suggested that a variety of concealment practices were used by governments.

The growth of off-budget expenditures has been used by successive governments as the main means to reconcile competing pressures. The major item of such off-budget expenditures has been Bank of Jamaica losses, with revamped Bank of Jamaica/government accounting proce-dures enabling the government to treat its interest obligations on government securities, and on IMF obligations and other balance of payments loans, as off-budget expenditures financed through the Bank of Jamaica overdraft.[3] Essentially the Bank of Jamaica meets these expenditures on behalf of government and reflects this in its accounts as advances to government. These items do not therefore appear in government expenditure accounts.

In the later 1980s, the Ministry of Finance increasingly used its Bank of Jamaica overdraft facility to finance public sector deficits. Through this mech-anism, since 1987, the fiscal deficit has been basically transferred to the BoJ. (USAID, 1992, p. 12)

This practice became particularly pronounced in the late 1980s by a new PNP government concerned to accommodate both the private sector and the IMF by recording a budget surplus. Although the public sector deficit appeared to improve, with the fiscal budget (net of interest and amortization payments) registering large surpluses from 1989 onwards, the growing lack of fiscal policy transparency has led many analysts to suggest that the fiscal improvement was more apparent than real (USAID, 1992). Table 4.3 supports this analysis, showing the correlation between the increase in the recorded fiscal surplus and the sharp increase in the government's debts to the Bank of Jamaica. The sums involved are substantial.

In addition to the inflationary and exchange rate pressures caused by the above erosion of monetary policy independence and the merging of fiscal and monetary policy, accountability of public expenditure man-agement has been severely undermined. The opaque nature of off-

Table 4.3 Government budget and overdraft with Bank of Jamaica (current J$ mn)

	Year												
	1978/79	1979/80	1980/81	1981/82	1982/83	1983/84	1984/85	1985/86	1986/87	1987/88	1988/89	1989/90	1990/91	1991/92
Due from government to Bank of Jamaica	64	427	615	540	821	1249	1687	2369	2553	4489	5158	5370	8280	19 780
Fiscal deficit/surplus	−364	−291	−434	−498	−326	−180	524	1066	1290	1662	567	2801	2658	1568

Note: Due from government includes: government agencies' overdrafts with the Bank; items in process of collection; advances to Consolidated Fund; exchange losses and interest paid, i.e. amounts advanced to cover exchange losses realized on repayment of government foreign liabilities, interest thereon, and interest paid on certificates of deposit.

Source: Bank of Jamaica *Reports*, various years.

budget expenditures, particularly those involving the Bank of Jamaica, has made it very difficult to evaluate fiscal performance. Persistently high inflation, excess liquidity, and downward pressure on the exchange rate, particularly in the early 1990s (Table 4.1) all suggest that the official fiscal deficit figures belie the true nature of fiscal policy.[4]

Other methods used by the government to conceal public expenditure from the IMF include: shifting expenditure to a highly unaccountable parastatal sector; resorting to the use of supplementary budgets later in the fiscal year; and failing to record transfers in kind from external agencies.[5]

Lack of financial accountability in the parastatal sector (statutory bodies, public corporations and state-owned companies) is of particular importance to the overall assessment of the accountability of public expenditure management because of ways in which parastatals have been used in Jamaica as a means of bypassing the normal checks and controls on central government expenditures (Mills, 1990, p. 344):

> In the 1980s parastatals were used to mask the fiscal position of Government. Initially funds were shifted to larger parastatals. When these came under scrutiny activities were moved to smaller bodies such as the National Housing Corporation and small Government companies like the Bauxite Trading Company and the Oil Trading Company. Funds were parked in these entities so that they were available for expenditure without being reflected in Central Government expenditure accounts. Many of these bodies were accountable to their Board but not to Parliament. (Personal interview, representative of Private Sector Organisation of Jamaica)

> Parastatals can get away with a lot because the Ministry of Finance control units are understaffed and weak. There is such a large number of parastatals that they are monitored by exception. (Personal interview with USAID staff)

Many of the activities of parastatals are inherently central government activities which have been shifted to parastatals in order to circumvent IMF budget targets and civil service pay ceilings. Occasionally this appears to be linked to the workings of clientelist politics. Lump-sum subventions are made to bodies which fall outside the central government system in order to escape direct accountability for the politically motivated use of public funds. The potential to use the parastatal sector to promote clientelistic public expenditures is furthered by the political nature of many parastatal boards. Board seats offer considerable patronage potential both via direct salaries and via the award of parastatal contracts to private companies in which board members might be majority shareholders.

The parastatal sector in Jamaica is one of the few areas where lax financial accountability can be attributed to an ambiguous legal frame-work of checks and controls rather than to the way in which a clearly specified scrutiny system is interpreted and implemented. There is no clearly defined system of checks and controls on the financial activities of these bodies and until 1992 there was virtually no adaptation of the legislation to allow proper parliamentary control. Under the 1959 Financial Administration and Audit Act (FAA Act), each parastatal must come under a ministry portfolio, with the minister responsible to parliament for the parastatal's activities. However, before the 1992 Amendment of the FAA Act, the definition of public bodies and their legal obligations was ambiguous. As a result the Accountant General and the Public Accounts Committee of parliament received very little information on the financial activities of parastatals, particularly those designated as public companies. The submission of audited accounts three to four years late, or the failure to submit at all, has been a constant issue raised in the Accountant General's annual report.

Understaffing of the Public Enterprises Division of the Ministry of Finance means that it has been unable to fulfil its supervisory duties. As a result, most parastatals are monitored only in exceptional circum-stances and no single institution has an overall picture of the impact of the parastatal sector on public expenditure. Monitoring by exception is hardly surprising given the lack of information on the exact number and nature of these bodies. Although the Prime Minister's Office recorded the existence of over 300 parastatals (Government of Jamaica, 1991), it was only able to name 114, whilst the Nettleford Commission was only able to identify half of these 114 (Nettleford, 1992, p. 14).

An important feature of Jamaica's public expenditure practices that has accountability implications is the use of supplementary budgets. The difference between initial budget estimates and revised budget estimates gives the size of the supplementary budget. Initial budget esti-mates acceptable to the IMF are often modified later in the fiscal year by supplementary budgets. This practice not only reflects fiscal indiscipline; it also reduces accountability since parliament is often required to provide *ex-post* approval for expenditure over-runs by voting through a supplementary budget. Table 4.2 gives the magnitude of such budgets and shows that the post-1989 PNP government has resorted to much larger supplementaries than the 1980–89 JLP govern-ment, supporting the commonly held view that the PNP is the party of weaker fiscal discipline. The sums involved in this practice are significant and by the early 1990s exceeded 20 per cent of the initial budget.

Practices such as using the Bank of Jamaica, shifting expenditure to parastatals and recourse to supplementary budgets have contributed to a fragmentation of public expenditure in Jamaica in a manner detrimental to accountability. One major facet of fragmentation has been the weakening of the Ministry of Finance. During the 1980s, for example, the Ministry was unable to retain top talent due to civil service salary limitations which were in place to help the government meet IMF expenditure ceilings.[6] The government responded to this dilemma by transferring ministry functions to statutory bodies who were able to pay higher salaries, such as the Bank of Jamaica, the National Planning Authority and the Revenue Board. This fragmentation of activities away from a weakened Ministry of Finance seriously undermined effective management, with the Ministry of Finance serving as little more than a cheque-writing and accounting centre. The use of special ministerial advisers who were paid high salaries outside the civil service system had similar effects.

Fragmentation has led to: duplication of functions and overlapping jurisdictions and authority; undermining of effective coordination and control of ministries by permanent secretaries and ministers; loss of financial accountability; and parallel personnel systems with differential salaries undermining morale, motivation and productivity in the central administration (Nettleford, 1992).

Institutional weakening of the Ministry of Finance and fragmentation of public expenditure-related activities has made it difficult for the government to formulate and implement a clear public expenditure strategy. The Ministry of Finance has been unable to provide strategic direction to, and coordinate the activities of, the large number of institutions involved in the formation, implementation and monitoring of public expenditure activities (TEDA, 1983). Lack of strategic planning of public expenditure reduces accountability in two ways: denying groups the ability to input to the planning process; and failing to provide a plan as a yardstick against which to judge actual expenditure outcomes. One lesson which emerges from this is that although overly centralized public expenditure management systems can undermine accountability, the Jamaican case has shown that fragmented systems can have the same effect.

The IMF's own head of its Fiscal Affairs Department, Vito Tanzi, has drawn attention to problems created by the use of budget targets, which he sees as 'quick fix' aggregate spending ceilings (Tanzi, 1989). He notes that governments have become increasingly adept at evading spending targets whilst IMF missions find it impossible to close all possible loopholes: 'the longer ceilings on macro variables are in use, the more ways countries learn to get around them' (Tanzi, 1989, p. 24). As we have seen in the Jamaican case, some of these ways involve a reduction in accountability. Tanzi also notes that when faced with IMF budget deficit targets, governments often meet these targets with inefficient across-the-board expenditure cuts in crisis management conditions. This chapter has argued that such a practice in Jamaica has reduced the transparency and accountability of public sector expenditure decision making. Tanzi argues that IMF missions should place less emphasis on budget deficit reduction targets and more emphasis on forging government commitment to expenditure ceilings and on the budgetary processes involved in trying to achieve the ceilings.

5. EFFECTS OF IMF PROGRAMMES ON THE ACCOUNTABILITY OF THE MINISTRY OF HEALTH'S BUDGET

Public expenditure decision making in the health sector reflects many of the general problems associated with IMF budget reduction targets identified in the analysis of Jamaica's overall state budgetary process. These problems include: a mark-up budget mentality; crisis management budget slashing which lacks transparency; resource allocation influenced by political clientelism; lack of broader participation in the decision-making process; and fragmentation of the budget. Particular features of the health sector have tended to amplify these problems. These features include the fact that the budget head accounts for a large proportion of public expenditure and yet tends to be disproportionately squeezed in times of budgetary hardship; crisis management is compounded by sector-specific crises such as disease outbreaks and national disasters; bargaining over resource allocation is made harder by the fact that over twenty distinct groups of staff work in the sector; building health care facilities is a high-profile way for politicians to promote clientelist networks; and historic mark-up budgeting is encouraged by the difficulty of unit cost measurements for health services in both developing and developed countries alike.

The initial stage of budget preparation in the primary health sector, as opposed to the secondary sector, is a fairly participatory process. In the former, health clinics are the starting point for budget preparation. At this early stage there is a strong budgetary input from operational staff working in the clinics who are able to articulate their objectives and resource needs. Preparation of the initial round of budget estimates in the secondary sector is a less participatory exercise. Hospital budgets are drawn up by the hospital administrative team and involve little dialogue with technical and operational staff engaged in care delivery.

In times of IMF-guided fiscal austerity, however, resources finally available often bear little relation to initial guidelines and the initial estimates are usually returned by the Ministry of Finance for cuts. This cutting process is often conducted under crisis management conditions which lack both transparency and participation. Decisions on estimate cuts are taken by the Ministry's headquarters staff, leading to complaints by line staff at parish and district level that there is no period of dialogue during which they can defend their programme estimates and headquarters can explain the rationale behind cuts. Awareness of this scenario encourages staff to submit inflated initial estimates based on mark-up costs which, in turn, reinforce the pattern. The upshot is that down-stream staff seldom feel that they own or are responsible for the budgets they are eventually expected to work with, an attitude inimical to accountability:

> There is a fairly good system for gathering up estimates from ministries but then revenue falls short such that unfulfilled expectations have been set up. This encourages ministries to overestimate in the next cycle. Hence, the Ministry of Health tends to submit an historical mark-up budget which is then torn apart by the Ministry of Finance operating under crisis management conditions. (Personal interview with Jamaica Ministry of Health staff)

Faced with a final budget allocation which often bears little resemblance to their initial budget estimates and which has often borne a disproportionate part of the IMF-guided expenditure reduction which has taken place during the past decade and a half, Ministry of Health staff have sought various extra-budgetary means of maintaining services, with external bilateral donors often willing to oblige. Donor-funded projects, for example, often employ people off-budget in order to be able to offer adequate salaries to attract high-calibre project managers. In addition, the political directorate, sensing the political costs of deteriorating social services, has used various programmes, such as the Social and Economic Support Programme (SESP) and the MPs' Constituency Fund, which fall outside the Ministry of Health's direct budget head, to finance health sector activities.

A final source of extra-budgetary resources are those funds raised voluntarily at local level by health sector staff and supporters. These 'unofficial' funds remain at parish level and are placed in private accounts with community leaders and health care workers as signatories. Although the sums involved are small, they represent an important source of flexible finance which can be used for urgent work. However, the cost of such flexibility is the bypassing of all the normal checks and controls on public expenditure management. The result of the use of extra-budgetary funds has been fragmentation of the health sector budget which has further reduced the transparency and accountability of public expenditure in the sector and has created immense planning and budgeting difficulties for the Ministry of Health. Often, such funds are channelled into suboptimal use influenced by political clientelism over which the Ministry of Health has little control and where account-ability is lax.

Sometimes the Ministry of Health's first involvement with extra-budgetary health projects is when a bill for work already carried out is presented. In some instances health staff have found it difficult to verify whether or not the work has been carried out or have not been satisfied that the work was necessary. In other instances, although Ministry of Health staff have been involved in identifying the project, they are not consulted over choice of contractors for the work. Instead contractors are chosen by politicians, leading to concern over the nature of bills sent to the parish administrator.

The correlation between expenditure outcomes and expenditure intentions in the health sector is another important dimension of accountability influenced by IMF fiscal austerity programmes. The his-torical correlation between GDP growth, fiscal performance and health sector expenditures suggest that in times of macroeconomic buoyancy and the associated budgetary expansion, such as the 1960s through to the mid-1970s, the health sector fared well, with the health budget increasing as a share of GDP. But in times of economic stagnation and IMF fiscal austerity, as from the late 1970s onwards, health sector expenditures often experience a disproportionate part of the expendi-ture cut-backs, regardless of the party in power and its ideological commitments to social welfare improvements. For example, the new post-1989 PNP government is committed to fiscal prudence as dictated by IMF budget targets. However, this has left the PNP unable to fulfil its election pledge to 'put people first' by increasing social welfare expenditures. This has reduced accountability in the health sector in that expenditure outcomes do not reflect the government's stated social welfare policies and intentions and instead tend to mirror fiscal pressures.

The above correlations are not unique to Jamaica. Many LDCs which have endured economic stagnation and fiscal austerity during the 1980s have likewise experienced declining state social welfare expendi-tures in terms of both shares and real absolute values (Cornia, et al., 1987; Mosley, et al., 1991). This can perhaps be explained by the fact that in almost all small open developing country economies the need for IMF-guided fiscal austerity has been closely associated with unsustainable balance of payments current account deficits. Because health is a tertiary sector which uses rather than earns foreign exchange, it tends to be a prime sector for public expenditure cut-backs. This view is shared by senior staff in Jamaica's Ministry of Health:

> Although on paper the Ministry of Health is given priority, this is not reflected in our allocations. There is an attitude that because health is a non-income-earning and foreign-exchange-using tertiary sector we should not get a large share of the pie. We constantly have to rationalise the need for healthy individuals for a vibrant productive sector. (Personal interview, Kingston, April 1993)

Low Ministry of Health priority during IMF austerity periods also takes the form of delays and in some cases failure to release warrants for approved expenditures, particularly non-salary recurrent expenditure items such as drug procurement. This reduces the operational efficiency of health sector investments and reduces accountability since it means that public expenditures approved by parliament are not efficiently executed. Considerable foreign exchange inflows from donors are also lost. Delayed release of warrants for Government of Jamaica counter-part funds and for investment expenditures from the Consolidated Fund, which are required before many donors can release their funds by way of reimbursement, mean that many externally funded projects have been held up for long periods of time. In fiscal year 1992/93, for example, the Inter-American Development Bank held US$58.2 million of undisbursed funds approved for health sector projects in Jamaica.

IMF fiscal authority programmes have also indirectly influenced some of the checks and controls on health sector expenditure. Examination of the annual Accountant General's reports for the past decade shows one general accounting problem which is specific to the Ministry of Health. Many medical personnel employed by the state also run private practices out of state hospitals and clinics. This is often done without properly charging private patients for the use of state-run services such as X-rays and laboratories. This abuse of the state health care system has intensified in recent years and has become an inducement to keep state medical personnel in the face of declining real salaries. As such, it can be seen as a side-effect of budgetary austerity, which, as with many such crisis management responses, not only undermines accountability in the use of public resources, but also, in the long run, may actually intensify the resource constraints facing the public sector.

One notable general feature of checks and controls on health expenditure is the degree of tension that exists between financial and administrative staff on the one hand and technical and operations staff on the other regarding the manner in which these checks and controls are used. Many technical and operational staff feel frustrated by the tendency of financial and administrative officers to see the budget as an end in itself rather than as a means to the end of delivering efficient health care services. The following view is common amongst doctors, health care workers and programme managers:

> The important issue is not that the budget is spent correctly and adds up, but that it achieves, in terms of care delivery, what it set out to achieve. This is the real meaning of appropriate and accountable expenditure. At present there are no incentives for improving performance. An individual who does not run up a budget overdraft is thought to be good regardless of the quality of their hospital. Most of our public expenditure rules and regulations are over 40 years old and are not appropriate for dealing with modern-day needs. As a result everyone is tied up in rules which prohibit rather than facilitate. (Personal interview, Kingston, April 1993)

This tension between financial and administrative staff, who see accountability in the form of a balance sheet, and operational and technical staff, who see it in terms of care delivery, tends to intensify in times of budget squeeze when a balanced budget becomes more essential to the former and when innovatory behaviour becomes increasingly necessary for the latter to maintain care delivery standards. These two views represent different interpretations of accountability, the balance sheet view reflecting a fairly narrow concept of administrative accountability involving detailed checks and controls on how money is spent, and the care delivery view representing a broader concept of political accountability whereby public servants are held accountable for the ability to deliver the standard of care promised by the political directorate within the constraints set by resource availability. The challenge is to find a system which provides a balance between both sorts of accountability in times of budget cut-backs.

The move from line item to programme budgeting introduced in the health sector in 1992/93 is an attempt to meet this challenge. Under the new system expenditure will be allocated to programmes, with programme officers given greater responsibility and flexibility regarding use of funds. Within this more decentralized system finance and administration staff at ministry headquarters will concentrate on monitoring and auditing overall programme performance using a performance audit rather than a simple book audit. Each ministry's corporate plan will provide the broad guidelines for performance audits by specifying the type and quality of services which it plans to deliver with the available physical and financial resources. The government also intends to introduce client evaluation committees into the programme budget framework. These will provide feedback for the performance audit from clients using public services, such as health facilities, as to whether programmes are meeting client needs. These reforms should also improve the strategic planning input to health sector budgeting. This in turn should make the priorities guiding the annual budget-slashing exercise more transparent to both operational staff and the general public, and offer scope for more participation in budget decision making via the indirect route of interest-group and health-staff input to plan formulation.

6.   CONCLUSIONS

External agencies such as the IMF and the World Bank have influenced public expenditure in Jamaica in three distinct ways: influencing the allocation of resources within the budget; advocating and supporting reforms to improve general financial management in the public sector; and setting macroeconomic targets under stabilization and structural adjustment programmes which affect the nature and outcome of the state budgetary process. Tensions and conflicts exist between these influences. Externally backed economic reform – macro and meso – can affect both negatively and positively the transparency and accountability of public expenditure management.

IMF public expenditure targets fall under the third type of influence. In Jamaica government actions to circumvent such targets contributed to numerous practices which undermined the accountability of public expenditure. This observation is supported by documentary evidence and by interviews with a large number of public sector officials involved in the budget formulation process in Jamaica. A detailed analysis of the health sector showed that many of the unaccountable modes of behaviour were pronounced within the Ministry of Health. Note, however, that these negative accountability effects of IMF budget targets were not the effects of the targets *per se*, but resulted from the imposition of such targets on a government which was not committed to meeting them. Although prompted by IMF expenditure ceilings, the unaccountable modes of behaviour are ultimately the responsibility of government. Another significant factor is that these IMF effects occurred within a domestic political context in which expenditure accountability more generally was weak, for the reasons outlined in Section 1. Hence, although the IMF had accountability effects, this should not divert attention away from the role played by domestic political irresponsibility.

Two important policy conclusions emerge from the observed impact of IMF budget targets on accountability. First, organizations like the IMF and the World Bank, which impose expenditure targets on LDC governments, need to devote considerable effort to forging commitment to such targets from the recipient government in order to ensure that such targets do not lead to unaccountable modes of behaviour. Such a commitment entails a sense of recipient government ownership of macroeconomic reform programmes. Second, external donors such as the IMF might consider whether externally conditioned targets for fiscal performance are impeding the development of accountable governance and whether conditions on the budget management and formation process might be more appropriate than budget ceilings.

The Jamaican study of accountability in the context of public expenditure management has shown that the relationship between good governance, in the sense of accountable public policy management, and the macroeconomy is complex and does not consist of unidirectional positive causal links from the former to the latter. Although the quality of governance can have an important impact on the efficiency of economic outcomes, equally, the way in which the macroeconomy is managed can affect, both positively and negatively, the quality of governance. In some instances macro-policies such as exchange rate liberalization can have a positive impact on the transparency of public expenditure management. In other instances macroeconomic policies that current economic orthodoxy regards as good, such as targets to reduce budget deficits, can have negative effects on good governance in the area of public expenditure management.

IMF- and World Bank-guided fiscal deficit reduction targets have led to conflicting external and internal pressures on government expenditure in Jamaica. This has contributed to budgetary practices that have directly reduced the transparency, the participatory nature, the efficiency and the overall accountability of the state budget process. Such practices have included: a crisis management approach to budget formulation; institutional fragmentation via the transfer of both budget functions and expenditures to non-government agencies such as the Bank of Jamaica and parastatals; and recourse to supplementary budgets towards the end of the fiscal year. Many of these practices have set up conflicts with the other traditional roles played by international institutions in the area of public expenditure, such as their role in supporting institutional reforms designed to improve the efficiency and the accountability of public policy management, an example being Jamaica's World Bank-supported Administrative Reform Programme.

The above conclusions have important implications for external agencies involved in LDC macroeconomic adjustment programmes. Good governance (including an open, participatory and accountable public expenditure process) is increasingly being regarded by such agencies as an important prerequisite for the success of macroeconomic reform (Wapenhans, 1994). The Jamaican case suggests that the relationship between good governance and macroeconomic performance is more complex, and that, at least in the area of public expenditure, there is no simple one-way causal link.

7. POSTSCRIPT

The PNP administration that came to power in 1989 expressed a desire to return to the more consensual, participatory and accountable policy-making style of the 1960s. This trend has been accelerated by the PNP government re-elected in 1993 under its new leader P.J. Patterson. Several significant reforms have been undertaken. A national planning council has been formed and similar councils are intended at the sectoral level.[7] Other innovations include the introduction of annual rolling corporate plans for each ministry, as part of the government's Administrative Reform Programme. These are designed to make ministries more responsive to client needs. They require a clear statement of policy targets within the context of a medium-term strategic plan for each ministry, which provides a potential avenue for interest-group input and may well help to improve policy transparency. They may also improve the line ministries' ability to contribute to the Planning Institute's work, including the drawing up of the three-year rolling PSIP.

The government has also established a Fiscal Policy Management Unit in the Ministry of Finance to coordinate policy formulation, analysis and monitoring. It hopes that the new unit will enable the Ministry to re-establish its leadership and will be an important step towards the institutionalization and depersonalization of all aspects of fiscal policy. In 1992 the Amendment of the 1959 Financial Administration and Audit Act was passed. This removed many of the ambiguities regarding the financial accountability of the parastatal sector. In 1993, the Coke Commission recommended restructuring of the Bank of Jamaica, including making it more independent of the Ministry of Finance and less accommodating of fiscal deficits. Commencing in April 1993, Bank of Jamaica advances to government also started to be liquidated and these Bank of Jamaica transactions were reflected in the central government budget. In 1991 the deliberations of parliament's Public Accounts Committee were opened to the media and the public and in the same year a more accountable form of programme budgeting was introduced. Although accountability has undoubtedly improved under the PNP government, an assessment of these improvements goes beyond the scope of this chapter. There is clearly potential here for future research.

NOTES

1. Acknowledgement: some of the material in this chapter draws on earlier work published as 'Effects of the IMF and World Bank on public sector accountability in Jamaica', in *Public Administration and Development*, **18** (1998), copyright John Wiley Ltd reproduced with permission.
2. Against this evidence should be weighed the fact that politicians and bureaucrats in developing countries often tend to use the multilateral institutions as scapegoats for disappointing outcomes.
3. In 1977 the Bank of Jamaica regulations, which had placed limits on government indebtedness to the Bank, were amended to enable the Bank to accommodate, virtually without limit, the fiscal deficit, largely through purchase of government securities.
4. Since 1993 external agencies as well as the local media and some government officials have focused attention on this transparency problem and attempts were made to reduce Bank of Jamaica losses and to eliminate the government overdraft at the Bank of Jamaica.
5. It should be noted that these practices are not only the result of IMF budget ceilings. The argument here is that IMF conditionality may contribute to such practices which are carried out in many countries, both developed and developing.
6. The difficulty in keeping top civil service talent exists in many developing countries, particularly in times of macroeconomic stress. In Jamaica this problem was exacerbated by the imposition of IMF budget ceilings.
7. The National Planning Council has representatives from: the Private Sector Organisation of Jamaica; Chamber of Commerce; Jamaica Exporters' Association; Manufacturers' Association; Bankers' Association; Small Businesses' Association; a range of government ministries and agencies; Planning Institute; Bank of Jamaica; trade unions; consumer groups and a range of other NGOs.

REFERENCES

Bank of Jamaica (various years), *Annual Reports*, Kingston.

Cornia, A., Jolly, R. and Stewart, F. (1987), *Adjustment with a Human Face*, vol. 2, Oxford: Clarendon Press.

Government of Jamaica (annual publication), *Economic and Social Survey*. Planning Institute of Jamaica, Kingston.

Government of Jamaica (annual publication), *Financial Statements and Revenue Estimates*. Ministry of Finance and Planning, Kingston.

Government of Jamaica (various years), *Report of the Auditor General on the Appropriation and Other Accounts of Jamaica*.

Government of Jamaica (1957), *A National Plan for Jamaica, 1957–67.*

Government of Jamaica (1978), *Five Year Development Plan, 1978–82.*

Government of Jamaica (1991), *Government Policy Statement on Administrative Reform*, 6 May, Kingston.

Harrigan, J. (1991), 'Jamaica', ch. 17 in Mosley, P., Harrigan, J. and Toye, J., *Aid and Power: The World Bank and Policy-Based Lending*, vol. II, pp. 311–61, London: Routledge.

Harrigan, J. (1995), 'Jamaica: mature democracy but questionable account- ability', ch. 3 in Healey, J. and Tordoff, W. (eds), *Public Expenditure Management Under Different Political Systems: Comparative Studies in Accountability*, London: Macmillan.

Harrigan, J. (1998), 'Effects of the IMF and World Bank on public sector accountability in Jamaica', *Public Administration and Development*, **18**, 5–22.

Healey, J. and Tordoff, W. (1995), *Public Expenditure Management Under Dif- ferent Political Systems: Comparative Case Studies in Accountability*, London: Macmillan.

Hyden, G. and Bratton, M. (eds) (1992), *Governance and Politics in Africa*, Boulder, CO and London: Lynne Rienner.

IMF, *Financial Statistics Yearbook* (various issues), Washington, DC: IMF.

IMF (annual publication), *International Financial Statistics Yearbook*, Wash- ington, DC: IMF.

Mills, G. (1990), 'The English-speaking Caribbean', ch. 13 in Subranariam, V. (ed.), *Public Administration in the Third World*, New York and London: Greenwood.

Mills, G. and Slyfield, M. (1987), 'Public service reform in Jamaica: human resource management', *International Review of Administrative Sciences*, **53**, 395–412, London: Sage.

Mosley, P., Harrigan, J. and Toye, J. (1991), *Aid and Power: The World Bank and Policy-Based Lending*, vol. 2, London: Routledge.

Nettleford, R. (1992), *Report of the Committee of Advisers on Government Structure*, Chairman R. Nettleford, presented to the Ministry of Finance and Planning, Government of Jamaica.

Private Sector Organisation of Jamaica (1992), *A Policy Framework for Eco- nomic Development in Jamaica II: A Progress Report*, Kingston.

Stone, C. (1989), *Politics versus Economics: The 1989 Election in Jamaica*, Kingston: Heinemann.

Stone, C. (1991), 'Power, policy and politics in independent Jamaica', in Nettle- ford, R. (ed.), *Jamaica in Independence: Essays on the Early Years*, pp. 19–53, Heinemann Educational.

Tanzi, V. (1989), 'Fiscal policy, growth and the design of stabilization programs', in Blejer, M.I. and Ke-Young Chu (eds), *Fiscal Policy, Stabilization and Growth in Developing Countries*, Washington, DC: IMF.

TEDA (Trade and Economic Development Associates), *Institutional Audit of Financial Management in Jamaica*, Washington, DC.

USAID (1992), *Study of Fiscal Policy in Jamaica*, Report prepared for the Government of Jamaica, Kingston.

Wapenhans, W. (1994), 'The political economy of structural adjustment: an external perspective', in Van Der Hoeven and Van Der Kraaij (eds), *Struc- tural Adjustment and Beyond in Sub-Saharan Africa*, London: James Currey.

World Bank (1992), 'Governance and Development', Washington, DC: World Bank.

5.   Public expenditure reform without policy change: infrastructure investment and health care provision under fiscal squeeze in Kerala

D. Narayana

1.   INTRODUCTION

It is well known that structural adjustment programmes (SAPs) under the auspices of the International Monetary Fund and the World Bank make a distinction between stabilization and structural reforms (Stewart, 1995). Stabilization under the Fund is dominated by demand-restraint measures, among which public expenditure cuts are the most pervasive (Stewart, 1995, Table 1.5). The structural reforms of the Bank concerned with long-run efficiency involve institutional and incentive measures.

The first and foremost reform measure introduced as part of an adjustment programme is the squeeze on public expenditure with no policy change at the sectoral level. Fiscal contraction is transmitted to the sectors in terms of a continuous decline in infrastructural spending and a fall in per capita social spending. As regards infrastructure spending, there is a naïve notion that the cut is implemented by closure of projects that are uneconomic. Thus 'a reduction in public investment at the initial stage of adjustment was often considered desirable because most of the adjusting countries had public investment programmes that were unsustainable, inefficient and burdened with projects of dubious economic and social merit' (Jayarajah et al., 1996, p. 81). A fall in per capita social spending, it is presumed, may not affect services to the vulnerable sections of the population if properly reallocated. But it has been observed that, 'first, ... most countries have made little effort to shift resources into primary education and basic health care services

106

that offer a higher rate of return and are more cost effective. Second, non-wage recurrent spending for supplies and maintenance has been severely underfunded' (Jayarajah et al., 1996, p. 49). Such an observed pattern of spending is then ascribed to poor public management.

Underlying these notions is the simplistic assumption that decisions regarding expenditure cuts in sectors are public management issues independent of political processes and separable from public policy (and politics). This chapter questions the naïve notion regarding the transmission of fiscal squeeze to the sectors and contributes to the growing literature which argues that public management cannot be separated from policy (and politics) (Mackintosh, 1995). The argument put forth is that public management needs to be viewed within the coordinates set by policy and that political processes decisively influence policy choices.

By the mid-1980s, the IMF and the World Bank had recognized the role of political factors in the success of adjustment: 'the success of adjustment measures may depend on the feasibility of building coalitions of those who benefit and on careful sequencing with respect to political as well as economic objectives' (World Bank, 1990, p. 115). It has further been accepted that development of social safety nets in the context of SAPs resulted both from concern with poverty and equity and also from a desire to overcome the political opposition to adjustment measures from both the poor and the middle class (Johnson, 1994). The Fund recognizes as much when an official says, 'in essence, the underlying rationale [of social safety nets] was the necessity to buttress the social and political acceptance of the adjustment effort' (Kopits, 1993, quoted in Vivian, 1995, p. 4). If design and implementation of adjustment has been accepted as a political process, then, by the same logic, transmission of fiscal squeeze to the sectors also needs to be viewed as a political process. The pattern of expenditure allocation observed would then be a result of these processes.

The chapter seeks to illustrate public expenditure management as a political process by taking two sectors, irrigation and health, in Kerala during the 1980s. Kerala should be of interest because in the context of development policy there is often talk of learning from Kerala's development experience (Drèze and Sen, 1995). In their view, Kerala's success in human development has been traced to 'the role of public action in promoting a range of social opportunities relating inter alia to elementary education, land reform, the role of women in society, and the widespread and equitable provision of health' (ibid., p. 51). Further, they argue that 'the political process itself has played an extremely important role in Kerala's experience' (p. 55). The share of total government expenditure devoted to social sectors – education, health, social security and so on – during 1974–90 has been over 40 per cent in Kerala whereas it was well below 32 per cent for all states put together (George, 1993; p. 101). And in the Indian system of governance the division of responsibilities between the central and the state governments is such that the exchange rate, bank credit, and food and fertilizer subsidies are the concern of the central government, and in the period under consideration were not the subject of rapid policy action (SAPs have been implemented since 1991 in India); but government expenditure at the level of the states was subject to a squeeze in the 1980s, prior to SAP. Hence the transmission of fiscal squeeze to the sectors could be studied in its pure and simple form in a state where the political process plays an important role.

This chapter analyses the ways in which the political process transmits the fiscal squeeze into the irrigation and health sectors in Kerala (Sections 3 and 4), following an elaboration of the nature of the fiscal contraction (Section 2). In the irrigation sector, fiscal squeeze is transmitted as a resource gap as the political process rules out closure of projects as a policy option. The gap is then sought to be closed by 'levering in' external assistance. The objective of gap closure leads to putting up those projects which can effectively fill the gap. Those projects which are relatively large, or are at the initial stage of implementation and hence require large funds, would then be put up for funding. Assistance often comes with a 'matching fund' condition which would then guide the management of own funds in the direction of allocating a higher proportion of these limited funds to the assisted projects and starving the other projects, thus defeating the very purpose of going for assistance. In fact, the larger the assistance the greater is the squeeze on non-assisted projects.

In the health care sector, a policy stance which binds the government to finance medical education and provide universal access to allopathic and Indian systems of medicine implies that the fiscal squeeze falls on the cost of drugs and other medical supplies. Such a situation, while providing universal access to health care services, sacrifices quality. As the political process concerns itself with issues of access and not specific aspects of quality, population groups conscious of quality of service go in search of it in the private health care sector. Such a movement not only weakens the 'voice' of political demand but also feeds into privatization in the health care sector. The creeping privatization goes against the very policy of public financing of medical education and universal access.

A point of clarification regarding the administrative system in India is in order at this stage. India has a federal structure of governance, with state governments enjoying considerable autonomy. According to the constitutionally mandated division of responsibilities, some sectors, such as irrigation and health care, are under the exclusive control of the states. Transfer of funds from the central government to the states is constitutionally mandated. State governments may incur public debt by borrowing from the central government, the Reserve Bank of India (the central bank) and other financial institutions, as well as the general public within the country. State governments already indebted to the central government need the prior permission of the latter to borrow. As fiscal deficits have been mounting in the 1980s and states have been under pressure to curtail expenditure, reforms such as tight fiscal constraints, targeting of social spending to primary provision, and use of public funds for 'levering in' external assistance have been familiar features of state-level public finance well before the implementation of SAPs in 1991.

2. FISCAL CRISIS IN KERALA

The tiny state of Kerala, situated in the south-western part of India, known the world over for its remarkable improvements in mortality and fertility rates, has been spending the bulk of public funds on infrastructure and social services. The government of Kerala had been running into recurrent fiscal crises throughout the 1980s. The problem became much worse in December 1987, and following prolongation of its overdraft beyond the mandatory seven-day limit, the Reserve Bank of India suspended Treasury payments on behalf of the government of Kerala. Tight control on treasury payments has been a common phenomenon ever since.

Almost all states in India face a fiscal crisis today. But the magnitude of the crisis is much greater for Kerala and is not of recent origin. Kerala had begun running budgetary deficits during the mid-1970s. Initially the amounts involved were small and deficits were less frequent. The 1980s saw the crisis grow in magnitude and frequency. Since 1983–84 (April–March), revenue expenditure has exceeded revenue receipts every year, and the magnitude of the deficit has tended to exceed 10 per cent of the revenue expenditure since 1987–88. In other words, day-to-day running of the government in Kerala has required borrowed funds for a long time now.

In the Indian context public borrowing has become one of the major instruments of financing the budgetary needs of state governments. The state governments have been borrowing, and for all states debt as a proportion of GDP has increased from 19.81 per cent in 1980–81 to 22.38 per cent in 1992–93. But in the case of Kerala, the outstanding debt as a percentage of state domestic product (SDP) has increased from 24.52 per cent in 1980–81 to 43.60 per cent in 1992–93. The large debt burden has given rise to an equally large interest liability in the revenue account of the state government. The interest outlay as a percentage of the total expenditure, which was well below 5 per cent until the early 1980s, had crossed the 10 per cent mark by the early 1990s. In the early 1990s, the figures for net interest outlay as a percentage of total expenditure and revenue expenditure were 8 and 10 per cent respectively for all states; for Kerala the figures were 11 and 14 per cent respectively (Table 5.1).

The difficult resource position of the 1980s has not led to a contraction of government expenditure. Revenue expenditure as a proportion of SDP has increased from 16 per cent in 1980–81 to 22 per cent in 1991–92 (Table 5.2). Total expenditure as a proportion of SDP has also increased,

Table 5.1   Some dimensions of fiscal crisis in Kerala

Year	Deficit in revenue account as a percentage of		Debt outstanding as a percentage of SDP		Net interest payment as a percentage of					
	RE	SDP	KE	AS	SDP (KE)	TE (KE)	RE (KE)	SDP (AS)	TE (AS)	RE (AS)
1980–81	–4.08	–0.66	24.52	19.81	0.87	4.20	5.39	0.31	1.69	2.59
1981–82	12.72	2.18	24.67	19.52	1.19	4.82	6.94	0.42	2.39	3.52
1982–83	3.42	0.52	24.46	20.40	0.98	5.05	6.42	0.44	2.41	3.42
1983–84	–5.86	–0.97	26.28	20.30	1.36	6.17	8.22	0.41	2.29	3.22
1984–85	–1.20	–0.20	27.86	21.14	1.35	5.72	7.89	0.57	2.96	4.16
1985–86	–5.13	–1.03	31.12	22.36	1.42	5.20	7.08	0.66	3.46	4.74
1986–87	–9.20	–1.79	29.25	23.32	1.72	6.52	8.52	0.92	4.61	6.28
1987–88	–10.93	–2.06	30.02	23.43	1.89	7.73	9.77	0.99	4.88	6.48
1988–89	–7.95	–1.57	27.97	22.12	2.17	8.63	10.56	0.99	5.22	6.70
1989–90	–10.90	–2.15	30.07	22.52	2.35	9.46	11.89	1.12	5.89	7.52
1990–91	–14.94	–3.21	33.74	22.89	2.40	9.37	11.20	1.32	6.83	8.66
1991–92	–11.33	–2.50	33.55	22.51	3.15	11.49	14.31	0.91	5.17	6.47
1992–93	–12.60	–3.58	43.60	22.38	3.71	10.93	13.04	1.31	7.75	9.64

Note: RE – Revenue expenditure; SDP – State domestic product;
KE – Kerala; AS – All states; NIP – Net interest payments;
TE – Total expenditure
Year is from April to March.

Source: Chakraborty (1995).

*Table 5.2   Trends in revenue expenditure, total expenditure and the
share of plan expenditure in Kerala (%)*

Year	RE/SDP	TE/SDP	(RE–NIP)/ SDP	(TE–NIP)/ SDP	Share of plan expenditure KE	AS
1980–81	16.14	20.71	15.27	19.84	31.67	32.47
1981–82	17.15	24.69	15.98	23.50	27.04	33.13
1982–83	15.26	19.41	14.28	18.43	27.03	33.19
1983–84	16.55	22.04	15.19	20.68	32.83	33.95
1984–85	17.11	23.60	15.76	22.25	28.10	32.57
1985–86	20.06	27.30	18.66	25.90	23.36	31.22
1986–87	20.19	26.38	18.47	24.66	24.76	34.35
1987–88	19.34	24.45	20.67	22.56	23.44	35.23
1988–89	20.55	25.14	20.80	22.97	22.70	33.01
1989–90	19.76	24.84	20.14	22.49	23.46	30.29
1990–91	21.43	25.61	20.81	23.21	22.50	30.12
1991–92	22.01	27.42	21.12	24.27	20.49	28.82
1992–93	28.45	33.94	21.52	30.23	21.16	29.23

Notes: As for Table 5.1.

Source: As for Table 5.1.

but the increase has been much smaller compared to the revenue expenditure. As government expenditure has been financed to an increasing
extent by public borrowing, the interest liability has also continued to
increase. This has an important implication. While the discretionary
part of the revenue expenditure has increased by about six percentage
points, that of total expenditure has tended to stagnate throughout the
1980s. Such a trend has left few resources for investment. This is under-
lined by the fact that in Kerala plan expenditure as a proportion of
total expenditure has shown a steady decline from over 30 per cent in
the early 1980s to around 20 per cent in the early 1990s. The picture
for all states has not shown such a trend; some states have been able
to maintain the share of plan expenditure in total expenditure at around
30 per cent (Table 5.2). Noting that plan expenditure in Kerala is largely
(over 50 per cent) capital expenditure and non-plan is largely (about
90 per cent) revenue expenditure, this means that public investment is
steadily falling in the state.

The decline in public investment is especially serious because the
SDP growth rate itself has been low in Kerala. The combined effect of
all these factors shows up in the trend in per capita plan outlays over
the long period of 1956–90. Per capita state plan outlay in Kerala, which
was higher than that of the all-state average until 1974, has been below
it since then. It was 14 per cent lower than the all-state average until

the mid-1980s and was 35 per cent lower in 1985–90 (George, 1993, p. 116).

3.   'LEVER IN' EXTERNAL ASSISTANCE AND 'LEVER OUT' MANAGEMENT

Irrigation is a state responsibility in the Indian set-up, but central plan assistance is provided for those projects cleared (technically by the Central Water Commission and financially by the Planning Commission) by the centre. But there are always a large number of projects at various stages of investigation and implementation by the states which have not been cleared by the centre. In Kerala, almost all the irrigation projects – numbering about ten – taken up before the formation of the state were situated in the districts of Trichur and Palakkad, which were the main rice-growing areas in a cash-crop-dominated economy. The 1960s and 1970s witnessed the initiation of a large number of projects – 18 in all – covering all the districts of the state. Two factors were seen to be at work: the severe shortage of the main cereal, namely rice, and its rising price in the state. Public investment in irrigation was thought to be the main policy instrument in the drive towards increased food production. There was popular demand for such investments by the elected representatives from all parts of the state. Whereas the delay involved in getting central clearance for projects initiated in the 1960s was about four years, it had increased to over eight years for the projects initiated in the late 1970s. More important; the number of projects not cleared by the centre had increased to seven by the end of the 1980s, pointing to poor investigation or difficult resource position.

All the irrigation projects taken up for construction up to the end of the 1950s had been completed by the early 1970s, the only exception being the Periyar Valley project, started in 1956, which was commissioned as late as 1993–94. Out of the 18 projects referred to above, only seven were in any meaningful state of implementation until 1975–76, as 99 per cent of the outlay of the sector was being spent on these projects (Table 5.3). In the mid-1970s three more projects – Chimoni, Muvattupuzha and Idamalayar – gained in importance, their share in the total outlay reaching 10 per cent by 1980.

The fiscal squeeze building up in the late 1970s led the state to go for 'levering in' external assistance for the sector. As external assistance was available only in the form of project funding (central assistance had also taken that form by the early 1970s, which had earlier been assistance to the sector as a whole), it became necessary to propose projects

Table 5.3   *Share of different projects in the plan expenditure in the irrigation structure – Kerala (selected years) (%)*

	1973–74	1976–77	1979–80	1982–83	1985–86	1988–89	1991–92	1993–94
Kallada	21	15	24	38	54	59	48	51
Group I	78	80	59	40	28	20	27	15
Group II	0	4	9	19	14	15	19	29
Group III	1	1	8	3	4	6	5	5
Total	100	100	100	100	100	100	100	100

Notes: Group I – Pamba, Periyar, Chitturpuzha, Kanjirapuzha, Kuttiadi, Pazhasi.
Group II – Chimoni, Muvattupuzha, Idamalayar.
Group III – Varamapuram, Kuriakutty, Chaliyar, Kakkadavu, Attappady, Karapuzha, Meenachil, Danasurasagar.

Source: Government of Kerala, *Economic Review* (various issues).

for funding. The Irrigation Department proposed one of the seven projects, namely Kallada – the investment requirement of which was larger than that of the other six put together – for World Bank assistance. The project received the International Development Assistance (IDA) loan of 52.3 million SDRs (special drawing rights) in July 1982. The estimated cost of the project at that point in time was Rs 1636 million and investment made until then was roughly Rs 645 million. The loan formed about 50 per cent of the remaining cost of the project.

The loan was utilized from 1982–83 to 1988–89. During this period the cost of the project had escalated to Rs 3135 million, and despite the rupee–SDR exchange rate increasing from 10.5628 in 1982–83 to 19.2619 in 1988–89, the loan formed only about 37 per cent of the investment made. The project has not been completed to date, despite the fact that over 50 per cent of the total irrigation investment of the state has been earmarked for it beyond 1988–89. The repayment of the principal began in 1992–93, amounting to 0.523 million SDRs, the interest payment during the year being 0.408 million SDRs and the interest payment up to 1992 being 3.817 million SDRs.

Ever since it was decided to propose the Kallada project for IDA funding the pattern of intrasectoral allocation within the irrigation sector in the state has moved in its favour. Initially, it was to establish the 'interest' of the state in the project because no project can hope to obtain external assistance if the state itself is not interested in it. At this stage the project showed a jump in its share of the total outlay from less than 20 per cent to over 35 per cent. During the assistance period its share ranged between 45 per cent and 68 per cent. The promotion of Kallada to centre-stage meant that little was left for the other projects. The exceptions were three projects initiated in the mid-1970s, which continued to receive a share in the total outlay of over 10 per cent – going up to 20 per cent in some years – throughout this period. The other six projects were virtually starved of funds; their share, which was well over three-quarters of the total outlay up to the late 1970s dropped below one-third. Some of these projects were at fairly advanced stages and required little money for completion. Let us take four of these projects which were finally completed in 1993. Pamba received no more than 2 per cent of the total outlay from 1986–87 to 1993–94; Chitturpuzha, around 1 per cent from 1980–81 to 1993–94; Kuttiadi, around 2 per cent from 1984–85 to 1993–94, except in two years when the allocation went up to 5 per cent. Kuttiadi was finally completed with a massive infusion of around 10 per cent of the total outlay in 1991–92.

It is evident that the 'levering in' of external assistance brought Kallada to centre-stage in the irrigation sector. All the other projects, which were at fairly advanced stages of completion, had to be kept waiting and some were finally commissioned with a delay of over ten years. The external assistance, instead of releasing funds for other projects, had drawn in funds from other projects leading to delay of all the projects. In the process debt incurred on the project had to be serviced from non-existent income flow.

At the macro-level, the scope for a government to control its spending generally exceeds its ability to ensure a rise in the receipts (see Section 1 above). Turning to the sectors, such an overall cut is the most difficult to implement at the level of the different projects. As projects are, at various stages of implementation, located at different places to benefit different population groups and as there are no guidelines for closing any, the aim is to bring projects to completion by mobilizing resources. Again, as no general support for the sector becomes available and as the form of assistance is project funding, the sector puts up for assistance those projects which fill the resource gap to the greatest extent. Projects which are large, at the initial stage of implementation, and characterized by fairly well-defined criteria for evaluation are put up for funding. The external assistance fills the resource gap for the large project, simultaneously widening the gap for all the other smaller projects owing to the 'matching' condition for assistance. Because the form of assistance is project funding the gap is not completely filled (not all projects are put up for funding or get assistance) and the overall gap gets translated into cuts in non-externally assisted project spending through the 'matching' condition of external assistance.

While the logic of levering in is clear, the policy leaves little space for management of the limited outlay of the sector, especially when other competing demands cannot be ruled out, as is evident from the allocations for the three projects initiated in the mid-1970s, leading to very ineffective use of funds and massive time and cost overruns of all the projects. It was to avoid such a situation that external assistance was sought in the first place.

4. CREEPING PRIVATIZATION IN THE HEALTH CARE SECTOR

The state of Kerala is well known the world over for its remarkable, decreases in fertility and mortality rates. The achievement is often attributed to the open-society characteristic of the state, where 'successive elections resulted in electors demanding educational and health services and in competing political parties offering to provide such services' (Caldwell, 1986). The state has been devoting the bulk of public funds on infrastructure and social services, and in particular on health. The investment on health is guided by three policy coordinates: a public medical institution (allopathic) in every *panchayat* (development administration unit equal to or larger than a revenue village), government-funded medical education, so as to ensure an adequate supply of medical personnel, and encouragement of traditional medical systems.

At the time of reorganization of the state in 1956, the southern Travancore–Cochin part of the state was far advanced in terms of government medical institutions in comparison with the northern Malabar, which had earlier been part of the Madras province. In 1960, while the districts south of Palakkad had one medical institution (allopathic) for less than 45 000 population, the ratio was one medical institution for over 65 000 population in the northern districts, the Kerala average being one institution per 50 000 population. The period 1960–75 witnessed two developments. First, the density of medical institutions increased rapidly to reach one institution per 25 000 population by 1975. Second, the interdistrict variation was greatly reduced, with almost all the *panchayats* in the state having at least one institution (Table 5.4). The period beyond 1980 witnessed further equalization and expansion. Following the recommendations of the Pai Committee in 1979, there was popular demand for the provision of equal facilities in all *taluk* hospitals and a medical institution for every 20 000 population (a *taluk* is a sub-district administrative unit). Note the government reply on these issues in 1981 (Government of Kerala, 1981), following

Table 5.4   Distribution of medical institutions (allopathy) by districts

Districts	1960	1965	1970	1975	1980	1985	1990
Trivandrum	53	57	53	80	91	97	121
Kollam	35	50	53	90	92	97	121
Alleppey	38	48	54	78	81	84	100
Kottayam	27	39	42	59	61	64	95
Idukki	14	19	16	41	46	50	59
Ernakulam	42	57	62	81	87	100	116
Trichur	38	62	62	86	87	105	113
Palghat	30	45	55	76	90	97	113
Malappuram	19	31	44	71	74	90	114
Kozhikode	14	23	31	60	59	67	87
Wynad	11	10	15	23	24	30	42
Kannur	20	26	33	72	72	84	97
Kasaragod	7	16	21	44	49	51	61
Kerala	348	483	541	861	913	1016	1239

Source: Government of Kerala, *Administration Reports of the Health Department* (various years).

the vociferous demand by the members of the subcommittee on social services of the state legislature:

> The High Power Committee in their report had suggested to improve the services of all Taluk hospitals and to bring them on an equal footing. The Committee had also recommended that the Taluk level hospitals should be provided with basic specialties like medicine, surgery, gynaecology and pediatrics and subspecialties like ENT, dental, eye, orthopaedic and STD. When these recommendations were implemented the present state of affairs would be completely changed and more or less equal facilities and status would be available in all of them. Steps had been taken to implement the recommendations of the High Power Committee. (p. 4)

Regarding the second issue, 'It was stated on behalf of the government that Pai's Committee had recommended that, in stages, a second dispensary may be started in each Panchayat having a population of 20,000 or more. The report, the committee was informed, was being considered by the government' (p. 13). There was gradual implementation of the policy and by 1990 most of the districts had one medical institution for about 20 000 population.

The expansion of facilities under the Indian system of medicine (*ayurveda*) has also progressed more or less on similar lines. The distribution of facilities across the districts was skewed in favour of the southern districts to start with. By the mid-1970s equality had been

Table 5.5 Distribution of medical institutions (ayurveda) *by districts*

District	1960	1970	1975	1981	1985	1991
Trivandrum	18	43	46	51	58	61
Kollam	24	35	42	45	40	46
Alleppey	28	39	50	49	41	46
Kottayam	16	19	23	29	31	35
Idukki			18	19	22	28
Ernakulam	30	42	34	43	50	58
Trichur	51	57	61	68	71	78
Palghat	22	34	44	45	46	54
Malappuram		24	45	48	54	61
Kozhikode	16	29	44	41	35	41
Kannur	15	39	75	66	38	46
Kerala	220	362	482	504	551	635

Source: As for Table 5.4.

achieved and the northern districts were comparable with the southern districts and the distribution corresponded with that of allopathic institutions. Whereas in the case of allopathic institutions a further expansion took place between 1980 and 1990 to achieve the Pai Committee norm, the expansion of *ayurvedic* institutions followed the earlier norm (Table 5.5).

It is evident from the deliberations of the 1981 committee that public accountability conforms to the three features discussed by Paul (Paul, 1992):

1. Government accountability to the public rested with the political leadership at the macro-level.
2. Public accountability has been on inputs and not on outputs.
3. Accountability is enforced in a top–down fashion. It is hardly ever that quality of care is discussed in any detail.

Kerala started its first medical college in 1951 with about 100 seats. The number of colleges had increased to five by the mid-1980s with about 750 seats for undergraduate training and about 200 seats for postgraduate specialized training in about 18 specializations. The number of teachers has increased from around 200 in 1960 to over 1000 in 1990. The standards of medical education in India are set by the Medical Council of India, which requires the observation of certain norms regarding the student–teacher ratio, infrastructure facilities and hospital beds, on which expenditure had to be incurred.

In a situation of developing fiscal crisis the health sector has escaped any sharp cut in expenditure. Government expenditure on health as a percentage of total government expenditure has shown a very mild decline since the late 1980s. Expenditure on health care as a percentage of total government expenditure, which was well over 5.2 until 1987–88, has shown a decline since 1988–89, reaching 4.04 by 1992–93. Per capita government expenditure on health care has also shown a mild decline in recent years from its peak of over Rs 40 (at 1981–82 prices) during 1985–86 to 1987–88. In the face of an expenditure squeeze and growth in medical education and facilities under the two systems of medicine, the share of allopathic medicine in total expenditure has fallen.

Expansion of medical education has come with a proportionate increase in expenditure on account of expanding facilities and teaching staff in accordance with the standards set by the Medical Council of India. Any failure on this count would have run the risk of losing recognition for the degrees awarded. The result is a steady increase in the share of expenditure on medical education in the total expenditure on curative services from 10.21 per cent in 1977–79 to 17.05 per cent in 1990–92 (Table 5.6). The steady expansion of services under the Indian system of medicine has led to its share in total expenditure going up steadily from less than 8 per cent in 1977–79 to about 13 per cent in 1990–92. The share of allopathic services has fallen steadily from over 70 per cent of the total in 1977–79 to about 58 per cent in 1990–92.

As the number of allopathic medical institutions has increased during this period by over 40 per cent, the expenditure has largely gone into pay and allowances. The share of pay and allowances, which was only 37 per cent in 1960, increased to 55 per cent by 1975 and further to 63 per cent by 1990. Such an increase has left little resources for medicines (the expenditure share of which fell from 39 per cent in 1960 to 25 per cent in 1990), or maintenance and up-grading of facilities (Sadanandan, 1993).

Table 5.6   Distribution (%) of expenditure on curative services

	1977–79	1980–89	1990–92
Allopathic medical services	70.16	67.06	58.32
Other systems of medicine	7.96	9.24	12.32
Medical education	10.21	12.89	17.05
Employees' state insurance	10.11	8.99	10.08
Direction and administration	1.56	1.82	2.45
Total	100	100	100

Source: Raman Kutty and Panikar (1995).

Thus while access to institutions and doctors has been improved, the supply of medicines and facilities has steadily come down. Such a situation in a period of demographic transition has led to the phenomenal expansion of private medical institutions. Kerala had 1016 medical institutions (allopathic) and about 32 000 beds under the government in 1986. This increased to 1249 institutions and 42 000 beds by 1994. The private sector had 3565 institutions with 49 000 beds in 1986, increasing to 4288 institutions and 68 000 beds by 1995 (Government of Kerala, 1986; 1996).

More than the numbers, it is the specializations and other facilities the private institutions offer that is an indication of the nature of demand that has not been met by the government institutions. In 1995, nearly 45 per cent of the institutions had in-patient facilities, 25 per cent had operation facilities, 40 per cent of the doctors had postgraduate degrees, and 30 per cent had at least one of the higher specializations. By 1986–87, of the total patients hospitalized, only 43.38 per cent in rural areas and 55.65 per cent in urban areas were hospitalized in government hospitals. These percentages must have decreased further by now. More importantly, in the rural areas this percentage did not show much of a variation across decile groups; in the urban areas among the poor a relatively higher percentage approached the government hospitals compared to the rich (Government of India, 1991).

The cut in overall public expenditure has been translated into the often-mentioned squeeze on recurrent non-wage expenditure of the curative services (allopathy). Two factors have led to such a development. First, medical education is not amenable to any cut in expenditure, as recognition of the medical degree is regulated by a national-level organization. Second, public accountability of the health care sector has largely been to the political leadership at the macro-level and has been in terms of inputs, such as number of health posts and number of specializations, and not in terms of processes or outcomes. Thus the emerging situation is one where there is an adequate supply of medical personnel and universal access to health care but quality of the service has gone on deteriorating.

The high differentiability of the product, its infrequent use (contrast with water supply, electricity, or telecommunication) and the easy availability of private health care services have considerably weakened the 'voice' response of the public. The 'exit' response has been further speeded up by the growing private practice by physicians employed in government service (Jayachandran, 1996), which would have brought down the cost differential between the 'voice' and 'exit' options further.

5. CONCLUSION

Does 'levering in' ease the fiscal crisis? As is evident from Section 2, this is a not an easy question to answer. It could in fact allow for the continuance of projects on which hard decisions were overdue and in the process accentuate the crisis. It does not allow for management of finances, as funds are tied to projects or priorities of donors and are not 'freely' available for the particular sector. In sectors such as health the issues are universal access and medical education and the policies addressing such issues set the path of expansion of services and the management space is defined by it. Stopping midway or redirecting resources on inadequately defined paths can lead to strong protests from deprived groups in an open society like Kerala.

A fiscal squeeze at the macro-level with no policy change at the sectoral level translates into a pattern of allocation of expenditure conditioned by the strategies adopted to close the gap, as in 'levering in', or the conditions set by outside forces influencing decisions within the sector, as in medical education. The question then is, should public sector expenditure reform begin at the macro-level and percolate down to the sectors, or should it begin at the micro-level, given the overall context, and add up to the macro-level. If the policy goal is simply a cut in total expenditure, then one could begin at the macro-level. If the policy goal is a better allocation of scarce resources among the sectors as well as within the sectors, then reform needs to begin at the micro-level and add up to the macro-level.

REFERENCES

Caldwell, J.C. (1986), 'Routes to low mortality in poor countries', *Population and Development Review*, **12** (2), June, 171–220.

Chakraborty, P (1995), 'Public debt of selected states: a comparative analysis,' unpublished M. Phil. dissertation submitted to the Jawaharlal Nehru University, New Delhi, Trivandrum: Centre for Development Studies.

Drèze, J. and Sen, A.K. (1995), India: Economic Development and Social Opportunity, Delhi: Oxford University Press.

George, K.K. (1993), *Limits to Kerala Model of Development*, Trivandrum: Centre for Development Studies.

Government of India (1991), 'NSS consumption survey, 44th round', *Sarvekshana*, **XIV** (3).

Government of Kerala (1981), *Subject Committee VI Social Services, Report*, Trivandrum: Secretariat of the Kerala Legislature.

Government of Kerala (1986), *Report of the Survey of Private Medical Institutions in Kerala*, Trivandrum: Department of Economics and Statistics.

Government of Kerala (1996), *Report on the Survey of Private Medical Institutions in Kerala*, Thiruvananthapuram: Department of Economics and Statistics.

Jayachandran, T.N. (1996), *Report of the Commission on Private Practice by Doctors in Government Service*, Trivandrum: Government of Kerala.

Jayarajah, Carl, Branson, William and Sen, Binayak (1996), *Social Dimensions of Adjustment: World Bank Experience, 1980–93*, Washington, DC: The World Bank.

Johnson, Omotunde E.G. (1994), 'Managing adjustment costs, political authority and the implementation of adjustment programmes, with special reference to African Countries', *World Development*, **22** (3), 399–411.

Kopits, George (1992), 'Towards a cost effective social security system', in ISSA, *Responding to Changing Needs: Developments and Trends in Social Security Throughout the World*, Geneva: ISSA.

Mackintosh, Maureen (1995), 'Competition and contracting in selective social provisioning', in Jessica Vivian (ed.), *Adjustment and Social Sector Restructuring*, London: Frank Cass.

Paul, S. (1992), 'Accountability in public services: it's voice and control', *World Development*, **20** (7), 1047–1060.

Sadanandan, Rajeev (1993), 'The role of government in the development of the health care system in Kerala', unpublished M. Phil. dissertation submitted to the Jawaharlal Nehru University, New Delhi, Trivandrum: Centre for Development Studies.

Stewart, F. (1995), *Adjustment and Poverty: Options and Choices*, London: Routledge.

Raman Kutty, V. and Panikar, P.G.K. (1995), *Impact of Fiscal Crisis on the Public Sector Health Care System in Kerala*, Trivandrum Achuta Menon Centre for Health Science Studies.

Vivian, Jessica (1995), 'How safe are "social safety nets"? Adjustment and social sector restructing in developing countries', in Jessica Vivian (ed.), *Adjustment and Social Sector Restructing*, London: Frank Cass.

World Bank (1990), *World Development Report 1990*, Washington, DC: World Bank.

6. Aid, financial decentralization and accumulation under economic reforms: theoretical reflections on the Tanzanian experience

Marc Wuyts[1]

1. INTRODUCTION

The concept of decentralization is most commonly applied to fiscal and management decentralization in the public sphere, which, in recent times, has often gone hand in hand with the greater reliance on public–private funding arrangements. This chapter, based upon the Tanzanian experience, develops a conceptual framework to look at a different but not unrelated aspect of decentralization: the decentralization of foreign aid to support private sector development under economic reforms. The issue here, then, is not how public funds can lever in private funding in social provisioning, but instead how the state can shift its influence over the allocation of non-tax sources of finance to support private sector development, particularly in commodity production. The concern of this chapter, therefore, is the relation between the process of decentralization in the *fiscalization of finance* (Amsden, 1997a, p. 474), on the one hand, and the nature of economic development, on the other, in a context where economic reforms aim to give impetus to the private sector's leading role in restructuring production.

The concept of the fiscalization of finance refers to the various ways in which the state or any other agent of public action (for example, donor agencies) exerts influence over the allocation of non-(domestic) tax sources of finance such as private or institutional domestic savings, money creation and credit allocation, or foreign grants and loans, in particular foreign aid, within the domestic economy. The fiscalization of finance can serve different purposes and, hence, assume different forms.[2] This chapter looks at the case of Tanzania, where foreign aid was the driving force behind the varied processes of fiscalization of finance. At first, the era of socialist development was characterized by a process of fiscalization of finance which involved its centralization by the developmental state behind the development of the public sector. But subsequently the economic reforms of the 1980s, and particularly the adoption of structural adjustment policies since 1986, heralded a new phase which involved the reallocation of finance in favour of private sector development. This latter process, however, did not imply the dismantling of the mechanisms of fiscalization of finance, but rather its restructuring and decentralization. More specifically, this chapter argues that this transition towards a more open market economy is not a spontaneous process, but one in which the state assumes an active role (whether explicitly or implicitly recognized) in shaping the nature of production within the economy at large through the influence it exerts over the allocation of finance.

The argument of this chapter is that the restructuring of the fiscaliz- ation of finance under economic reforms is perhaps one of the most important determinants in shaping the new regime of accumulation in the making. More specifically, the shift in emphasis from aid as invest- ment support towards aid as balance of payments support – first as commodity import support and, subsequently, as budget support – played an important role in shaping the nature of the mechanisms at work and the outcomes to which they give rise. It is argued that, in the case of Tanzania, the mushrooming of 'informal sector' activities, the apparent stagnation in traditional exports after a brief recovery, and the plight of formal sector manufacturing are not unrelated events, but are at least in part determined by the specific nature of the processes of financial restructuring, import liberalization, and the decentraliz- ation of finance. The latter mechanisms, it is argued, restructured the competitiveness of different economic activities in general, and, more specifically, that of labour-intensive accumulation in the 'informal sector'. The argument is that, to secure its competitiveness at minimally viable levels of real wages, accumulation within the informal sector came to rely on the relative cheapening of wage goods made possible by cheap imports of manufactured goods. The dynamics of the informal sector, therefore, cannot be properly understood without reference to the financial mechanisms through which these imports were financed. Finally, it is argued that these processes at work had adverse conse- quences for the production of traditional export crops and for domestic formal manufacturing (in particular, the production of manufactured wage goods).

The main concern of this chapter is theoretical. Its aim is to posit a hypothesis about the relation between financial mechanisms under

economic reforms and the nature of informal sector accumulation in
Tanzania. To do so, it draws upon the existing literature for part of the
empirical evidence needed to sustain the arguments made, but it does
not engage in further empirical analysis. Its purpose is, then, in the light
of available arguments and evidence, to generate a plausible hypothesis
which undoubtedly needs further empirical investigation.

Section 2 looks at the relation between processes of fiscalization of
finance and the character of economic development in Tanzania since
the late 1960s. It deals with the relation between the changing forms of
foreign aid and changes in the nature of production before and after
the economic reforms of the mid-1980s. In particular, it pinpoints the
growth in informal sector production and the increased reliance of
households on multiple diversified sources of income, both formal and
informal, as one of the most characteristic features of recent economic
development in Tanzania. This provides the setting for Section 3, which
puts forward a theoretical framework to come to grips with the dynamics
of the so-called informal or second economy in its interaction with
processes of financial restructuring. Section 4 concludes with a brief
statement of the main argument of the chapter and argues that the
observed dynamics of the growing informal sector is not without its
costs: in particular, the relative stagnation of the production of traditional cash (export) crops, on the one hand, and the demise of formal
manufacturing industry, on the other.

2. AID, THE FISCALIZATION OF FINANCE, AND ECONOMIC DEVELOPMENT IN TANZANIA

In its economic development since the late 1960s, Tanzania (like many
other developing countries) witnessed a *transition* from a strategy of
state-centred import-substituting industrialization to one characterized
by the outward-looking private-sector-centred liberalization of the
economy propelled by structural adjustment policies initiated since
the mid 1980s.[3] There are two processes of change within this broader
context of transition which concern the argument of this chapter. One
process is macro in scope and financial in nature, and concerns the
changing role of foreign aid in Tanzania's economic development. Of
specific importance here are the effects of the shift in the composition
by type of aid under economic reforms: from the near-exclusive reliance
(with the exception of food aid) on project aid towards the increased
use of commodity import support and, subsequently, budget support
(Doriye et al., 1998). The other process is micro in scope and relates to

the changing nature of production as the source of livelihoods, and concerns the apparent growth in informal sector activities accompanied by the much greater reliance of households, rural and urban, on multiple and diversified sources of income, both formal and informal, in the wake of the economic reforms of structural adjustment (Maliyamkono and Bagachwa, 1990; Booth et al., 1993; Sarris and Van den Brink, 1993; Jamal and Weeks, 1993; Raikes and Gibbon, 1996; Bryceson, 1997; Bagachwa, 1997). It is the purpose of this chapter to investigate the linkage between both these processes from the perspective of the changing nature of accumulation in Tanzania. Table 6.1 is a time chart which pinpoints the key features (relevant to the argument in this chapter) of economic development and the role of foreign aid therein in Tanzania, both before and after the economic reforms of the mid-1980s.

To start with the macro-financial side, there are mainly three broad types of foreign aid: project aid, programme aid and technical assistance, the last of which is often linked to project aid and is of less concern to the argument here (White, 1998a). Apart from food aid (an early form of programme aid), project aid as *investment support* tended to be the dominant form of aid up to the early 1980s. Typically, in Tanzania, donor agencies would directly finance the foreign exchange costs of an investment project, requiring the local partner to raise local finance to meet local resource costs (Wuyts, 1994, p. 167). The direct beneficiaries of project aid were either the state or parastatal enterprises. If, as was generally the case, domestic public savings fell short of the amount required to fund local resource costs, the public sector would rally additional funds either by laying claim on institutionalized private savings, or, more commonly, through money creation.[4]

From the mid-1980s, under the impulse of the economic reforms, *financial* programme aid, which included debt relief, commodity import support and subsequently (during the 1990s) budget support, gained in importance. Import support can either take the form of commodities or of foreign exchange and can either be allocated administratively or through market-based mechanisms (White, 1998a). In contrast with project aid, programme aid sought to alleviate the foreign exchange constraint on recurrent expenditures (intermediate or private and public consumer goods) to allow for fuller utilization of existing capacity (White, 1998a, p. 71). The earlier form of commodity import support predominantly involved the administrative allocation of commodity support by donors to particular sectors of the economy or to specific enterprises. Later on, the emphasis swung gradually towards the market-based allocation of foreign exchange. In 1988, the open general licence scheme was introduced, in which aid in cash was set aside to fund

Table 6.1 The role of foreign aid in Tanzania's economic development

Period	Development strategy	Types of foreign aid	Key features
1967–80	Aid-financed and state-led import-substituting industrialization	Project aid as investment support	• Project aid propelled deficit financing through money creation to finance local (counterpart) costs of investment • Growth in formal wage employment • Relative rise of prices of food versus those of cash (export) crops • Falling export volumes • Capacity creation crowds out its utilization
1980–85	Crisis management and creeping economic reforms • minor devaluations • own import support scheme	Donor fatigue • withdrawal of IMF support	• 1980/3: severe import compression, goods famine and parallel market inflation • Erosion of formal sector incomes through inflation
1986–90	Structural adjustment policies • exchange rate devaluation • import liberalization • emphasis on output recovery	Shift towards aid as import support	• Improved availability of 'incentive goods' • Improved capacity utilization in industry • Mild export volume recovery
1990 onwards	Public sector reforms and financial restructuring	Further shift towards aid as budget support	• Cheap imports of wage goods • Informal sector growth • Increased household reliance on multiple sources of income • Demise of formal sector employment • Decline in formal manufacturing output • Stagnation in traditional exports

imports of raw materials and spare parts. Subsequently, as the scheme grew in size, the system moved from an expanded positive list of eligible items to a negative list of items which could not be imported with aid moneys. This process went hand in hand with the process of exchange rate unification (between the official and parallel markets). In 1991 the parallel market in foreign exchange was legalized with the opening up of foreign exchange bureaux, and unification of the exchange rate was finally achieved in 1993.

By about 1990, the emphasis in aid allocation had shifted towards budget support as donors became increasingly concerned with social expenditures and poverty alleviation programmes. Budget support is a form of aid akin to untied import support in cash (White, 1998a, p. 82). To obtain import support (whether allocated administratively or through market mechanisms and whether in commodities or in foreign exchange), the beneficiary (private or public) is required to pay the countervalue in local currency, which is subsequently channelled to the government budget as additional non-tax revenues aimed to reduce the budget deficit. The massive depreciation of the real exchange rate in the late 1980s meant that these countervalue payments had become a major source of revenue. Changing donors' concerns meant that they sought to tie the use of counterpart funds to social expenditures.

The dual move towards market-based allocation of programme aid and towards the greater preoccupation with social expenditures meant that donor agencies became less concerned with earmarking (or with imposing restrictions on) the types of goods which could be imported with foreign aid. The outcome of these changes was that formal sector manufacturing, trade or services ceased to have exclusive (or, at least, preferential) access to the foreign exchange provided by programme aid.

How then did these changes in emphasis on different types of aid affect the wider economy? And, more specifically, how did these macro-changes affect the nature of production in the economy? Obviously, these changes did not proceed in a vacuum, but were part and parcel of a wider process of transition towards an outward-looking, more market-based economy. The point is, however, that restructuring of foreign aid and of its accompanying financial processes played an important role in affecting the nature of the outcomes in terms of restructuring production.

The period before structural adjustment, from the late 1960s to the crisis of the early 1980s, was characterized by a state-led aid-propelled process of import-substituting industrialization and basic needs provisioning. The underlying model of development was not exceptional, but largely rooted in the literature on economic development of the 1950s, 1960s and early 1970s. More specifically, development was to take place within a Lewis-type process of import-substituting industrialization based upon the expansion of *formal* wage employment in industry, services and larger-scale agriculture within a dual-economy framework in which the peasantry, characterized by a surplus population, supplied cash (= export) and food crops as well as migrants into formal employment. The informal sector was seen to constitute a shock absorber and a temporary (or perhaps, probabilistic) abode between rural out-migration and formal employment in industry and services. The economy, therefore, was depicted as consisting of three sectors: agriculture, the largely state-owned or parastatal formal sector, and the mainly urban informal sector (Jamal and Weeks, 1993, p. 30). In the tradition of two-gap models, aid as investment support was seen to promote economic growth of the formal sector by augmenting available savings and relieving the foreign exchange constraint. Finally, there was a strong belief in the capacity of the state to direct development and to compensate for market failures. To this effect, the state sought to *centralize* financial resources behind its strategy of import-substituting industrialization in which the public sector was to play the leading role. Foreign aid acted as the pivot in the process of the centralization of the fiscalization of finance. First, aid directly financed the foreign exchange costs of investment projects. And, second, by channelling institutionalized private savings to the government budget and (more importantly) through money creation, the state sought to obtain the necessary counterpart funds to finance the local costs of investments.

The distinctive feature of this process of import-substituting industrialization in the Tanzanian context was that *capacity creation* in the formal sector depended largely on the availability of foreign aid as investment support, while *capacity utilization*, which required imported intermediate inputs, depended on the country's capacity to earn foreign exchange through the exports of cash crops (Wangwe, 1983; Lipumba et al., 1989).[5] The question then arises whether or not capacity creation went hand in hand with its utilisation. Lipumba et al. (1989) showed that in reality capacity creation and its utilization went in opposite directions, particularly during the late 1970s and early 1980s (which also witnessed falling levels of output). Wuyts (1994) argued that the processes which propelled capacity creation adversely affected the growth in export earnings and, consequently, led to falling capacity utilization in the formal sector.

In a nutshell, the argument runs as follows. Investment implied growth in consumer demand. First, as investment projects involve local expenditures on wages, the rise in investment (particularly, during the investment boom of the second half of the 1970s) brought in its wake an increased demand for consumer goods (the multiplier effect). Second, as new investments (factories, hospitals, schools, and so on) came on stream, employment increased along with installed capacity, thereby increasing the demand for consumer goods out of wage income. In Tanzania, a low-income country, a significant portion of the increased demand for consumer goods consists of the demand for food. The growing demand for marketed surpluses of food led to the rise in the price of food (first in parallel markets, followed by official markets). Under a regime of a fixed exchange rate, food prices rose relative to those of cash crops, provoking a fall in export volumes (from the mid-1970s onwards) due to the shift in peasant production from cash to food crops. Declining export earnings affected the import capacity of consumer goods and, more importantly, of intermediate inputs and raw materials.

The rise in the price of oil during the late 1970s and early 1980s made matters worse. In fact, the share of the imports of (non-oil) intermediate inputs in total imports fell dramatically. Consequently, capacity utilization in the formal sector (industry and services) fell sharply, while capacity creation continued unabated (up to 1980) under the impulse of foreign aid. This, in turn, had two adverse effects. First, it led to severe shortages of manufactured 'incentive' goods which adversely affected agricultural production in general, and officially marketed production in particular. Second, shortages of goods, both food and manufactured consumer goods, and severe price inflation (particularly in parallel markets upon which most people came to depend) led to the rapid erosion of real wages in the formal sector. To counter the erosion of real incomes, households increasingly turned to diversifying their sources of income by engaging in parallel market production or trade.

The investment drive behind import-substituting industrialization, therefore, resulted in an undermining of its own momentum by pitching capacity creation against its utilization. As this tension mounted, 'donor fatigue' and disenchantment with Tanzania's economic policies ended the investment boom in 1980, leaving the economy to cope with further import compression and the consequent 'goods famine' of the early 1980s. Household diversification strategies emerged as a way of survival during these crisis years and would subsequently, as economic reforms took effect, take on a new momentum and become more widespread with the increase in employment in the growing informal or second economy, both rural and urban.

The economic reforms from the mid-1980s onwards heralded a radical break with the past. The initial key features of this break were import liberalization, real exchange rate depreciation and the start of a second aid boom (after the period of 'donor fatigue' during the crisis years of the early 1980s) in which the composition of aid shifted in favour of programme aid (in particular, commodity import support). Two aspects of these features are of relevance to the argument here. First, early reforms in 1984 (before structural adjustment) introduced the so-called 'own exchange imports scheme', which opened the door to imports financed by foreign exchange balances (and incomes) held abroad by residents with no questions asked as to the source of such earnings, most of which resulted from unrecorded (parallel market) exports (Doriye et al., 1998, p. 215; Sarris and Van den Brink, 1993, pp. 51–2). In fact, as shown by Sarris and Van den Brink (1993, p. 30, Table 7, and p. 52, Table 15), during the period 1985–88 these unrecorded exports were consistently somewhat larger in value than official export earnings. Second, the immediate concern of donors at the time was to restore capacity utilization in manufacturing and services and to revive rural production and trade through the greater availability of manufactured consumer goods and implements (so-called 'incentive goods') in the rural areas. The initial key mechanism through which this was achieved was the shift towards commodity import support based upon the material allocation by donor agencies of commodity imports to parastatal and private enterprises (for example raw materials and intermediate inputs) and to specific sectors (for example fertilizer, medicines). During the late 1980s, (formal) manufacturing output and export volumes witnessed a modest recovery (Raikes and Gibbon, 1996, Doriye et al., 1998). Moreover, food prices on the parallel market declined markedly, in part due to the improved weather conditions in the second half of the 1980s (Sarris and Van den Brink, 1993, pp. 116–45).

Hence, in this initial period of economic reforms, the formal manufacturing sector (mainly parastatal, but also private enterprises) received a brief breathing space as import support directly aimed to boost its output. This initial short-term concern with rapid output recovery meant that less attention was devoted to counterpart payments as a potential source of budget support. The scheme was initially administered by the Treasury which *de facto* operated a parallel credit scheme inasmuch as many beneficiaries of commodity import support delayed (or failed) to pay the counterpart payments in domestic currency. As the real exchange rate kept depreciating, the size of these credits rose dramatically in domestic currency. It was only at a later stage, when donor attention shifted towards social expenditures, that the question of repayment of these debts became prominent on the policy agenda. In this early phase, therefore, the emphasis of aid policy lay with increasing capacity utilization rather than with industrial restructuring. Yet the economy was rapidly moving from a phase in which *quantity rationing* widely prevailed to one in which *price rationing* was to become the dominant feature. As argued below, the growth of the informal sector and its linkage with cheap manufactured imports was to play an important role in affecting this transition, for which the manufacturing sector was ill prepared.

Economic analysis of Tanzania during the 1990s has witnessed a growing awareness that one of the most distinctive features of the post-reform era has been the growth of the second or informal economy, coupled with increased reliance of households, both rural and urban, on multiple and diversified sources of income, both formal and informal, as a means to secure a livelihood (Maliyamkono and Bagachwa, 1990; Booth et al., 1993; Sarris and Van den Brink, 1993; Jamal and Weeks, 1993; Raikes and Gibbon, 1996; Bryceson, 1997; Bagachwa, 1997; Economic and Social Research Foundation and The Business Centre, 1997). Bagachwa, for example, argues that not only has wage labour come to assume an increasingly important role in the rural economy since 1980, but also that about 80 per cent of rural wage incomes were earned in the so-called informal sector (Bagachwa, 1997; pp. 139–40).

In fact, contrary to the predictions of the Berg report (World Bank, 1981); structural adjustment appears not to have led to the recovery and growth of traditional export crop production, but instead to growth of the informal or second economy. With respect to rural development, for example, Booth et al. pointed out that 'while economic liberalisation seems to have contributed new dynamism of village economies, it certainly has not done so by the route of "classic" structural adjustment – incentive-led recovery of traditional agricultural exports' (1993, p. 67). Instead, they argue that

> the evidently expanding activities . . . look much more like extensions of the processes of rural commercialisation and diversification . . . survival strategies from an earlier era now boosted by the availability of incentive goods and fuelled by the new income flows generated by a poorly understood mixture of factors including illegal natural resource exports and the restoration of foreign aid. (p. 68)

The issue at hand, then, is to come to grips with this 'poorly understood mixture of factors' which generated the growth of this second economy.

Broadly speaking, the second economy is referred to as 'economic activities that are unregistered and exist outside state regulations' (Engberg-Pedersen et al., 1996, p. 43). In the Tanzanian context, however, this definition would include most of rural production, particularly that derived from peasant production. Hence, it is more common to distinguish three sectors: (1) formal sector production (for example, large-scale manufacturing or construction), (2) peasant agricultural production, and (3) informal or second economy production, both rural and urban. The last sector refers to the widespread appearance, particularly over the last two decades, of 'income diversification' activities. In rural areas, informal sector non-agricultural activities span a wide spectrum including 'water, firewood, charcoal and fodder sales, the food and beverage trade, especially beer brewing, trade and transport activities, tailoring, brickmaking, carpentry, metal working, mineral excavation, leather goods production, and pottery' (Bryceson, 1997, p. 5). Informal sector mining of gold, rubies and gemstones such as tanzanite, for example, appears to have been a particularly fast-growing sector which, in the mid-1990s, involved somewhere upward of 300 000 persons, and up to a million if all those living in mining towns are included (Raikes and Gibson, 1996, p. 277). Urban informal sector activities equally involve a large range of mainly (but not exclusively) small-scale activities. In this case, however, it is customary also to include fringe urban agricultural activities.

This definition of the informal sector is not always theoretically very satisfactory, but often reflects a concern to draw boundaries for empirical investigation. However, these boundaries matter inasmuch as the activities thus delineated have manifested certain dynamic features over the last two decades which are worth investigating in their own right. As stated, one feature is that these activities remain unregistered and operate largely outside state regulations. But it would be erroneous to take this to mean that these activities do not depend on state policy, or, more importantly, that they do not rely on resources the allocation of which is largely influenced by state policies or donor activities. On the contrary, this chapter argues that the dynamics of the informal sector cannot be understood without taking explicit account of its interactions with financial processes and, more specifically, with the decentralization in the fiscalization of finance in general, and of foreign aid in particular. To tackle this question is the purpose of the next section.

3.   TOWARDS A THEORY OF INFORMAL SECTOR ACCUMULATION UNDER ECONOMIC REFORMS

This section tries to come to grips with the comment made by Booth et al. (1993, p. 68) concerning the 'poorly understood mixture of factors' which accounted for the evidently expanding income flows in the informal economy. This study pointed to the importance of the restoration of foreign aid and the availability of consumer goods as vital ingredients in this overall mixture. To establish the link between these ingredients and the dynamics of the informal sector, however, it is necessary to investigate the nature of capital accumulation in this sector.

The question of capital accumulation in the informal sector is often ignored because informal sector activities are seen to be largely labour-intensive.[6,7] Capital, therefore, is not explicitly included as a factor of production, let alone as a source of finance. This is a major shortcoming in the analysis of informal sector production. The fact that production is labour-intensive by no means implies that capital accumulation does not take place. This chapter argues instead that accumulation within what are commonly called 'informal sector' activities can, given the labour-intensive nature of most of these activities, best be depicted as a process of accumulation of *capital as the wage fund*. Hayami explains this Ricardian concepts as follows:

> Capital in his [= Ricardo's] view was the 'wage fund', defined as the sum of payments to labour in advance of the sale of commodities produced by the labour applied, as well as the payments for the purchase of tools and structures complementary to the use of labour. Therefore, the demand for labour increases proportionally with the increase in the wage fund. (1997 pp. 67–8)[8]

Capital accumulation under labour-intensive production, therefore, implies that savings are ploughed back into the expansion of the wage fund to allow for the increase in production.[9] Or, alternatively, that savings generated in the rest of the economy are channelled to informal sector production to expand the wage fund. In the Tanzanian context, it can be argued that both processes are at work. In the discussions during a workshop held in Dar es Salaam in August 1997, J. Semboja, a Tanzanian economist, remarked that 'many of the owners of the informal sector were located in the formal sector', a statement which quite plausibly suggests that the formal sector, including the public sector, is a major source for channelling material resources and finance to the informal sector, often (but not always) within the confines of kinship relations (Tripp, 1997).

Two aspects of this form of capital accumulation need further elaboration. First, given the largely unregulated nature of labour markets in the informal sector, an important requirement in securing competitiveness of its production is that labour is highly flexible and, hence, that wage costs are truly variable in nature. That is, labourers are only employed when orders exist or the market is secured and profitable, and laid off otherwise. This ability to keep labour costs flexible has two implications. First, the irregular employment of labour only works as a cost-reducing mechanism if sunk costs in infrastructure or specialized equipment are kept minimal, since such investments would otherwise remain idle. Hence the more volatile the demand for output, the less likely it is that major investment costs are tied up in production.[10] Second, the cost of adjustment in terms of insecurity and income generation falls squarely on the labourer, particularly when markets are volatile. This may help to explain why households pursue strategies of diversification rooted in both formal and informal production which, in rural areas, also embraces food production, with the aim to minimize the insecurity and risk.

In gemstone mining, for example, employment in the mining areas fluctuates markedly with the price of gemstones. The opening up of new mining areas as well as fluctuations in the demand for gemstones can alter the balance significantly between demand and supply, and, hence, lead to large price fluctuations which, in turn, affect employment levels as workers are laid off or recruited. Furthermore, in many mining areas, employment tends to be seasonal as well, since mine workers often engage in food production during the peak periods in the agricultural season. This is particularly important since, given that many of these mining towns are located in remote areas which are difficult or costly to reach, localized inflation of food prices is often a common feature (Wangwe et al., 1997).

A second feature of informal sector accumulation is that the consequent growth in employment in the informal sector, and the expansion of the wage fund it brings in its wake, propels the growth in the demand for *wage goods*, the goods and services consumed by workers in the informal sector. It follows then that the *availability* and the *cheapening* of wage goods, and the financial mechanisms which make this possible, will play an important role in shaping the viability and competitiveness of labour-intensive informal sector production.

This point can best be shown through the adaptation of a convenient analytical framework developed by Amsden (1997b, p. 124) which

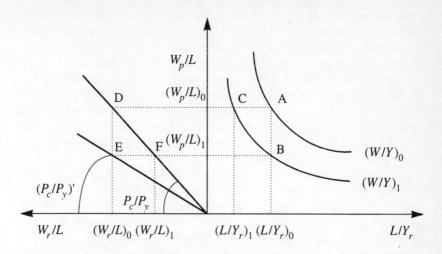

Notes: Y   = value of the output;
     Y_r = real output (output deflated by its price, P_y);
     W   = nominal wage bill;
     W_r = real wage bill (wage bill deflated by the price index of wage goods, P_c);
     W_r/L = the real wage;
     W_p = product wage bill (wage bill deflated by the price of output, P_y);
     W_p/L = the product wage;
     L   = labour;
     L/Y_r = the inverse of labour productivity;
     W/Y = unit wage costs.

Figure 6.1   Labour productivity, real and product wage, and unit wage costs

assumes that labour is the only factor of production. Amsden (who ignored the importance of the relative price of wage goods *vis-à-vis* the price of the output produced within the informal sector) was concerned with investigating the relationships between the inverse of labour productivity, the real wage, and unit wage. To take explicit account of the role of relative prices, however, the framework is extended by including the product wage as well. In contrast with the real wage, which deflates the nominal wage by the price index of wage goods, the product wage deflates the nominal wage by the price of the output produced. Figure 6.1 graphically depicts the relevant set of relationships which are explained more rigorously and completely in the Mathematical Appendix.

The right-hand side of Figure 6.1 features the product wage on its vertical axis and the inverse of labour productivity on its horizontal axis. Since both are deflated by the price of the output produced, it follows that the product of both variables equals the corresponding unit wage costs. Each curve in this quadrant depicts loci where unit wage costs are equal to a given constant. Each curve, therefore, is said to be a rectangular hyperbola since, for any point on this curve, the product of its corresponding coordinates on the vertical and horizontal axes equals the same constant. That is, movements along a curve keep unit labour costs constant, while curves located closer to the origin represent lower unit labour costs which can be taken as an indicator of the greater competitiveness of the industry.

The left-hand side features the product wage on its vertical axis and the real wage on its horizontal axis. The rays through the origin on the left-hand side have a slope equal to the ratio of the composite price of wage goods, P_c, to the price of commodity Y, P_y, and, hence, translate changes in the real wage rate (on the horizontal axis) into changes in the product wage (on the vertical axis). If the relative price of wage goods *vis-à-vis* that of the output produced falls, from (P_c/P_y) to $(P_c/P_y)'$, the ray will rotate downwards to the left.

Assume now that point A in Figure 6.1 depicts the initial position of the industry producing good Y. There are three ways in which unit labour costs can be reduced:

- by increasing productivity (a change from A to C in Figure 6.1)
- by reducing real wages (a change from A to B due to a move from D to F)
- by cheapening the cost of wage goods (a change from A to B due to a move from D to E).

Amsden (1997, pp. 124–5) only considered the first two cases. She argued that an industry can lower its unit labour costs either by moving in the direction of C (increasing productivity), or downwards toward point B (by reducing the real wage), or some combination of both. This latter case implies that the move from A to B goes hand in hand with a move from D to F on the left side of Figure 6.1. That is, unit labour costs are lowered due to a fall in real wages.

But the move from A to B in Figure 6.1 can also be brought about as a result of the relative cheapening of the price of wage goods, from (P_c/P_y) to $(P_c/P_y)'$, a move from D to E on the left side, leaving real wages unchanged. This is the third case. Such a situation can arise if productivity in the domestic wage goods sectors increases or if cheap imports of these goods substitute for local production.

It is the argument of this chapter that the situation depicted analytically by case 3 is relevant to understanding the drive behind the expansion of informal sector activities in Tanzania. As the economy moved from quantity rationing to price rationing in a context where relative prices were changing dramatically as a result of the steep depreciation of the real exchange rate, the viability and competitiveness of labour-intensive production depended on its capacity to keep unit wage costs low, though not wholly at the expense of real wages. Indeed, labour-intensive production, even if real wages are low, is not necessarily cheap or competitive. Much depends on labour productivity, which is generally low with labour-intensive production. Unit wage costs can therefore be high, notwithstanding relatively low real wages. But there is an obvious limit to the reduction of real wages since workers have to subsist one way or the other. In conditions where real wages fell significantly before and during the economic crisis of the early 1980s, the scope for a process of accumulation based on the continued reduction of the real wage was rather limited. However, import liberalization and increasingly flexible access to aid-funded foreign exchange allowed for cheapening wage goods through greater reliance on imports.

Under the impulse of these imports, the domestic market for consumer goods effectively *bifurcated*, with its upper tier catering for quality products demanded by higher income earners, and the lower tier catering for wage goods the demand for which sprang from the expansion of informal sector employment. In textile and clothing sectors, for example, the lower tier consists of the imports of cheap cloth and second-hand clothing, the latter of which are often refitted in the informal sector (De Valk and Mbelle, 1990; Semboja and Kweka, 1997). The required growth in imports was made possible initially by the introduction of the own-funded import scheme, and subsequently by the added availability of programme aid as sources to finance required import needs.

It was these imports which then played a key role in securing the competitiveness and viability of the expansion of this informal sector. More specifically, cheap manufactured imports served two purposes with respect to informal sector accumulation: (1) they provided so-called 'incentive goods' to boost agricultural production, including the supply of marketed food surpluses, and (2) they lowered the price of manufactured wage goods consumed within the informal sector. The latter mechanism directly cheapens wage goods. The former mechanism does so indirectly. It is nevertheless important because, at lower levels of real income, expenditure on food constitutes a major share in workers' expenditures on goods and services, and, hence, the prices of foodstuffs are major ingredients in the determination of workers' cost of living.

In the Tanzanian case, the relative lowering of the price of basic food-stuffs (or, at least, of preventing its price from rising) is directly linked with that of the availability and cheapening of manufactured basic consumer goods and farm implements and inputs 'incentive goods'. As argued earlier, in the period before the economic reforms of the mid-1980s it was the decrease in the availability of incentive goods due to import contraction as a result of falling export volumes that adversely affected the supply of marketed surpluses of food (Sarris and Van den Brink, 1993, pp. 124–5; Wuyts, 1994, pp. 179–87). With the economic reforms of the mid-1980s, however, the availability of incentive goods improved as a result of increased local production propelled by import support and because of direct imports. The consequent revival of rural production and trade, aided by favourable weather conditions, meant that food prices in the parallel markets (upon which the majority of workers depended) fell during the second half of the 1980s, notwith-standing price increases in the official markets (Rugumisa and Semboja, 1985; Sarris and Van den Brink, 1993, (pp. 116–45).

4.   CONCLUSION

During structural adjustment, Tanzania witnessed the rapid develop-ment of its second or informal economy. Household livelihoods increasingly came to depend on diversification strategies involving employment in both the formal and the expanding informal sector, characterized by a wide range of largely labour-intensive activities. The development of the informal sector is often depicted as a spontaneous process propelled by survival strategies of individual households. More specifically, this growth of the informal sector is seen to be located outside the purview of fiscal and financial processes within the 'official' economy. This chapter argues that this assumption is erroneous: it cannot be assumed that labour-intensive production is necessarily cheap, competitive, or even minimally viable. It is important, therefore, to analyse the broader macro-context which conditions the development of this sector. More specifically, this chapter argued that the supposedly spontaneous dynamics of the informal or second economy are directly linked with the processes of decentralization of the fiscalization of finance in general, and of foreign aid in particular. The importation of cheap wage goods to which these processes of decentralization of finance gave rise was identified as the key mechanism which fuelled informal sector accumulation and its competitiveness.

But this process was not without costs. First, formal domestic manufacturing industry was largely caught unawares by this trend and, given its precarious financial plight (made more acute by the restructuring of the banking system in the 1990s), largely unable to adjust to these changing conditions (Wangwe et al., 1996; Semboja and Kweka, 1997). The bifurcation of consumer demand under structural adjustment meant that much of its output lost its market due to insufficient quality to satisfy the upper tier of the market, on the one hand, and its inability to compete with cheap imports of consumer goods, on the other hand. Not surprisingly, formal manufacturing seeks protection (Semboja and Kweka, 1997), but this conflicts with the interest of informal sector accumulation which relies on the imports of cheap wage goods. In the absence of an explicit industrial strategy backed by financial policies and aimed at restructuring formal sector industry to be able to produce cheap wage goods, it is difficult to see how this tension can be resolved.

Second, the dependence of informal sector accumulation on imports is clear, given the widespread prevalence of imported basic consumer commodities in rural and urban areas. This impetus towards greater import dependence has undoubtedly been propelled by a process of decentralization of foreign aid. What is less clear, however, is whether the informal sector can generate the necessary export earnings to finance its own dependence on imports. It is likely that unrecorded exports have grown, perhaps significantly. But, in contrast, traditional exports appear, at best, to have stagnated.

Third, this stagnation of traditional exports may not be unrelated to the dynamism of the informal sector. Rural households seek to balance their activities between the production of food and cash crops and employment in the informal sector in ways which give them security, minimize risks, and generate cash income as well as income in kind. The increased attractiveness of informal sector activities under the impulse of the economic reforms draws labour away from farm production. Traditional cash crop production is likely to be more adversely affected by this withdrawal than food crop production since the growth in informal sector employment also propels the domestic demand for marketed surpluses of food.

These points raise the important question of the sustainability of the process of informal sector accumulation. The danger indeed exists that the observed dynamism of the informal sector is largely dependent on the economy's continued dependence on the current pattern of foreign aid.

MATHEMATICAL APPENDIX

The relationships depicted in Figure 6.1 can be more formally derived as follows.

Let

W = nominal wage bill
L = labour
P_c = the composite price index of wage goods
W_r = real wage bill: $W_r = W/P_c$ (6.1)

Y = value of output of commodity Y (say, an export product)
P_y = the price index of Y.
Y_r = real output: $Y_r = Y/P_y$ (6.2)

and, hence,

$$\frac{W}{L} = \text{nominal wage rate} \tag{6.3}$$

$$\frac{W}{P_c \cdot L} = \text{real wage rate} \tag{6.4}$$

$$\frac{L}{Y_r} = \begin{array}{l}\text{labour input per unit of output (the inverse of}\\ \text{labour productivity)}\end{array} \tag{6.5}$$

$$\frac{W}{Y} = \text{unit labour costs} \tag{6.6}$$

Note that

$$\frac{W}{Y} = \left(\frac{W_r}{L}\right) \cdot \left(\frac{L}{Y_r}\right) \cdot \left(\frac{P_c}{P_y}\right) \tag{6.7}$$

which shows that the unit cost of labour not only depends on the real wage and on (the inverse of) real output per head, but also on the price of wage goods relative to the price of output of the commodity in question.

Taking logarithms of both sides of equation (6.7), and differentiating with respect to time (t), yields an expression in rates of change, as follows:

$$\left[\frac{dW}{W}\frac{1}{dt} - \frac{dY}{Y}\frac{1}{dt}\right] = \left[\frac{dW_r}{W_r}\frac{1}{dt} - \frac{dL}{L}\frac{1}{dt}\right] + \left[\frac{dL}{L}\frac{1}{dt} - \frac{dY_r}{Y_r}\frac{1}{dt}\right] + \left[\frac{dP_c}{P_c}\frac{1}{dt} - \frac{dP_y}{P_y}\frac{1}{dt}\right] \tag{6.8}$$

Amsden (1997b, p. 124) ignored the last term on the right-hand side in equation (6.8) and, hence, also in equation (6.7). More specifically, she appears to assume that the ratio P_c/P_y remains constant. She overlooks, therefore, the effect of changes in relative prices on unit labour costs. More specifically, equation (6.8) implies that, other things being equal (in particular, the real wage), a fall (rise) in the price of wage goods relative to the price of output will lead to a fall (rise) in unit labour costs.[11] Amsden did not consider this possibility.

It is possible to depict this relative price effect graphically. To do this, equation (6.7) can be rewritten as follows:

$$\frac{W}{Y} = \left(\frac{W}{L \cdot P_y}\right) \cdot \left(\frac{L}{Y_r}\right) \tag{6.9}$$

Next, define

$$W_p = \frac{W}{P_y} \tag{6.10}$$

as the product wage bill, the wage bill deflated by the price of the output. And, hence,

$$\frac{W}{Y} = \left(\frac{W_p}{L}\right) \cdot \left(\frac{L}{Y_r}\right) \tag{6.11}$$

where W_p/L is the *product wage*. Note, furthermore, that

$$\left(\frac{W_p}{L}\right) = \left(\frac{W_r}{L}\right) \cdot \left(\frac{P_c}{P_y}\right) \tag{6.12}$$

Equations 6.11 and 6.12 can now jointly be depicted graphically as shown in Figure 6.1.

Assume, furthermore, that P_c is a weighted geometric mean of $P_{c:f}$, the price of food, and of $P_{c:m}$, the price of manufactured consumer goods (and basic services), as follows:

$$P_c = P_{c:f}^{a} \cdot P_{c:m}^{(1-a)} \; ; 0 < a < 1 \tag{6.13}$$

where the coefficient a equals the relative weight of food in the average worker's budget in the initial period (Wuyts, 1988, p. 655). And, consequently,

$$\frac{d\frac{W_r}{L}}{\frac{W_r}{L}} \cdot \frac{1}{dt} = \left(\frac{d\frac{W}{L}}{\frac{W}{L}} \cdot \frac{1}{dt}\right) - \left(a \cdot \frac{dP_{c:f}}{P_{c:f}} \cdot \frac{1}{dt}\right) - \left((1-a) \cdot \frac{dP_{c:m}}{P_{c:m}} \cdot \frac{1}{dt}\right) \tag{6.14}$$

which shows that the effect of food prices on the real wage rate will be greater, the higher the weight of food in the average worker's budget. The argument in the chapter, however, was that the last two terms of equation (6.14) were not unrelated in the case of Tanzania. The cheapening (and availability) of manufactured consumer goods not only had a direct impact in terms of cheapening wage goods, but also an indirect impact in so far as it stimulated the production of marketed surpluses of food and, hence, kept the inflation of food prices in check (and even lowered food prices in the parallel markets in the mid-1980s).

NOTES

1. Institute of Social Studies, The Hague, The Netherlands. The analysis presented in this chapter forms part of a broader research endeavour which combines earlier work on the impact of foreign aid on Tanzanian economic development (Wuyts, 1994; Doriye *et al.*, 1998) with ongoing research on the dynamics of the informal economy (Wuyts, 1998). The latter work took place as part of the UNCTAD project on *African Development in a Comparative Perspective*. I am indebted to Yilmaz Akyuz and Charles Gore for inviting me to take part in this project, and to Samuel Wangwe, director of the Economic and Social Research Foundation (ESRF) in Dar es Salaam, for the opportunity to spend more time at ESRF to undertake this research. I am furthermore indebted to Yilmaz Akyuz, Charles Gore, Maureen Mackintosh, Benno Ndulu, Rathin Roy, Bridget O'Laughlin, Semboja Hadji Hatibu and Samuel Wangwe for incisive comments and criticisms on the argument in this chapter.
2. Amsden (1997a; p. 474), for example, argues that, in East Asia, these off-budget financial resources approximately doubled the share of government spending in GDP, and looks at the way in which these resources were used to fuel processes of industrialization in East Asia. In Japan, she argues, these resources were mainly directed towards small-scale enterprises, physical infrastructure and social welfare (in particular, housing), while in South Korea they were used to build heavy industry.
3. The key features of structural adjustment policies are by now sufficiently well known to require further elaboration. For an excellent exposition of these policies and their application in the African context, see, for example, Tarp (1993).
4. Using econometric evidence, Doriye and Wuyts (1992), for example, showed that domestic bank borrowing (= money creation) by the government was positively related to the volume of project aid received by the government. An increase in project aid, therefore, would generally bring in its wake an increase (and not a decrease) in money creation to finance the increased budget deficit (to meet the costs of local resource use of the aid-funded investments). Wuyts (1994) showed, furthermore, that during the 1970s, aid and domestic savings showed a positive correlation, indicating that a larger inflow of aid (as a percentage of GDP) went hand in hand with a larger savings ratio.
5. More formally, let Y be the output of formal sector, Y_c its capacity output and u its degree of capacity utilization. Hence,

$$Y = u \cdot Y_c$$

    taking logarithms and differentiating with respect to time, yields

$$\frac{dY}{dt} \cdot \frac{1}{Y} = \frac{dY_c}{dt} \cdot \frac{1}{Y_c} + \frac{du}{dt} \cdot \frac{1}{u}$$

which shows that the growth rate in output of the formal sector equals the sum of the growth rates in capacity output (which depends on aid-financed investment) and in capacity utilization (which depends largely on export earnings to finance intermediate inputs). The possibility can then arise that the first term on the right-hand side increases while its second term decreases. This raises the additional question to what extent and in what circumstances the increase in the former may provoke the decrease in the latter.

6. A more detailed discussion of the literature on the informal sector in Tanzania can be found in Wuyts (1998).

7. This explains, for example, why Sarris and Van den Brink write the production function of the informal sector as follows:

$$X_u = K_u L_u^{\beta}$$

where K_u summarizes the contribution to informal sector production of 'other primary factors', and L_u denotes the labour employed in this sector (1993; p. 161).

8. An interesting example concerns investment in informal mining in Tanzania. Typically, pit owners employ about 50 workers before the pit starts operating, after which up to 150 workers may be employed. Hence the infrastructural investment itself requires the advance of a wage fund, which subsequently needs to be augmented when production starts (Wangwe *et al.*, 1997)

9. My recent stay at Peacock Hotel, a new venture in Dar es Salaam, provides an interesting example. The four lower floors of the hotel were then in full operation, the fifth floor was under construction, while the other top floors (with only the basic skeleton in place) awaited further work. This suggests that a considerable part of the investment is financed through prior savings by ploughing back retained profits into construction.

10. I am indebted to Sam Wangwe for this point. Volatile markets (such as prevail in the export of gemstones or in domestic construction), therefore, will tend to reinforce the labour-intensive nature of production and its reliance on flexible employment.

11. Obviously, equation (6.8) also reveals that, other things being equal (in particular, the real wage), a fall in the consumer price index which is matched by a proportional fall in the price of the output (such that the last term in equation (6.8) equals 0) leaves unit labour costs unchanged, but competitiveness will be enhanced since, for given real wages, nominal wages will be lower, and so will the price of the output produced. Such a situation would arise if the price of the output of the commodity in question were determined by a fixed mark-up over prime (labour) costs. In this case, it is the productivity increases in the wage goods sectors of the economy (or cheaper imports) which renders the output of the commodity Y more competitive.

REFERENCES

Amsden, A.H. (1997a), 'Editorial: bringing production back in – understanding government's economic role in late industrialization', *World Development*, **25** (4), 469–80.

Amsden, A.H. (1997b), 'A strategic policy approach to government intervention in late industrialization' pp. 119–44 in Solimane, A. (ed.), *Road Maps to Prosperity: Essays on Growth & Development*, Ann Arbor: The University of Michigan Press.

Bagachwa, M.S.D. (1997), 'The rural informal sector in Tanzania', pp. 137–54 in Bryceson and Jamal (1997).

Booth, D., Lugangira, F., Masanja, P., Mvungi, A., Mwaipopo, R., Mwami, J. and Redmayne, A. (1993), *Social, Economic and Cultural Change in Contemporary Tanzania: A People-Oriented Focus*, Stockholm: SIDA.

Bryceson, D.F. (1997), 'De-agrarianisation in sub-Saharah Africa: acknowledging the inevitable', pp. 3–20 in Bryceson, D. and Jamal, V. (eds), *Farewell to Farms: De-agrarianisation and Employment in Africa*, Leiden: Africa Study Center, Research Series 1997/10.

Bryceson, D. and Jamal, V. (eds) (1997), *Farewell to Farms: De-agrarianisation and Employment in Africa*, Leiden: Africa Study Center, Research Series 1997/10.

De Valk, P. and Mbelle, A. (1990), *Textile Industry under Structural Adjustment in Tanzania (1980–1988)*, mimeo, The Hague: Institute of Social Studies.

Doriye, J. and Wuyts, M. (1992), *Aid, Adjustment and Sustainable Recovery: The Case of Tanzania*, Working Paper No. 6, School of Oriental and African Studies, Department of Economics, University of London.

Doriye, J., White, H. and Wuyts, M. (1993), *Fungibility and Sustainability: Import Support to Tanzania*, Stockholm: SIDA.

Doriye, J., White, H. and Wuyts, M. (1998), 'Tanzania', pp. 195–221 in White (1998b).

Engberg-Pedersen, P., Gibbon, P., Raikes, P. and Udsholt, L. (eds) (1996), *Limits of Adjustment in Africa*, Oxford: James Currey.

Engberg-Pedersen, P., Gibbon, P., Raikes, P. and Udsholt, L. (1996), 'Structural adjustment in Africa: a survey of the experience' (Part One), in Engberg-Pedersen et al. (1996).

Economic and Social Research Foundation (ESRF) and The Business Centre (TBC) (1997), 'The parallel economy in Tanzania: magnitude, causes and policy implications', ESRF Discussion Paper Series No. 11, Dar es Salaam, Tanzania: ESRF.

Hayami, Y. (1997), *Development Economics*, Oxford: Clarendon Press.

Jamal, V. and Weeks, J. (1993), *Africa Misunderstood*, London: Macmillan.

Lipumba, N., Ndulu, B., Horton, S. and Plourde, A. (1989), 'A supply constrained macroeconometric model of Tanzania', *Economic Modelling*, October, 354–75.

Maliyamkono, T.L. and Bagachwa, M.S.D. (1990), *The Second Economy in Tanzania*, London: James Currey.

Raikes, P. and Gibbon, P. (1996), 'Tanzania' (Part Two), in Engberg-Pedersen et al., *Limits of Adjustment in Africa*, James Currey, UK.

Rugumisa, S. and Semboja, J.J. (1985), 'Possible redistributional effects of recent policy changes in Tanzania: some thoughts on the 1984/85 government budget', *Zimbabwe Journal of Economics*, January.

Sarris, A.H. and Van den Brink, R. (1993), *Economic Policy and Household Welfare during Crisis and Adjustment in Tanzania*, New York and London: New York University Press.

Semboja, H.H. and Kweka, P. (1997), 'Import liberalization, industrialization and technological capacity building in Sub Saharan Africa: the case of the garment industry in Tanzania', ESRF Discussion Paper Series, Dar es Salaam: ESRF.

Tarp, F. (1993), *Stabilization and Structural Adjustment: Macroeconomic Frameworks for Analysing the Crisis in Sub-Saharan Africa*, London: Routledge.

Tripp, A.M. (1997), *Changing the Rules: The Politics of Liberalization and the Urban Informal Economy in Tanzania*, Berkeley: University of California Press.

Wangwe, S.M. (1983), 'Industrialisation and resource allocation in a developing country: the case of recent experiences in Tanzania', *World Development*, **11** (6).

Wangwe, S.M. et al. (1997), 'Small-scale mining and mineral/gemstone cross border trade and marketing in Tanzania', ESRF Discussion Paper Series, Dar es Salaam: ESRF.

Wangwe, S.M., Semboja, H.H. and Lecomte, H.B. (1996), 'Exit procedures and economic transformation', ESRF Discussion Paper Series No. 10, Dar es Salaam: ESRF.

White, H. (1998a), 'Different types of aid', pp. 69–108 in White (1998b).

White, H. (ed.) (1998b), *Aid and Macroeconomic Performance: Theory, Empirical Evidence and Four Country Cases*, London: Macmillan, in association with the Institute of Social Studies,

World Bank (Berg Report) (1981), *Accelerated Development in Sub-Saharan Africa*, Washington, DC: IBIRD/World Bank.

Wuyts, M. (1988), 'The food balance and economic growth: an appraisal of FitzGerald's reformation of Kalecki', pp. 649–68 in *Development and Change*, **19** (4).

Wuyts, M. (1994), 'Accumulation, industrialization and the peasantry: a reinterpretation of the Tanzanian experience', *The Journal of Peasant Studies*, **21** (2), January, 159–93.

Wuyts, M. (1998), 'Informal economy, wage goods and the changing patterns of accumulation under structural adjustment', Study No. 2 in *African Development in a Comparative Perspective*, September, Geneva: UNCTAD, United Nations.

PART II

Policy and Regulation in Privatizing Systems

7. Informal regulation: a conceptual framework and application to decentralized mixed health care systems

Maureen Mackintosh

1. INTRODUCTION: RETHINKING SOCIAL SECTOR REGULATION

This chapter[1] argues for a rethinking of the concept of regulation within social sectors, with particular reference to health care. There is an emerging literature[2] on the regulation of mixed social sector provision, that is, social sector services provided by a mix of private, public and voluntary sector organizations. Governments in low- and middle-income countries that had previously monopolized or dominated provision of health care and education are increasingly liberalizing and encouraging the entry of private sector providers alongside existing or new charitable provision. At the same time, as Chapter 1 of this book outlined, aid donors are encouraging both governmental decentralization and devolution of decision making to semi-autonomous or independent agencies. These coexisting processes of decentralization and mixed public/private provision require new thinking about institutional processes of effective regulation.

The concept of regulation dominant in the economic literature – whatever its strengths and limitations may be in the arena of utility regulation for which it was designed – is inappropriate when transferred to the regulation of decentralized mixed social sector production. In its place, this chapter proposes a concept of regulation of social provision that encompasses informal regulatory processes alongside, and intertwined with, formal rule setting. As a consequence, it further argues for a process of regulatory design that incorporates the objective of effective informal regulation.

The chapter proceeds by comparing two economic models of the

149

regulatory process. One is the now conventional model of the independent public interest regulator, analysed in terms of principal–agent contracting (explained in Section 3), drawing on an individualist version of institutional economics. The other is a cooperative model of regulatory process set out in Section 4. The latter model conceives of regulation as a process with evolutionary elements, where learning and norm-formation occur. The exposition draws on game-theoretic formulations of the regulatory problem that allow a much larger role for culture and norms than do conventional models of regulation.

The chapter thus argues for an alternative theoretical approach to underpin research and policy making in social sector regulation, moving away from the starting point generated by the current theoretical literature on utility regulation. It proposes a broader and more context-specific concept of regulation for the sphere of social provision. Effective regulation needs to be understood as a mix of formal regulatory rules and informal patterns of behaviour. It follows that regulatory design must be rooted in local culture, and in the shared promotion of culturally appropriate self-reinforcing elements of ethical professional behaviour.

2. THE REGULATORY CONTEXT IN SOCIAL SECTORS

As Chapter 1 discussed, several different types of economic decentralization are being actively promoted by multilateral and bilateral donor agencies as methods of restructuring and reducing the public sector in low- and middle-income countries. These changes, taken together, are generating a big change in the regulatory context in social sectors such as health and education. The major changes, with particular reference to health care, are the following.

Public spending on social sectors has faced a severe fiscal squeeze in many countries,[3] and the problems of public sector service providers are often compounded by receiving less than budgeted income. The World Bank's preferred response has been a tight targeting of social spending to primary provision in health care and education, plus some 'safety net'-style activities such as social funds (World Bank, 1993; Vivian, 1995). These proposals are associated with the promotion of privatization of a large part of curative health care, and greater reliance on charitable provision. Many low- and middle-income countries had already seen rapid increases in private health care provision in the 1980s, under pressure of rising demand, and in the 1990s there was a further round of liberalization in health care, particularly in African countries (Bennett et al., 1997b).

This increasing acceptance of mixed public/private provision in social sectors has been associated with some managerial decentralization and contracting-out of remaining publicly supported social provision. There has been some creation of cost centres within public services, and some establishment of contractual or semi-contractual relationships between central government funding bodies ('purchasers') and those spending the funds ('providers'). Across the boundaries of the public health care sector, there has been a rise in contracting-out of publicly funded services to private and voluntary suppliers (Mills, 1997). In health care there has so far been little direct divestiture of public provision to the private sector in developing countries (ibid.). But health care providers in low-income countries increasingly survive through a mix of public, charitable and (official and unofficial) funding.[4]

These organizational reforms have been promoted internationally, as Chapter 1 noted, as a 'leading-edge' set of reforms (Nunberg, 1992) for the public sector world-wide.[5] More recently, the World Bank (1997, p. 87) has recognized that these reforms are institutionally demanding and may be 'unworkable' in some low-income-country contexts without a strengthening of institutional capability. However, there continues to be donor pressure to employ aid funding within an organizational framework of semi-autonomous or autonomous projects. There are exceptions to this trend, in the form of programme support, but project-focused aid continues to reflect a widespread distrust of direct government provision (Mackintosh, 1995).

Many countries with a past commitment to public sector health care provision free of charge at the point of use have turned to the liberalization of private provision, acceptance of autonomous NGO and mission provision, and a painful recognition of inability to guarantee access to even primary provision in health care and education. In this context the 'new public management' ideas can appear to offer institutional mechanisms for handling the demanding mix of centralization and decentralization implicit in social sector reform programmes: contractual frameworks for decentralization, and project accounting frameworks for user-charging systems. This has helped the new public management framework to take on the status of a conventional wisdom: a management model prescribed by consultants for implementation in stages. These prescriptions can have an aura of coherence the reforms lack on their home turf – in the UK, for example – where the reforms have been more thoroughly experimented in practice and their contradictions more closely examined.[6]

Taken together, the advantages generally proposed for the conventional model of social sector reform, encompassing fiscal capping and targeting, the 'new public management', and the liberalization of private sector provision are: spending control, cost reduction, innovation at local level to produce higher-quality and more responsive services, and higher total levels of service provision. The model is of a mix of 'quasi-market' semi-contractual relations between 'purchasers' and 'providers' within the state, and a market – no quotation marks – for service provision locally and nationally.

Social sector reform programmes of the competitive-state type therefore generate a new need for regulation – national or local – of the behaviour of social sector providers. There are two interrelated regulatory issues.

First, the private providers require regulation. As the World Bank notes (1997, p. 88), 'greater use of market mechanisms must be accompanied by effective regulatory capacity'. The Bank goes on to record the failure to regulate private health care delivery in many developing countries, a failure well documented in other studies (McPake, 1997; Kumaranayake, 1996). Private provision (like public provision) may or may not be of good quality; and it may or may not provide some level of access for those unable to pay. Furthermore, many governments retain a commitment to ensuring some level of complementarity between provision by different sectors. There are therefore good reasons for government rule setting – such as quality standards and licensing – and incentive creation. Making these rules and incentives 'stick' is another matter – addressed further below.

Similar issues arise *within* the public sector once a separation of 'purchasers' and 'providers' has been instituted. This separation is often characterized as a separation of 'policy' (a purchaser concern) and 'management' (by providers in response to contractual incentives). It introduces a new need for a regulatory role within the state, to monitor and shape the behaviour of public providers in line with government policy. This need is well recognized by many policy makers in low-income countries; as one government official put it, discussing health sector reform: 'regulation is very poorly developed in the public sector' (Mackintosh and Tibandebage, 1998).[7]

The conventional wisdom on social sector reform thus assigns an important role to regulation: 'Government becomes regulator and enabler rather than direct service provider' (Batley, 1997). But there is still a notable lack of depth of discussion of effective regulatory mechanisms in social sectors. The World Bank's 1997 report examines social sector reform but excludes the social sectors from its discussion of regulation. It notes (1997, p. 88) that 'The difficulties of regulation are even more daunting in social services' than in other sectors such as infrastructure, and (ibid., p. 67) that increased 'voice' from citizens can improve service quality. But the report offers little help to governments seeking to make social sector regulation work. This chapter aims to contribute to addressing this notable gap in the policy literature, drawing on research in health care. The argument questions Batley's widely shared formulation: not the need for regulation in the social sectors, but the implied assumption that regulation is a function solely of government, and that the government regulates best if it retreats from provision.

3. PROBLEMS WITH PRINCIPAL–AGENT MODELS OF REGULATION

'Regulation' has a distinctly narrow meaning in the current Anglo-American economic literature. It is generally taken to mean the formal setting of rules by a (presumed) public interest regulator, structured to provide appropriate incentives and backed up by legal sanctions. Much recent writing on privatized utility regulation takes that definition of regulation for granted, seeing no need to problematize it.[8]

Given this definition of regulation, the objectives and instruments of the regulator are typically analysed in a top–down fashion, using the principal–agent framework and the theory of incentive contracting.[9] This approach models both the internal and 'boundary' economic relations of government as a central 'principal' facing decentralized 'agents': that is, policy departments or 'purchasers' contracting with devolved agencies and independent firms. Extensively applied to the regulation of private utilities (as well as to employment relationships within the firm), the framework is now being applied to government itself (Tirole, 1994; Barrow, 1996).

The model characterizes the principal as capable of defining the required outputs – but unable to achieve them by simple fiat. Instead, the principal has to contract with agents who are self-interested, and may well not share the principal's aims. The agents know more than the principal, for example about their costs or how much effort they are putting in, and about the quality of the output they are supplying: that is, there is a problem of 'asymmetric information'.

Therefore, in this model, the government principal (the regulator) has to try to specify incentive contracts to align the motivations of the agents as closely as possible with the regulator's objectives. One of the key choices is between high-powered and low-powered incentives; the choice will depend on the nature of the risk and the capacity of the different parties to bear risk. High-powered incentives shift risk to the agent, while low-powered incentives leave risk with the principal. Performance-related payments are high-powered, as are fixed-price contracts. Conversely, salaries and cost-plus contracts are low-powered. Key conclusions of the literature are that where it is hard to identify individual contributions to output, where there are many aspects of the environment over which the agent has no control, where only some objectives can be monitored, or there is no way to measure output effectively, incentives should be low-powered. Furthermore, low-powered incentives are efficient where the principal is much more capable of bearing risk than the agent.

This literature predicts quite well the areas of regulatory activity where high-powered incentives are likely to be effective. The British approach to utility regulation is widely regarded as setting hard contracts: pricing rules are set for several years ahead, and interim changes evoke principled protest.[10] Large private power utilities have substantial leverage over their own business environment, and can be expected to behave self-interestedly, and to respond angrily but effectively to enforced price reductions. Similarly, the high-powered incentives embodied in competitive contracting-out at fixed contract prices are most suitable for easily specified and monitored activities. And indeed, the market-like reforms in UK public services have been least controversial in manual services such as refuse collection from households, where a hard contractual environment can be efficient (Walsh, 1995).

Beyond those areas, specifying efficient contracts becomes, in principle and in practice, much more problematic. There are a number of reasons for this, all relevant in different degrees to social provision such as health care.

First, the problem of asymmetric information is particularly serious in the social sectors. For most utilities, consumers and independent monitoring agencies can in principle assemble a great deal of relevant information about the service they are getting. It is not difficult technically to specify what constitutes a good service.[11] Social sectors, however, tend to have more vulnerable and less well informed consumers, faced with well informed professional providers. The extent of such asymmetric information is a matter which can be influenced by policy – a point returned to below – but very substantial levels of information will remain solely in the hands of providers, both public and private. Furthermore, difficulties of monitoring providers' behaviour imply that

contracting systems in social sectors tend to generate escalating transactions processing and monitoring costs.

A second relevant problem is the higher level of uncertainty that
tends to prevail in social sectors. The distinction is not complete: in this,
as in other relevant aspects, the water industry doubtfully fits the standard utility model, given the high externalities and uncertainty
associated with water supply.[12] But the health sector, for example, faces
high levels of both systemic and individual uncertainty. That is, the
demands on the health care system include unpredictable epidemics
and other emergencies, to which the system needs to be able to adapt
as they arise – including the effects of uneven fiscal pressure. And
individual health care professionals face high levels of uncertainty
requiring professional judgement and collaborative problem solving.

Given this mix of uncertainty and asymmetric information, incentive
contracting theory suggests that high-powered incentive contracts
should be avoided because they will have perverse incentive effects.
Strikingly, however, applications of the 'new public management' framework in social sectors have nevertheless tended to move towards higher-
powered incentives within the public sector and in contracting-out.
Performance pay, payment by results and fixed-price year-on-year contracts are all quite common features of reformed social sectors. So are
contracts which, while looking low-powered, are not: for example,
health care contracts priced at predicted average cost per case, but with
an uncertain case mix.

The predicted perverse incentives have not been hard to find in the
health and education sectors.[13] When payment is partly for 'output' in
education and training, for example payment for numbers of students
passing or attaining certain grades, then grades tend to inflate and/or
students needing a lot of teaching are selected out. When, as in the UK
health care reforms, the contracting process focuses primarily on cutting
costs, then eventually providers will cut costs at the expense of quality,
however reluctant they are to do so. In general, if contracts require
achievement of measurable targets based on data that can be manipulated at provider level, eventually providers' staff will manipulate them.

The reactions of social sector staff to these incentives focus attention
on a third problem with the incentive contracting model in the social
sectors. The quality of social services in the public or private sectors
only remains high so long as those working in the sectors seek to serve
the interests of the clients, such as patients or students. The more people
respond manipulatively to perverse incentives of the type just described,
the less they respect the principal who is funding them. This induces
professional cynicism: the more playing such games with the 'purchaser'

works, the more people's commitment to a service for its own sake can be eroded. Such cynicism can rebound on commitment to the patient or student.

Finally, the social sectors pose particular problems over equity of access and private payment. Theories of regulation built on the principal–agent framework tend to generate a preference for payment systems as close as possible to commercial charging practices. Access problems for the poor, it is often proposed, should be solved not by internal cross-subsidy but by cash transfers to those unable to pay (Burns et al., 1995). This strategy is, however, of limited feasibility in high-income countries, let alone in the weak fiscal context of low-income populations, and charging can undermine access by the poor.[14] Yet health care and education services are investments in human capital with strong public goods elements, as well as services essential to human capabilities or well-being.

This set of problems puts serious pressure on lower-level social sector managers in contract-based systems. Such managers face in practice two contradictory sets of pressures and instructions. On the one hand, the new public management, in its principal–agent contractual formulation, leaves policy, including policy on equity of access, in the hands of central purchasers, and construes providers as self-interested. That orientation is reinforced by managers' having to compete – on cost – for contracts.

On the other hand, the new public management claims local responsiveness and multiple income sources as one of its strengths. This claim can be fulfilled only if managers develop some initiative of their own, and respond to local populations and alternative sources of funding, not just to the initial funding principal. Such initiative leads in turn to strategic behaviour at local level. For example, if local managers respond to local pressure for improving access by looking for scope for cross-subsidy – and if formal contracting rules tend to exclude cross-subsidy, as they often do – managers may be led towards concealment, eroding the information available in the system.

A key source of many of these problems with the principal–agent model of regulation in social sectors is the lack of sufficient attention to the motives of both regulator and regulated. The incentive-contracting model of regulation simply assumes that the regulator reflects the public interest: it pays no attention to the motives of the regulator (Helm, 1994). The regulated providers, whether in the public or private sectors, are thought to be wholly self-interested; in the private sector, this is assumed to mean profit-seeking; in the public sector, it tends to be assumed that the providers respond chiefly to material incentives. It is increasingly recognized in the UK that both of these assumptions are unsatisfactory, and that a move towards lower-powered or 'softer' contracting, that recognizes professional commitment and the extent of asymmetric information, is desirable in the public services.[15] The next section argues that to make regulated decentralization work in the social sectors, this principal–agent framework may need to be abandoned in favour of a framework that encourages the pooling of information and resources to solve problems as they arise.

4. REGULATION AS A COOPERATION PROBLEM (1): ASSURANCE AND REGULATION

An alternative and more appropriate way of modelling the regulation problem in social sectors may be as a problem of *cooperation* rather than one-way incentive setting. In the privatized utility setting, cooperation between regulator and regulated is generally understood as a problem to be avoided, that is, as evidence of regulatory 'capture', although some level of collaboration between the two sides is clearly necessary to get the system to work (Helm, 1994).

However, in the social sectors such as health care, it is not even clear that a sharp distinction between regulator and regulated makes sense. Given the set of problems just described, it might be better to see regulation as a *system* problem: a substantial level of mutual regulation needs to be achieved. For example, health care providers such as hospitals need to be assured that formal regulatory mechanisms, for example licensing, are honest as well as enforced. Good provider organizations in all sectors need to be assured that good-quality provision will be recognized, even where it cannot be exactly monitored. Providers need to be encouraged to collaborate with each other to resolve problems (such as sustaining effective training), and to take a collaborative attitude to relations with patients. Governments need to be able to believe the data they get, and to identify poor provision. Patients need to be able to complain effectively. What is needed, then, is effective collaboration among the main actors in the system, for some agreed ends.

Suppose therefore that we model regulation not as a one-way principal–agent problem but as a problem of sustaining cooperative behaviour in situations of mutually incomplete information, where all sides have a stake in the outcome. One well-known way to model such a cooperation problem is as an 'assurance game' (Sen, 1973; Collard, 1978). An assurance game is a game with multiple equilibria such that the equilibrium chosen by the parties to the game depends upon their expectations of each others' behaviour – or, to put the same point another way, on the

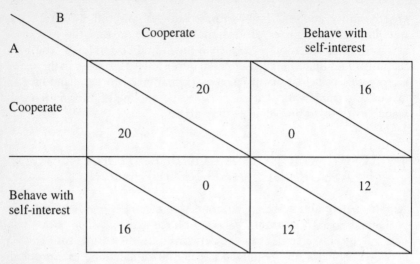

Figure 7.1   An assurance game

level of 'assurance' they have that the other parties will behave in the way they prefer. The pay-off matrix in Figure 7.1 shows a simple example of such a game for two players, A and B.

In this simple one-off game, if A thinks B will behave collaboratively, then so will A. If A thinks B will act in a self-interested manner, then so will A. The motivations are symmetrical, and the game has two equilibria, the top left and bottom right quadrants. Where the players end up depends on the probabilities they attach to each other's actions. If A believes that B will collaborate more than 75 per cent of the time, then, with the pay-offs shown, A will collaborate too, since in that case the expected value for A of collaborating is higher than A's expected pay-off from behaving self-interestedly. The same argument works for B. The specific numbers in Figure 7.1 are merely illustrative of the relevant patterns of pay-offs. The pay-offs are symmetrical for the two parties but that is not fundamental either – indeed in many situations asymmetric pay-offs would be more plausible.

Games such as this are useful in so far as they offer illuminating frameworks of thought for policy making. The attraction of the assurance game framework of thought is that – unlike principal–agent theory – it does not assume that agents behave in a wholly self-interested fashion. Instead, it leads us to ask how people acting within the system think others are motivated, what influences those views, and what the implications are for the system as a whole. Thus it allows us to bring the regulator also within the framework as an actor whose motivations must be specified.

Applying this assurance game framework, we can tell quite a plausible story about regulation of a mixed health care system. We can think of the players as different health care providers who need to work together; as the government (purchaser and regulator) facing the providers as a group; as patients faced with particular providers; and so on. This game then illustrates a system where the highest output is available if people behave collaboratively. The pay-off to each player in Figure 7.1 is largest if both cooperate. The next best is for everyone to behave self-interestedly (the bottom right-hand corner in Figure 7.1): the health care system functions, but a lot of resources are wasted, say in bargaining, monitoring and litigation costs. Worst for each party is if they try to collaborate while the other behaves self-interestedly; then the system delivers little in total, but what is left goes mainly to the self-interested party. That sole self-interest pay-off is not large enough, however, to make this choice preferable for any player to the mutually collaborative outcome if it can be achieved.

The assumption behind such a game-theory framework is that the 'players' act independently; they cannot make prior agreements about behaviour. It is worth noting that there is a trade-off, in this framework, between pay-offs and probabilities. If the pay-off to each from both behaving self-interestedly – 12 in Figure 7.1 – falls, then a lower probability of collaborative behaviour from the other party will be sufficient to induce collaboration. A fall in the pay-off to being to sole party to behave self-interestedly – 16 in Figure 7.1 – has the same effect, while a rise in that pay-off increases the need for assurance.

In such a framework, suppose that by 'self-interested' behaviour we mean the unmixed pursuit of personal material advantage. And by 'cooperative' behaviour we mean behaviour that combines concern with material reward with commitment to clinical standards and to responding to patients' needs. What then determines expectations and behaviour? One quite plausible answer is professional norms. If the norm is self-interested behaviour, the system will stick at the lower pay-offs of the self-interest equilibrium. Shared professional ethics may get you to the upper left quadrant, by generating a well-founded belief by each 'player' that the other will behave cooperatively. The system will then settle at the mutually cooperative equilibrium, since norms of cooperative behaviour then become self-reinforcing, given that no alternative is better for any player.

However, if one player's expectations of the other's behaviour are lowered, that player may jump first into self-interested behaviour in

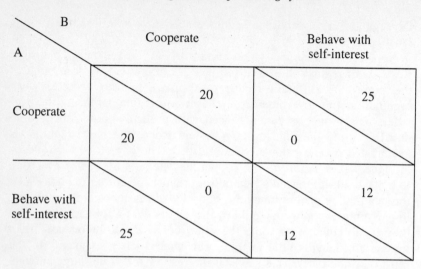

Figure 7.2   A prisoners' dilemma game

order to avoid being 'suckered'. So the system will flip to the lower-level equilibrium. Similarly, the higher level equilibrium would be desta-bilized if the individual pay-off to behaving instrumentally while the other cooperated went up sharply: above 20 in Figure 7.1 the game becomes a one-shot prisoners' dilemma and the bottom right quad-rant becomes the sole equilibrium (as for example in Figure 7.2).[16]

There is nothing new about the view that professional working relationships in services such as health care are better modelled as collaborative than as competitive. Maynard (1991), in a critique of the theoretical economic basis of the British health service reforms, pointed out that such collaboration is essential and that it may be induced by expectations of others, as in the assurance game, or by a sense of duty, when people do what is best for others because they think it right, rather than because they expect others to act in such a way that it makes it worth while for both. Such other-regarding preferences could also emerge because of professional norms, and would give us a game in which collaborative behaviour was the dominant strategy (as in Figure 7.3). But this seems a less plausible framework for thinking about professional collaboration than an assurance framework where norms influence behaviour by influencing expectations, and hence behaviour emerges from a mix of expectations and calculation.

So how are professional norms shaped? In the burgeoning economic literature on this subject, there are basically two stories about the emergence of such social norms. One sees all economic actors as acting

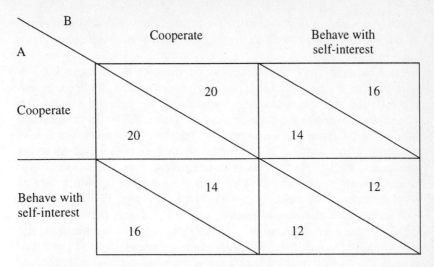

Figure 7.3   A game with other-regarding pay-offs

calculatively on material self-interest, and points out that collaborative behaviour may still occur if people interact with each other repeatedly. People may base their behaviour on experience of others' behaviour in the past, and on a calculation that it is in the other party's interest to continue to collaborate. This can sustain a cooperative outcome even in a prisoners' dilemma game, so long as it is repeated indefinitely. Individual agencies may get to know each other and develop a reputation for acting collaboratively. Then they may continue to collaborate even if the one-off individual pay-off from suddenly turning uncooperative rises: once you cheat you lose your reputation, and that is true of the other parties too. The long-term expected benefits of collaboration continue to outweigh the one-off 'temptation benefits', so people do not cheat (Kreps, 1990). This situation can *look* like a situation of shared professional ethics (Lyons and Mehta, 1997) – indeed it could even develop into that.

This brings us to the other story about professional norms, one which is much less orthodox in economists' terms. This story says that people's behaviour is not only influenced by self-interested calculation, but by other factors. One influential set of such factors, sociologists and social psychologists suggest, is identification with a peer group. There are different ways of interpreting such a sense of identity for the purposes of economic analysis. One version is to label this as a different type of rationality, such as 'expressive rationality' (Hargreaves Heap, 1988). This means that what one does may be expressive of the kind of person one wishes to be or how one wishes to present oneself. Such expressions of a sense of self may in turn emerge from membership of a peer group such as a profession.

Such professional ethics can also be thought of as some kind of 'gift exchange', where people give up opportunities to behave self-interestedly, and get something tangible – but non-negotiable – in return, such as social standing or 'regard' (Offer, 1997). Or professional ethics can be thought of as forms of 'routine' behaviour, which save constant calculation and are sustained so long as most members of the group also hold to them. This last approach sees people's capacity for calculation as much more limited than the standard economic model, so that they tend to hold on to what 'works' (Simon, 1978).

It seems most plausible to assume that in social sectors such as health care, people may operate on a mixture of group identification and individualistic calculation, and shift their behaviour as their perceived material pay-offs and the importance of ethics to professional standing change over time. They may have moments when they sit down and work out their own material interests in detail, and other periods when they operate on routine. The assurance game provides a useful framework of thought because it is, as shown above, a game with two equilibria. It suggests that a mixture of the structure of pay-offs – which affect people's calculations via their impact on the expected values of cooperating or behaving self-interestedly – and shared ethical norms – which affect expectations about behaviour – determine the choice of strategy and hence the equilibrium. Furthermore, the game-theory framework suggests that articulating ethical norms can help the system to work: identifying the non-material benefits of cooperation can provide 'focal points' in a common professional culture to help choose an equilibrium (Schelling, 1960; Mehta, 1993).

The next section considers the implications of this mixed approach to behaviour for regulatory intervention.

5. REGULATION AS A COOPERATION PROBLEM (2): CULTURALLY SPECIFIC INSTITUTIONAL DESIGN

> ... there is no one problem of cooperation: the problem is always how a given set of people are to cooperate. (Williams, 1989, p. 13)

If social sector regulation involves cooperation, and professional norms are relevant to the extent of cooperation, then the problem of designing effective regulatory structures has a strong element of cultural specificity. The health services literature emphasizes, for example, that health care is highly culturally embedded, and hence health care systems cannot easily be transferred from one country to another.[17] Thus particular incentive systems – for example paying doctors a salary – are seen in some countries as entirely compatible with professional behaviour, in others as entirely unacceptable. Cultural embeddedness also suggests path-dependence: that is, the initial conditions and direction of a system strongly influence its continuing characteristics. It also suggests that formal elements of regulation – rules and payments systems – need to be compatible with and sustained by informal culturally specific principles and expectations.

I propose to call the elements of a regulatory process that do not consist of explicit rules, but concern the sustaining of mutually fulfilled expectations, *informal regulation*. One can therefore understand cooperative regulatory processes as a mixture of formal rule setting and explicit contractual agreements, or *formal regulation*, and of informal understandings and established behaviour patterns, the latter based in norms, ethics and mutually understood principles.

If we accept an important role for such informal regulatory behaviour, then there can exist a need for deliberate regulatory design in the field of informal as well as formal procedures. This – like the rule setting – cannot be an activity determined solely by one party. It seems more useful, indeed, to consider informal institutional design as a process more akin to a *conversation*, as Dryzek (1996) suggests. Participants in, say, a particular health care system share a number of assumptions, ideas and meanings given to particular interventions. They share, in other words, a discourse.

Dryzek (1996, p. 109) defines a discourse as encompassing an ontology, ascription of agency and motive, and some taken-for-granted relationships. Such discourses make knowing and deciding possible, by removing the (impossible) requirement to rethink every action from first principles. A shared discourse underpins the reliance people may put upon the words of others; its shared meanings are constitutive of a situation, since they allow people to make sense of it.

When institutional contexts change, for example when health care systems are partially privatized, people seek to develop new discursive understandings. 'Discourse' here is thus being used, not in an embracing, Foucauldian sense, where people's ideas and behaviours appear almost entirely the product of a hegemonic discourse, but, following Dryzek, as something much more open to human influence and intervention, though substantially 'outside' of individuals. Participants in health care systems may frequently operate within more than one discourse in this sense, but competing discourses will be particularly evident in periods of sharp institutional change.[18] Dryzek suggests that we should see the informal aspects of institutional design as the reshaping, reinforcing or undermining of particular discourses over time.

There are other related ways of conceptualizing the informal elements of intra-organizational behaviour in the economic literature on working relationships between private firms. An example is the concept of corporate culture. Kreps (1986) suggests that corporate culture is an element of a firm's reputation, telling you what 'kind' of firm you are dealing with, and allowing employees and customers to understand 'how we do things here'. It operates as an institutionalized assurance that it is not in the interests of the firm to shaft individual clients in unforeseen circumstances, and the assurance carries weight because it both suits the firm's long-term interests and is embodied in the procedures and known behaviours of the firm.

Another parallel literature considers the problems of constructing a 'governance structure' for interfirm relations in Eastern Europe that will encourage collaboration and also organizational and technical learning, including the collaborative resolution of disputes: 'A governance system should not only provide monitoring and incentives for performance. It should also encourage experimentation, adoption and diffusion of better practices' (Kogut, 1996). There is a clear link between this industrial literature and the discourse framework. Sabel and Prokop (1996), for example, argue that internationally, manufacturing firms are developing long-term joint working relationships involving rethinking and reworking projects over time. In such relationships, they argue, prices become 'boundary conditions', not the key issue for negotiation, and precise specification of output is replaced by 'discursive standards' of competence to respond to challenges. Partners 'learn by monitoring' as the project progresses. It may be that, if we are looking for a metaphor for working relationships within a health care system, this notion of 'collaborative manufacturing', with its emphasis on shared innovation, and a lack of concern with the precise assignment of property rights, is a better metaphor than hard contracting stories.

The collaborative manufacturing metaphor implies that one cannot treat the governance structures as separate from and above the firms themselves: 'To monitor such relations, it seems that a governance structure would have to become in effect one of the collaborators, exchanging information on like terms with the others. There are indeed signs that this is occurring' (Sable and Prokop, 1996, p. 166). The parallel in the social provision case is arguably the role of government. The government needs to see itself, and to act, as a communicative partner, whose actions are open to scrutiny, if it is to be respected by good independent 'provider' institutions. The implications of this in the health care context are discussed in Section 6.

What would it mean, then, to treat the process of informal regulation as the creation and sustaining of a shared discourse? Discourses function effectively where feedback between understandings, resultant expectations and experiences are mutually reinforcing. So participation in developing an informal regulatory system implies helping to develop shared understandings of the nature of inter-organizational relationships.

Consider the two economic models in the previous sections. They treat these relationships quite differently. The first model views the relationships between funder or regulator and 'providers' as contractual transactions among self-interested parties: indeed it imposes that language on the parties. It then asks, what are the incentives embodied in these transactions and will they work in the sense of persuading the providers to do as the funder or regulator wishes?

The second, 'assurance', model leads us to ask, to what extent are these relationships 'transactions' at all? In other words, do we understand – do we wish the participants to understand – these relations as exchange? It is in the nature of the meanings of exchange in the twentieth century's economy that we tend to understand exchange relations as something-for-something swaps: in this case, cash or operating licences for evidence of 'performance'. We also invest 'exchange' with meanings about the ethics of strategic and arm's-length behaviour: it is generally felt to be acceptable to behave self-interestedly in exchange, but not in relation to – whom? Parents? Children? Vulnerable patients? Those *funding* vulnerable patients? The answers are culturally specific, but the questions make sense in a wide range of market contexts.

The discursive construction of the working relations within systems of social provision therefore matters. If a new public management framework constructs the regulatory relation as a contract, it invests it with new meaning. Some theorists (for example Macneil, 1980) label open-ended working relationships as 'relational contracting'. The danger, however, with the contracting language is precisely that it does carry the implication of self-interested exchange. Alternative discursive constructions, such as professional partnerships, longer-term 'gift' relationships where the something-for-something relationship is softened and not all the returns are material, or collaborative joint ventures, have different real effects. The gift relationship framework can alert us to the danger of assuming self-interested behaviour in a collaborative culture, and thereby creating a self-fulfilling prophecy.

Discourse therefore matters, and is open to manipulation, as the new public management has amply demonstrated. The effects are not always predictable, however, and managers who too openly try to manipulate or impose a language for their own ends can discover how hard it is to control the interpretations put by subordinates on a new language (Mackintosh, 1997a). This is why a 'conversation' is a good metaphor, and why context is key. Discourses change by accretion of conversations and experience. Where one set of shared meanings becomes dominant, is reinforced by experience, and has come to seem at least partly proper and natural, then the kind of stable inter-organizational culture has emerged that can provide a focal point for choosing an equilibrium in – say – and assurance game. The nature of the culture – collaborative or competitive – will determine which equilibrium will be chosen.

6.   INTERVENING IN INFORMAL REGULATORY DESIGN

To examine what this conceptual framework might mean for intervention in regulatory design, consider a hypothetical but plausible example:[19] a health care system in a low income country moving from public sector vertical integration (at low levels of funding and quality) to a mixed system with private investment and public sector managerial decentralization. All health care providers, whether funded by aid, taxes or payments, or a mixture of all three, face financial risk. They need to raise funds and to define their activities. Public clinics and hospitals are poorly supplied, and user fees have been instituted. The government licensing system for doctors and clinics is not robust, and training systems have been running down. Private for-profit clinics are springing up in better-off areas, and there are some well established charitable hospitals whose relation to the public sector system is uneasy. Aid funders prefer their own projects and vertical programmes to putting money into the public system. There is strong pressure on the government from multilateral institutions to retreat almost completely from supporting hospital care, putting very limited public funds into primary and preventive care.

Such large changes, following a history of declining quality of provision and falling morale in the sector, pose a considerable policy challenge. Path-dependency (defined in the previous section) implies that the first few years will establish some of the initial conditions of the system. This includes investment patterns, and culture and behaviour in the independent sectors and the public sector, and these conditions will bring consequences for many years to come. Policy needs to focus on influencing those initial conditions. A complicating factor, however, is that policy objectives too are path-dependent. What people think is possible and right depends in part of what they know and have seen.[20]

What then should be the regulatory role of government? The conventional view, stemming from the principal–agent model and implied by the 'new public management', would be for government to retreat to a role of licensing and standard setting, plus contractual funding for remaining publicly supported primary providers. However, one among many problems with this approach is that it does nothing to improve government behaviour itself. Formal rules and contractual obligations, if they are to be obeyed in letter and spirit, need to be legitimate with those who must conform. Such rules need a strong measure of prior acceptance and preferably a lobby in their favour.

An alternative, suggested by the assurance model, would be for the government to see itself as a partner with other funding and supplying bodies, and with the public, in trying to establish as good a system as is possible in the circumstances. Informal regulatory design involves a conversation between such 'speakers' about the terms on which the health care system should be developed.

This way of thinking about regulation can be illustrated by pursuing the hypothetical example introduced at the beginning of this section. Consider first the independent sector. There are various patterns of private provision and private health care market which might emerge, and which it is to be is initially at issue. Diversity of provision increases; commercial and non-profit provision coexist in primary and secondary care. Commercial investment rises sharply in the early stages of reform; and donors will continue to fund some preventive and community health care via local NGOs. A range of proposals are put forward for private and non-profit health insurance systems, some of them provider-based.

These developments open up alternative possible roads through privatization. Insurance or prepayment systems may be more or less individual; more or less employer-based; wholly voluntary, or compulsory for some categories. Private providers may be more or less interested in quality, more or less focused on profit seeking. Competition may emerge which is price-based or quality-based in different segments of the market. Perhaps the greatest danger, illustrated by 'polarized' Latin American systems (Frenk, 1993), is the solidification of low–quality – and not really very cheap – private provision for the poor, and of very expensive private provision for the well-off, generating very high medical incomes. Once solidified, the former is hard to break, and the latter can be impossible ever to generalize.[21]

Trying to prevent this kind of polarization requires regulation, based on generating agreement about the *kind* of private sector to be created. If a shared objective can be developed within the system that polarization should be minimized, then one way to think about the role of government is that it should use its limited public resources as *leverage* to influence the nature of quality and access. This means using government funds, not to complement and set rules for private and voluntary provision, but in negotiating mode, to develop working relations with providers. Here are some examples.

Health care systems tend to work best – and most cheaply – when they include an effective primary care system that also acts as 'gatekeeper' to expensive specialist treatment. But privatization often creates large numbers of unregulated private dispensaries, some of poor quality and poorly integrated into the broader system. How can regulation help? Close formal regulation of each provider is unrealistically expensive, though formal licensing can be associated with unsignalled inspections bringing a threat of withdrawal of a licence.

Trying to stimulate public pressure on dispensaries is one available form of informal regulatory intervention. Can the patients become much more actively critical users of the services: can expectations be raised and people encouraged actively to complain? Countries vary enormously in the extent of public pressure exerted on health care providers, and experiences such as that of Kerala suggest that political support for public pressure can be effective.[22]

A second approach is to try to construct public/private alliances with good dispensaries to agree norms for treatment and charging, which can then be widely publicized. Attempts can be made to increase self-policing in the sector – perhaps through a professional association structure – such that good dispensaries develop a material and professional interest in driving out undercutting by low-quality providers. All of these strategies mean involving patient groups and dispensaries in interactive regulatory mechanisms, rather than treating regulation as a role for government alone; but it also identifies a role for government in building professional associations.

Here is a second example. Liberalization tends to undermine two public good elements of a health care system. The emphasis on competition tends to reduce information flows in the system, since providers emphasize commercial confidentiality, share information less freely, and come to see little return from providing information to government.

And training provision is also threatened, since the private providers may not think it in their interests, or their job, to train. In privatizing systems, information has strategic uses, and it is in the interest of the commercial sector to 'poach' staff. In addition, access to the system by the poor can worsen.

In these circumstances, a 'negotiating' approach to the use of government funds and legal powers can help. Instead of treating government financial inputs to private institutions as contractual support, the public sector can go for explicit joint ventures, where limited government funding gains specific commitments to training, openness, treatment of those unable to pay, and collaborative behaviour, and the government too has obligations to sustain its agreed commitments and to share information. Funding can thus be explicitly aimed at generating regulatory information and mutual learning.

More generally, this framework suggests that regulatory systems should aim to reduce – or not to create – perverse incentives; to build in (or not lose) available mechanisms of social openness, cross-subsidy, risk pooling, and cost ceilings; to ensure that institutions created are in principle generalizable if incomes rise sufficiently. Most generally, this framework suggests that the best way to conceptualize a developing mixed health care system is as a joint venture where the boundaries between sectors are deliberately 'blurred' – a sharp alternative to conceptualizing it as a network of increasingly 'hard' contracts. The 'joint venture' allocates much of the new investment to the private sector, but the government contributes some revenue funding, and can use its legal (and political) powers to influence the evolution of the system strongly so long as it can establish legitimacy.

Regulation, in this framework, is therefore three-way: government, providers and public, orchestrated by the government, but also by providers' associations and by campaigns and lobbies for patients. For example, the government can use strong sanctions against bad providers if it works closely with good providers to develop acceptable regulation and to create a lobby in its support.

In this framework, too sharp a funding/providing distinction is, furthermore, undesirable, in contrast to the contractual model. Since providers engage in price discrimination and strongly influence access, they must be involved in experiments with local prepayment and mutual risk pooling. If the public are involved in local health care pre-payment schemes, then the same organizations can be used to scrutinize the quality of care received. Non-material incentives – especially professional and public recognition – can be explicitly built into the system alongside reasonable payment for work done. Unpaid mutual sharing of facilities and information can be positively encouraged, as can cross-subsidy.

One can conceptualize this 'negotiating' use of funds in terms of the assurance framework. Collaborative behaviour in that framework can be achieved by a mix of suitable pay-offs and a sufficient level of assurance. Assurance can be sustained by professional norms rooted in non-material concerns: professional standing, time to do research, a role in policy, a quality assurance label, public approval. Regulatory intervention can change the material pay-offs by, say, rewarding schemes that improve access. It can also improve assurance by improving mutual understanding and institutional mechanisms to sustain mutually agreed standards.

This line of thought on regulation is strongly at odds with the implicit ethical basis of the principal–agent contracting framework. It blurs the notions of principal and agent, and as a result undermines the principle that all agents should be treated even-handedly. By contrast, it proposes alliances, supports some kinds of 'insider' behaviour within the system, and proposes a deliberate attempt to establish shared understandings among limited numbers of regulatory participants. This regulatory approach is not of course unproblematic, but it may do better in sustaining quality and widening access in a commercializing health care system.

The framework also suggests an agenda for policy-oriented research. This involves investigation of the culture and motivations of health care providers in different sectors, and a contribution to a collaborative process of defining shared regulatory goals. Informal regulatory design can never start from scratch, but has to grow out of existing cultural assumptions, not least in order to challenge some of them effectively. So there is a role for interpretative research that investigates existing discourses, and enables reflection on existing assumptions, in order to build regulatory interventions upon those understandings.

7. CONCLUSION

The concept of a cooperative approach to regulation, with a strong element of informal regulatory process, rejects by implication the sharp divides between policy and management, and between management and regulation, inherent in the new public management. Cooperative regulation can be effective only if providers share ethical and practical responsibility for the quality of the system: government regulators cannot police it alone. Policy can seek to reinforce desirable behaviour at the provider level, but the government has to recognize that it needs to open itself up to desirable outside pressure and informal regulatory behaviour from other members of the system.

Systems of social provision, such as health care, work best if they attract people whose motivations are a mixture of material and professional. Purely materialistic behaviour can be highly inefficient. Mutually reinforcing ethical and professional behaviour is harder to create than to sustain once created – that was a key point being made by the assurance game. The challenge for policy in a liberalizing health care system is to try to encourage ethical and professional ways of working and institutions which will sustain them, piecemeal, but with a sense of direction over time.

Finally, the discussion of informal regulation suggests several tentative conclusions concerning the design of regulatory intervention, as follows:

- Regulation must have a strong element of inter-institutional collaboration, in which the government is one partner among many, despite acting as the formal rule setter.
- Formal rules and informal regulatory mechanisms must be mutually compatible; if they conflict, formal rules are unlikely to be effective.
- Informal regulatory mechanisms must be culturally appropriate, and grow out of or challenge existing cultural meanings in recognizable ways.
- Regulatory design should assume that participants can be motivated by a mix of adequate payment and other forms of ethical and professional standing.
- Information is key to effective regulation, and increasing information availability should be a key objective of regulatory collaboration.

NOTES

1. Earlier versions of this chapter were presented at a seminar organized by the Economic and Social Research Foundation in Dar es Salaam, Tanzania in November 1996, and at the conference on Public Sector Management for the Next Century in Manchester in June 1997. I am grateful to Graham Dawson, Anne Mills, Rathin Roy, Paula Tibandebage, Sam Wangwe and Marc Wuyts for comments on those earlier versions. The current text is the sole responsibility of the author.
2. The World Bank (1993) identifies the importance of regulating privatizing health care systems; Kumaranayake (1996) surveys the literature on regulation in the context of health care reform and liberalization in low-income countries; Bennett et al. (1997b) argue for the need for effective regulation of mixed health care systems;

Mogedal et al. (1995) make this case for the African health care context; Barrow (1996) and Tirole (1994) apply current economic theories of regulation to social sectors in high-income countries.

3. The papers by Tibandebage and Narayana in this book (Chapters 5 and 8) document the fiscal squeeze on health care in Tanzania and Kerala respectively.

4. Current research in Kerala and Tanzania by the author, Paula Tibandebage and D. Narayana identifies this phenomenon sharply. User fees are now widespread in African public hospitals (Gilson, 1997), as is informal private payment. See also Tibandebage, Chapter 8.

5. Mackintosh (1995) surveys evidence on the emergence of a consensus on this reform 'model' and its promotion.

6. See also Chapter 1; Mackintosh (1997b) makes this case for health care with reference to the NHS reforms; see also Walsh (1995), Clarke and Newman (1997), Stoker (1999) for surveys of some of the strengths and weaknesses of the 'new public management' in the UK.

7. This paper draws on current research funded by the UK Department for International Development. The content does not reflect DFID official policies or practices but represents the views of the authors alone.

8. See for example, Bishop et al. (1996); an exception is Helm (1994), who recognizes the limits on the institutional separation of regulator and regulated, and the need to consider the motivations of the regulators themselves. This is also the definition used in Kumaranayake (1996).

9. The classic exposition is Laffont and Tirole (1993). A text providing an accessible exposition of some of the ideas is Milgrom and Roberts (1992).

10. An example is the row that erupted in 1994 when the UK electricity regulator altered existing price-capping regulations in the face of new information about electricity distributors' profits exposed by a takeover bid. The regulator was widely accused of breaking contractual commitments and undermining confidence in regulatory stability.

11. The political will to enforce it is another matter: see Schofield and Shaoul Chapter 9 in this volume.

12. Schofield and Shaoul (Chapter 9) examine the problems of water industry regulation based on the UK experience.

13. Mackintosh and Smith (1996) discuss the problem in UK health care, with examples of the type of problems summarized here.

14. Gilson (1997) documents this effect of health care charging in the African context.

15. See, for example, a number of papers in Flynn and Williams (1997).

16. Those familiar with game theory will know that cooperative outcomes can be attained when a prisoners' dilemma game is repeated indefinitely. See below.

17. Fuchs (1993), for example, makes this case for the USA and Canada. Mackintosh (1995) surveys some of the evidence on cultural diversity in health care.

18. Such discursive conflicts can be researched through fieldwork. Mackintosh (1997a, 1999) analyses competing economic discourses in the context of local government quasi-market reforms in England.

19. This is simply a plausible scenario drawn on the basis of observation and available research such as Bennett et al. (1997a). It refers to no country in particular.

20. The differences in framework of thought on policy between most European and most US health care commentators is a striking illustration of this fact.

21. An impression reinforced by the failure of the US health reforms proposed by the first Clinton administration.

22. Sen (1992); see also Narayana, Chapter 5 in this book. The role of public pressure in health care regulation in Kerala is the subject of current research by Narayana.

REFERENCES

Barrow, M. (1996), 'Public services and the theory of regulation', *Policy and Politics*, **24** (3), 263–76.

Batley, R. (1997), 'Overview of the role of government research', *Government and Adjustment Newsletter*, Issue No. 4, Birmingham.

Bennett, S., McPake, B. and Mills, A. (eds) (1997a), *Private Health Providers in Developing Countries: Serving the Public Interest?*, London: Zed Books.

Bennett, S., McPake, B. and Mills, A. (eds) (1997b), 'The public/private mix debate in health care', in Bennett et al. (1997a).

Bishop, M., Kay, J. and Mayer, C. (eds) (1996), *The Regulatory Challenge*, Oxford: Oxford University Press.

Burns, P., Crawford, I. and Dilnot, A. (1995), 'Regulation and redistribution in utilities', *Fiscal Studies*, **16** (4), 1–22.

Clarke, J. and Newman, J. (1997), *The Managerial State*, London and Thousand Oaks, CA: Sage.

Collard, D. (1978), *Altruism and Economy: A Study in Non-Selfish Economics*, Oxford: Martin Robertson.

Dryzek, J.S. (1996), 'The informal logic of institutional design,' in Goodin (1996).

Flynn, R. and Williams, G. (eds) (1997), *Contracting for Health: Quasi-Markets and the National Health Service*, Oxford: Oxford University Press.

Frenk, J. (1933), 'The public/private mix and human resources for health', *Health Policy and Planning*, **8** (4), 315–26.

Frydman, R., Gray, C. and Rapaczynski, A. (1996) (eds), *Corporate Governance in Central Europe and Russia. Volume 1 Banks, Funds and Foreign Investors. Volume 2. Insiders and the State*, Budapest: Central European University Press.

Fuchs, V. (1993), *The Future of Health Policy*, Cambridge, MA: Harvard University Press.

Gilson, L. (1997), 'The lessons of user fees experience in Africa', *Health Policy and Planning*, **12** (4), 273–85.

Goodin, R.E. (ed.) (1996), *The Theory of Institutional Design*, Cambridge: Cambridge University Press.

Hargreaves Heap, S. (1988), *Rationality in Economics*, London: Routledge.

Helm, D. (1994), 'British utility regulation: theory, practice and reform', *Oxford Review of Economic Policy*, **10** (3).

Kogut, B. (1996), 'Direct investment, experimentation and corporate governance in transition economies', in Frydman et al. (1996).

Kreps, D. (1986), 'Corporate culture and economic theory', reprinted in Buckley, P.J. and Michie, J. (eds) (1996), *Firms, Organisations and Contracts*, Oxford: Oxford University Press.

Kreps, D. (1990), *Game Theory and Economic Modelling*, Oxford: Clarendon Press.

Kumaranayake, L. (1996), 'The role of regulation: influencing private sector activity within health sector reform', paper presented to the Development Studies Association annual conference, Reading, September.

Laffont, J.-J. and Tirole, J. (1993), *A Theory of Incentives in Procurement and Regulation*, Cambridge, MA: MIT Press.

Lyons, B. and Mehta, J. (1997), 'Contracts, opportunism and trust', *Cambridge Journal of Economics*, **21** (2), 239–57.

Mackintosh, M. (1995), 'Competition and contracting in selective social provisioning', *European Journal of Development Research*, **7** (1), 26–52.

Mackintosh, M. (1997a), 'Economic culture and quasi-markets in local government: the case of contracting for social care', *Local Government Studies*, **23** (2), 80–102.

Mackintosh, M. (1997b), 'Managing public sector reform: the case of health care', *DPP Working Paper*, No. 37, Milton Keynes: Open University.

Mackintosh, M. (1999), 'Two economic discourses in the new management of local governance: "public trading" and "public business"', in Stoker 1999.

Mackintosh, M. and Smith, P. (1996), 'Perverse incentives: an NHS notebook', *Soundings*, **4**.

Mackintosh, M. and Tibandebage, P. (1998), 'Economic analysis of an emerging mixed health care system, and implications for management and regulation: initial themes and issues of research design', ESRF *Discussion Paper*, Dar es Salaam, April.

Macneil, I. (1980), *The New Social Contract: An Enquiry into Modern Contractual Relations*, New Haven, CT: Yale University Press.

Maynard, A. (1991), 'Incentive contracts', in Lopez, G. (ed.), *Incentives in Health Systems*, Berlin: Springer-Verlag.

McPake, B. (1997), 'The role of the private sector in health service provision', in Bennett et al. (1997a).

Mehta, J. (1993), 'Meaning in the context of bargaining games: narratives in opposition', in Henderson, W., Dudley-Evans, T. and Backhouse, R. (eds), *Economics and Language*, London: Routledge.

Milgrom, P. and Roberts, J. (1992), *Economics, Organization and Management*, New Jersey: Prentice Hall International.

Mills, A. (1997), 'Contractual relationships between government and the commercial private sector in developing countries', in Bennett et al. (1997a).

Mogedal, S., Hodne Steen, S. and Mpelumbe, G. (1995), 'Health sector reform and organizational issues at the local level: lessons from selected African countries', *Journal of International Development*, **7** (3), 349–67.

Nunberg, B. (1992), 'Managing the civil service: what LDCs can learn from developed country reforms', *World Bank Policy Research Working Papers*, No. 945, Washington, DC.

Offer, A. (1997), 'Between the gift and the market: the economy of regard', *Economic History Review*, **L** (3), 450–76.

Sabel, C.F. and Prokop, J.E. (1996), 'Stabilization through reorganisation', in Frydman et al. (1996).

Schelling, T. (1960), *The Strategy of Conflict*, Cambridge, MA: Harvard University Press.

Sen, A.K. (1973), *On Economic Inequality*, Oxford: Clarendon Press.

Sen, G. (1992), 'Social needs and public accountability: the case of Kerala', in Wuyts, M., Mackintosh, M. and Hewitt, T., *Development Policy and Public Action*, Oxford: Oxford University Press.

Simon, H.A. (1978), 'Rationality as process and as product of thought', *American Economic Review*, **68** (2), 1–16.

Stoker, G. (ed.) (1999), *The New Management of British Local Governance*, Basingstoke: Macmillan.

Tirole, J. (1994), 'The internal organization of government', *Oxford Economic Papers*, **46**, 1–29.

Vivian, J. (1995), 'How safe are "social safety nets"? Adjustment and social sector restructuring in developing countries', *European Journal of Development Research*, **7** (1), 1–25.

Walsh, K. (1995), *Public Services and Market Mechanisms: Competition, Contracting and the New Public Management*, Basingstoke: Macmillan.

Williams, B. (1989), 'Formal structures and social reality', in Gambetta, D. (ed.), *Trust: the making and breaking of cooperative relationships*, Oxford: Blackwell.

World Bank (1993), *World Development Report 1993: Investing in Health*, Washington, DC: The World Bank.

World Bank (1997), *World Development Report 1997: The State in a Changing World*, Washington, DC: The World Bank.

8. Charging for health care in Tanzania: official pricing in a liberalized environment

Paula Tibandebage

1. INTRODUCTION: USER FEES AND MARKET PRICES

As noted in Chapter 1, the policies of liberalization, privatization and decentralization of the management of public funds frequently go hand in hand within the process of economic reform. In the social sectors, this has altered the policy framework for public sector provision by creating competing providers and market processes in social provision in some localities. This changing institutional framework requires in turn a shift in policy thinking which is still in its early stages in many countries. This chapter examines one aspect of this broad set of policy problems: the issue of charging for health services in a liberalized health care system.

There is now a considerable literature on user fees for public sector health care in low-income countries. In the African context, where user fees have been extensively introduced in government health care facilities in the wake of economic liberalization, this literature is well summarized by Gilson (1997). This survey examines the evidence on the impact of user fees on access to services, and on the finance and quality of services provided to patients. The survey of issues of fee system design, however, nowhere mentions the existence of competing providers as an influence on fee setting. A separate literature explores informal charging by public health care employees (Asiimwe et al., 1997), but this does not yet appear to have influenced the user fees research. There is clearly a gap in the policy literature concerning the implications for public policy towards user fees of health care liberalization and of the resultant, if patchy, market competition between public, private and voluntary facilities that this brings in its train.

This chapter utilizes data from a survey of private health facilities carried out in Dar es Salaam in 1997 to address this gap. Section 2 outlines the health care liberalization which has occurred in Tanzania in the 1990s. The effect of liberalization has been to create considerable competition in health care in the urban centres, especially in the largest city, Dar es Salaam, raising the question of the role of public sector services in this environment, and the considerations that should influence public sector pricing policy. The survey data, together with other recent research, permit some comparisons between prices charged within the non-government sector, and between pricing in the government and non-government sectors, for selected services. Section 3 examines these comparisons, with a view to drawing implications from the evidence so far for emerging patterns of charging and competition in health care in Tanzania.

Section 4 then re-examines the role of 'cost sharing' in its current form, that is, user fees in government health facilities. The main argument is that existence of price competition in the health care market indicates that the different sectors – public, private and voluntary – should be viewed as interacting within what appears to be an increasingly segmented urban health care market. If one role for the public sector is to ensure access to services by those with no ability to pay, then both the services and fee levels, including exemptions, need to be set with a view to creating such a safety net. Section 4 considers public sector pricing policy, both in terms of the type of possible forms of collaboration between government and non-government sectors and in recognition of alternatives available to users seeking access.

2. ECONOMIC PRESSURE AND HEALTH CARE LIBERALIZATION IN TANZANIA

Socioeconomic Background

The socioeconomic situation in Tanzania is characterized by a large agricultural sector, accounting for over 40 per cent of GDP and employing about 80 per cent of the labour force. The contribution of the industrial sector to GDP declined from 10.2 per cent between 1980 and 1984 to about 8 per cent between 1990 and 1994 (Wangwe et al., 1998). The majority of the population live in rural areas. Starting from a very low initial level at independence, the country made steady progress in the 1960s in economic growth and in meeting basic needs of the population. With the promulgation of the Arusha Declaration in 1967 Tanzania adopted a philosophy of socialism and self-reliance.

Implementation of this philosophy included nationalization of what were regarded then as the 'commanding heights' of the economy; this leading role for the public sector included a government semi-monopoly in health care, the only permitted independent providers being religious foundations.

The gains in standards of living and economic achievements of the initial period were undermined towards the end of the 1970s by macro-economic crisis. Budgetary and balance of payments deficits, a growing debt burden, and increasing inflationary pressures were associated with falling output. The capacity of the economy to support delivery of basic social services thus came under strain. Some of the achievements in the delivery of education, health and water supply in the 1960s and 1970s began to be reversed, reducing the quality of delivery of these basic services.

In response to the economic crisis and under the influence of the multilateral financial institutions, the Tanzanian government adopted economic reforms, moving towards economic liberalization and encouragement of private sector development. The economic reforms have been associated with a modest recovery in economic growth, with average real growth of 4 per cent annually for the period 1986–96, compared to 2 per cent in the first half of the 1980s (ESRF, 1997).

However, this improvement in economic performance implied fiscal and budgetary reforms that put a cap on the government's capacity to increase the finance going to basic social service. As a result, the health sector's share in the total government recurrent budget spending remained virtually constant at about 8 per cent over the period 1989/90 to 1993/94. Health expenditure as a percentage of GDP also remained almost stagnant, ranging between 2 per cent and 3 per cent over the same period (World Bank, 1994).

In Tanzania, donor funds constitute a large proportion of health care financing. In 1994 donor spending was estimated to total 1.7 times government spending (World Bank, 1996). Donor funding is devoted mainly to preventive services and primary health care (87 per cent in 1994), while the government health sector recurrent budget is allocated proportionately more to curative services.

Recent data furthermore show a trend decline in donor funding, in general and in the share of donor funding going to health care, trends which are likely to continue. An example is donor support to the National AIDS Control Programme (NACP), one of the programmes in the health sector receiving substantial donor support. Data from the programme (MOH, 1995) on donor expenditures show that global and multi/bilateral funds from the World Health Organization (WHO) channelled to HIV/AIDS control decreased from US$2 444 753 in 1992 to US$1 967 232 in 1993. UNDP funds (bilateral) to the same programme fell from US$272 680 in 1992 to US$231 176 in 1993 and to US$129 658 in 1994. This trend appears to be similar to that of donor financing in other developing countries. For example, expenditure data on HIV/AIDS control by donors in all developing countries show that the funds allocated decreased from US$60.9 billion in 1992 to US$54.5 billion in 1993 (Mann and Tarantola, 1996).

A similar declining trend is portrayed when we examine donor support to the health sector as a whole. For example, in 1994, donor funding to the health sector as a percentage of total donor support to the social sectors was 52 per cent, falling to 44 per cent in 1995. In 1996 it rose slightly to 48 per cent but was still below the 1994 level (Ravicz et al., 1996).

This declining trend in donor funding is raising concern about the sustainability and development of the Tanzanian public health care system. There is a perceived need to mobilize more local resources so as to reduce donor dependence. Although donor financing has prevented the situation in the health sector, particularly at the level of primary health care, from deteriorating even further, it has not succeeded in putting in place a sustainable capacity to manage the sector when donor support comes to an end.

Thus, despite the government's continued commitment to providing basic social services to its people, its commitment in terms of allocating adequate funding has been insufficient. The quality of health services has continued to decline. In recognition of this decline, cost sharing in the public sector, in the form of user fees, was introduced with a view to alleviating the problem of severe shortage of drugs and essential medical supplies in government health facilities. It is also in this context, and in the spirit of implementing the economic liberalization policy within the *Social Sector Strategy* (URT, 1995b), that private for-profit practice was reintroduced in health care in 1991 following the amendment of the 1977 Act which had banned private for-profit practice (URT, 1991).

The Public/Private Mix in Health Care Delivery

Health care provision in Tanzania is undertaken by various parties, including the government, private providers and religious organizations, and the public/private mix has shifted sharply since 1991 to an extent not well reflected in the statistics. The public health care delivery system has a central–local government structure. The Ministry of Health

(MOH) is responsible for policy formulation and development of guide-lines for implementation of the national health policy. At the regional level, each region has a regional hospital and a district hospital for each of its districts. Health facilities operated by churches have long supplemented government services. Many district hospitals in the country are owned by churches and designated to operate as govern-ment health facilities. These receive government subsidies in the form of grants intended to cover the recurrent budget. Other mission facilities receive smaller amounts of subsidy in the form of bed grant or personnel grant.[1]

According to the 1995 *Health Statistics Abstract* (URT, 1995a), 42 per cent of the 183 hospitals were owned by government. Of the 273 health centres and 3286 dispensaries, 93.8 per cent and 70 per cent respectively were owned by the government. The 1996 figures (URT, 1996a) show a small increase in the number of government health facilities and a faster increase in private facilities, resulting in small declines in the share of government-owned hospitals, health centres and dispensaries in the system.

In 1996 voluntary organizations owned 41 per cent of the hospitals, 7 per cent of the health centres and 17 per cent of the dispensaries. The big increase in independent provision was in the for-profit sector. For-profit private practice is now growing at a relatively high rate following the 1991 Amendment Act no. 26. Two *Health Statistics Abstracts* (URT, 1995a, 1996a) show an increase between 1995 and 1996 in private hospi-tals from about 5 per cent to 10 per cent of total hospitals, an increase from 0.3 per cent to 2 per cent of health centres in private ownership, and from 7 per cent to 9 per cent in the proportion of dispensaries privately owned. The private sector is thus playing an increasing role in health care provision. Recent studies in Dar es Salaam and Kilimanjaro indicate furthermore that official government figures grossly under-estimate the number of private health facilities (Munishi et al., 1995; Tibandebage et al., forthcoming). Private provision of social services has expanded fast since it began to be promoted in the context of the *Social Sector Strategy.*

Some parastatals also own health facilities. In 1996, 9 per cent, 1 per cent and 7 per cent of the total number of hospitals, health centres and dispensaries respectively were owned by parastatal enterprises. There are also many traditional healers and traditional birth attendants (TBAs), of whom 40 000 and 32 000 respectively were identified in the early 1990s (URT, 1992). The non-government health care sector is thus complex, rapidly changing and rather poorly documented.

The increase in the number of health facilities, public and private, has not brought easily accessible health care for the whole population. Over 82 per cent of the rural population remain over 6 kilometres from the nearest hospital and almost 50 per cent of the people living in the rural areas live more than 4 kilometres from the nearest health centre. The shortage of drugs and other essential supplies oblige some people to cover even longer distances in search of medical services. There is only one health facility per 100 000 people, with a population of 896 people per hospital bed (URT, 1996a). Demographic indicators also remain unimpressive, although relatively better than some of the countries in Sub-Saharan Africa. In 1994, the infant mortality rate (IMR) was estimated at 92 deaths per 1000 live births, and maternal mortality rate (MMR) at around 342 deaths per 100 000 births (World Bank, 1994). Diseases such as malaria, respiratory infections, water-borne diseases such as cholera and typhoid and HIV/AIDS continue to be leading killers of the people.

3. CHARGING FOR HEALTH SERVICES IN THE PRIVATE AND PUBLIC SECTORS

The Importance of Private Payment

Much more than half of the spending in the formal health care system in Tanzania is funded from non-government sources. A 1994 study on the burden of disease, cost-effectiveness and health policy by a team led by the World Bank with researchers from five Eastern African countries (Eritrea, Ethiopia, Kenya, Tanzania and Uganda) (World Bank, 1996) calculated that donor expenditures accounted for about a third of total health-related expenditures in 1994, and government spending only about 20 per cent, and private out-of-pocket expenditures contributing most of the rest (see Table 8.1).

World Bank data also illustrate the scale of underfunding of health

Table 8.1   Summary of total health-related expenditure by source, 1994

Source	Total amount (Tsh)	% of total
Government	19 918 414 890.00	20.8
Donor	34 046 652 800.00	35.5
Private	41 855 115 300.00	43.7
Total	95 820 182 990.00	100.0

Source: World Bank (1996).

care. The Bank (World Bank, 1995) estimated that government and donors combined spent about Tsh 1512 per capita per year, and individuals an average of about Tsh 1863 per year. Employers' contribution were estimated at about Tsh 50 per capita and contributions by religious missions Tsh 59 per capita. This adds up to Tsh 3468 (about US$7) per capita annually, out of which over half is contributed by households. With the cost of the minimum public health package and essential clinical health services estimated to be US$12 per capita in a low-income country (World Bank, 1993a), the Tanzania health system is thus severely underfunded, with total public spending on health care at less than 25 per cent of the minimum recommended spending, and a heavy reliance on private household spending.

The majority of the population in the country continue to seek health care in government health facilities. Provision there was 'free' until 1993 when cost sharing in the health sector was introduced in the form of user fees. The word 'free' refers to the fact that services were in principle provided free of charge. However, in practice patients had, even before the introduction of user fees, incurred some expenses in government health facilities, and the data just cited take account of this fact. Mujinja and Mabala (1992) showed that 28 per cent of the patients in their study had paid some money to whoever was attending them in government hospitals during their most recent visit.

'Cost sharing' in the health sector became effective in 1993 and 1994 when user fees for referral, regional and district hospitals were introduced, as one way of dealing with the problem of underfunding in the health sector. 'It is estimated that if all eligible patients and services are charged, a total of approximately Tsh 6.85 billion (approximately US$14 million) could be generated per year' (DANIDA, 1995). This calculation assumes, however, that price changes will not affect utilization, an assumption discussed further below.

People also seek treatment in not-for-profit (voluntary) and for-profit private health facilities where they pay for services. Charges in the former type of facilities are usually lower than in the latter, which is profit-oriented. The not-for-profit private health facilities, mainly owned and run by religious bodies, have traditionally complemented government services, especially in rural areas and at district level. Two of the four referral hospitals in the country are also owned by religious institutions supported by government subsidy. Whereas in some Sub-Saharan African countries such as Zimbabwe, Namibia and South Africa there are established insurance schemes whereby workers in the formal sector with insurance have access to private health care, such insurance schemes are still lacking in Tanzania, making it difficult for even those with stable jobs to afford private care. In Zimbabwe, 74 per cent of the payments by medical aid services go to care given by private practitioners. Insurance schemes are hard to extend to the poor, though some experiments with pre-payment schemes are discussed below.

Charging in the Health Care Market

The basis for setting prices remains unclear for all types of health facilities in Tanzania: government, voluntary and for-profit private. In government health facilities, the fee schedules indicate that drugs are charged at 50 per cent of the real cost, but the basis of this calculation is unclear. No information is available on the criteria used to set other user fees, such as consultation fees and in-patient charges. Mujinja and Mabala (1992), in a study which examined pricing mechanisms of user charges in non-governmental health facilities in Tanzania, showed great variation in pricing policies. In 81 per cent of the sampled facilities, prices were set by the head of the facility. In the remaining 19 per cent, prices were set by bodies such as workers' committees, a parent organization or a provider attending the patient. In most of the facilities in the study (92 per cent) a price list was available. The mission facilities have freedom to set prices: they are not bound by government user fee schedules. There is as yet no systematic evidence on private sector price-setting behaviour, though initial discussions with private providers[2] suggests the expected mix of cost-plus calculations and estimates of what the market will bear drawing upon observation of competitors' prices.

This chapter cannot, therefore, examine directly how prices are currently determined. Rather, it uses data from a survey carried out in Dar es Salaam of private (both for-profit and not-for-profit) health facilities (Tibandebage et al., forthcoming) to analyse the pattern of prices in the non-government private health care system by ownership (voluntary/not-for-profit vs private for-profit), by level of health facility (dispensaries vs health centres and hospitals) and by location (in this case, district). The chapter then examines official user fees in government facilities and compares prices in the non-government sector with prices in the public sector with a view to re-examining the role of user fees.

Pricing in the Private Health Sector

The survey of private health facilities examined, among other things, prices for different services and treatments, such as consultation fees and prescription drugs including anti-malaria drugs and antibiotics. The

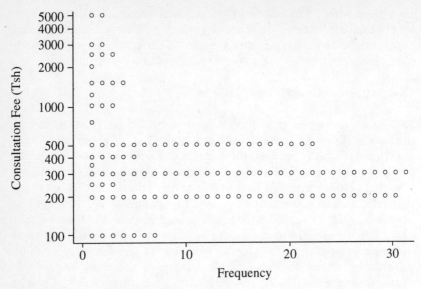

Figure 8.1   Consultation fees, all facilities

study covered a total of 137 non-government health facilities (not-for-profit private and for-profit private). For the purposes of this chapter, the facilities have been divided into two main groups by ownership ('business', and religious and NGOs) and two main groups by level of health facility (hospitals, health centres and clinics as one group and dispensaries as another group). The 'business' group consists of facilities owned by doctors and other medical staff, businessmen and limited companies, while the 'religious' group includes facilities owned by religious organizations and a small number of NGOs. Figure 8.1 presents a dotplot showing the distribution of consultation fees for all observations. Given the granulated nature of the data, dotplots give the clearest presentation of the prices as recorded. The figures are drawn on a logarithmic scale to make inspection of the lower range of charges easier.

Figure 8.1 shows quite a high concentration of consultation fees, with a high proportion of facilities charging Tsh 200–300. These data suggest the existence of price competition. Figure 8.2 is a dotplot of consultation fees by type of health facility. A comparison of consultation fees between the two types of owners also suggests the existence of price competition, and indicates some market segmentation.

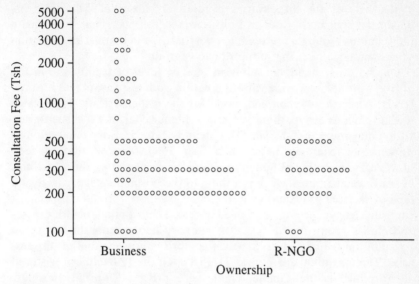

Figure 8.2 Consultation fees by ownership

Figure 8.2 indicates a fair degree of concentration of prices in both ownership categories, with a median fee of Tsh 300 in both cases. Although there is more variation in fees for business facilities, in both categories there is a concentration of prices between Tsh 200 and 500. The mean consultation fee of the facilities in the business category is significantly higher than the mean consultation fee in the religious category.[3] The business category has a tail of high-charging facilities: about 15 per cent of facilities were charging Tsh 1000 or above for consultation, while no religious facility charged at that level.

Many of the higher charges, however, are in the hospital and clinic sector. In both sectors, business and religious/NGO, dispensary consultation fees were generally lower than consultation fees for hospitals, health centres and clinics treated as a group. The median hospital and clinic charge, at Tsh 750, was more than twice the Tsh 300 median dispensary charge for the sample as a whole.[4] So it is worth comparing charges by level of facility in each category. At the higher end, the contrast in pricing policy between the business and religious sectors is striking. Within the religious category there is considerable concentration of prices at both hospital and dispensary level. The median and mode for the hospitals, health centres and clinics group is Tsh 500, while that for the dispensaries is relatively lower at Tsh 300.[5] The maximum consultation fee at both levels is Tsh 500. Thus hospitals in the religious group do not seem to overcharge, and there is an indication of consistency of pricing in the religious group.

On the other hand, consultation fees by level of facility within the business group show wide variation within both dispensary and hospital levels. While the median and mode for the dispensaries is Tsh 300, as in the religious group, there is a tail of higher charges for dispensaries, with a maximum of Tsh 3000. The mean is Tsh 452. An examination of dispensaries charging more than Tsh 1000 for consultation fees, however, reveals that although registered as dispensaries, these facilities either have attributes which put them in the hospital category (size and type of services provided) or in the clinic category (providing specialist care such as gynaecology and paediatrics). The hospitals, health centres and clinics group in the business category had a much higher mean consultation fee of Tsh 1142, which is more than twice that of dispensaries. The maximum charge was Tsh 5000. Of the 12 facilities registered as hospitals in the sample, eight were private for-profit (business category). These had a modal consultation fee of Tsh 5000, with a mean of Tsh 1956.

Consultation fees are one of the elements of price that is easiest for the potential patient to understand and compare. The survey also elicited price data for a range of treatments. Of these, chloroquine tablets for malaria treatment displayed the price distributions by ownership shown in Figure 8.3 for those facilities providing this information.

As in the case of consultation fees, prices for chloroquine tablets for both types of owners are concentrated at the lower end of the distribution, but the distribution for the for-profit facilities has a number of facilities making much higher charges. As the distribution in Figure 8.3 suggests, religious organizations and NGOs charge less on average and within a narrower range. Businesses had a significantly higher mean charge of Tsh 622 compared to Tsh 231 for religious facilities[6] (median charges Tsh 200 and Tsh 150 respectively). About 8 per cent (10 out of 82) of for-profit facilities appear to have charged Tsh 1000 and above for chloroquine tablets. It may be that some of these apparently very high charges for tablets reflect problems with accurate reporting of prices, since not all survey respondents clearly distinguished prices of tablets and injections; however, the generalization that there is a group of higher-charging business facilities seems likely to be robust.

The concentration of observations in Figure 8.3 does suggest something of a going price for a dose of chloroquine of around Tsh 150. A similar impression of a – much higher – market price norm emerges

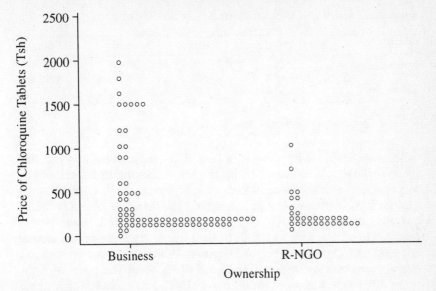

Note: R-NGO = Religious and NGO.

Figure 8.3 Charges for chloroquine tablets, by ownership

from the prices given for standard antibiotic treatments. The median and modal prices for the sample as a whole for two common antibiotic treatments was Tsh 1200; this was also the median price one of the antibiotics in both sectors, and for the other in the business sector; the other median price in religious facilities was Tsh 950. The higher charges, again, were mainly in the business category.

The preceding analysis suggests the existence of a relatively high degree of price competition in the non-government health care market in Dar es Salaam, a market which offers some choice for users. The degree of effective choice will depend on income levels, but users can and do move between providers depending on their perception of quality care and the trade-offs between quality and price, given their income levels. The high degree of concentration of consultation fees, whereby 73 per cent of the facilities charged Tsh 300 or below, suggests the market at dispensary level to be price-sensitive. A similar comment applies to charges for chloroquine tablets. There are, however, some higher-level facilities in which clients appear not to be price-sensitive, thus willing to pay more for consultation and treatment, perhaps because they believe the higher prices to be an indicator of quality of care.

Table 8.2   Mean and median consultation fees by district

District	No. of facilities	Mean	Median	Std dev.
Temeke	19	284	300	88
Ilala	45	499	300	620
Kinondoni	53	722	300	1054

Source: Tibandebage et al. (forthcoming).

The data employed here were collected at the facilities surveyed, and there is thus little evidence of the impact on pricing of clients' ability to pay. One relevant piece of evidence, however, is the differentiation of pricing by district of Dar es Salaam. Of the three districts, Kinondoni has a concentration of higher-income residents (as well as some poor areas), while Ilala, which extends to semi-urban areas, covers the central city and includes a number of hospitals. While there are no data for average incomes by district, Temeke is likely to be the poorest of the three districts: it has more rural areas (27 villages, while Kinondoni has 19 and Ilala 9), and has the highest proportion of people aged 5 years and above who have never attended school (33.5 per cent as compared to about a quarter in the other two districts). Temeke also has the lowest proportion of people with piped water within the house and the lowest proportion of flush toilets (URT, 1996b).

If prices – and perhaps quality of care – respond to income levels, then one would expect differences in charges by district. As Table 8.2 shows, Kinondoni district did indeed have the highest mean consultation fee of Tsh 722 while Temeke district had the lowest mean of Tsh 284.

Kinondoni district has more hospitals and health centres in the sample than other districts, and these, as shown earlier, charge higher fees than dispensaries: 50 per cent of the hospitals and 70 per cent of the health centres (seven out of ten) were in Kinondoni district. Temeke district, which has the lowest mean, had only two hospitals and one health centre in the sample. While the median consultation fee for all three districts is the same (Tsh 300), Figure 8.4 shows an interesting pattern in the consultation fees, with the spread increasing from left to right.

Comparison with Official User Fees in the Public Sector

According to the Ministry of Health cost-sharing operations manual (MOH, 1994), cost sharing had four main objectives:

1. *Generating additional revenue* The revenues generated were

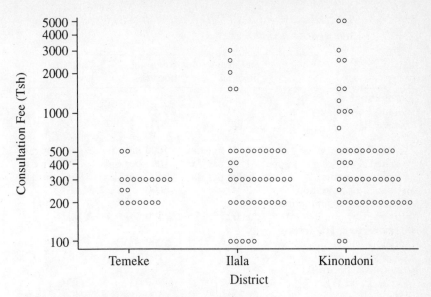

Figure 8.4   Consultation fees by district

expected to be additional to the regular budget allocation to the
health sector. A fee schedule outlining the type of services to be
charged and the fees for each service at different levels and grades
was prepared and implemented.

2. *Improving availability and quality of health services* Revenues col-
    lected as user fees were to be retained by the collecting facility and
    spent on items related to improving the availability and quality of
    services.

3. *Strengthening the referral system and rationalizing the health
    services* It was expected that user fees would, among other things,
    reduce patients' tendency to bypass low-level facilities by minimi-
    zing the problem of unavailability of services at these levels.

4. *Improving equity and access to health services* The fees were set at
    low levels, indicating a consideration of the ability to pay by users
    rather than the actual cost of providing those services, and there
    was provision of exemptions defined by disease types and patient
    characteristics.

   The manual, like the research literature on user fees, does not differentiate the objectives of user fees according to the existence of
competing provision from other sectors, nor does it discuss the level
of fees in those terms. The fees were set to be uniform nationally,

Table 8.3   Selected current rates (Tsh) for user fees: referral, regional and district hospitals

Item	Referral hospital	Regional hospital	District hospital
Consultation*			
Grade I and II	500	300	200
Grade III	300	200	150
Admission:			
Grade 3 Patients	2000 flat rate	1000 flat rate	500 flat rate
Grade 2 Patients	1500 per day	1000 per day	750 per day
Grade 1 Patients	3000 per day	1500 per day	1200 per day
Specialized examinations	3000	3000	3000
Medical board examinations (to be paid by employers)	20 000	20 000	20 000
BS, urine, stool, HB testing			
Grade I and II	700	200	200
Grade III	300	100	100
X-ray (per exposure)			
Grade I and II	1000	700	500
Grade III	700	500	400
Extraction or filling of permanent Teeth			
Grade I and II	1000	800	500
Grade III	500	500	500
Major surgery (general anaesthesia)			
Grade I and II	15 000	10 000	5000
Grade III	3000	2000	1000
Minor surgery (local anaesthesia)			
Grade I and II	3000	2000	1000
Grade III	1000	500	300

* As per original fee structure recommended by the MOH in July 1993.

Source: Ministry of Health, printed fee schedule, 1996.

varying by level of facility. Table 8.3 shows a sample of current rates (1998) for user fees in referral, regional and district hospitals. As expected, given the emphasis on discouraging bypassing of the lower levels, user fees are higher at the referral hospital level relative to regional and district hospital level.

A comparison of consultation fees between government hospitals (as set out in the user fee schedule) and the non-government hospitals in the Dar es Salaam study show some big differences. Consultation fees in government health facilities were set out in the original fee structure in 1993 as Tsh 300 (grade I and II) and Tsh 200 (grade III) and Tsh 200 (grade I and II) and Tsh 150 (grade III) at regional and district hospitals respectively. By comparison, consultation fees in non-government hospitals recorded in the Dar es Salaam study were between Tsh 500 and Tsh 2000. The median hospital consultation fee in the study was Tsh 750, and the mean fee was Tsh 1354, with a standard deviation of 1458, indicating a large variation in consultation fees among non-government hospitals. Similarly, while the fee for extraction of permanent teeth in government district hospitals was set at Tsh 500, fees for extraction of teeth in dental clinics in the Dar es Salaam study were between Tsh 1500 and 6000.

The substantially higher prices in non-government hospitals suggests confidence within the private hospital sector – including religious facilities – that people will pay more for perceived higher quality, and in the for-profit sector substantially more. It also suggests that in Dar es Salaam there exists a segmented market, with the less well-to-do unable to seek medical care in relatively expensive facilities.

Other charges which were compared and found to be substantially higher in the Dar es Salaam study include those for X-rays. While the highest official fees for one exposure of X-rays in government district hospitals were Tsh 500 and 400 for grades I and II, and grade III respectively, fees for X-rays in the private hospitals in Dar es Salaam ranged between Tsh 2500 and 20 000. While the gap in prices appears large, anecdotal evidence suggests that substantial informal under-the-counter payments to technicians in government facilities are particularly common for technical services such as X-rays, which are often in short supply in the public sector. One would expect, however, that given the big gap, cost incurred will still be much higher in the private sector, informal payment notwithstanding.

Analysis of these price differences depends on judgements about the differences in quality of provision in the two sectors, and about the extent to which patients can and do move between providers. This in turn requires evidence from interviews with patients and prospective patients. The research is continuing in Dar es Salaam. There is, however, evidence from other studies which suggests similar charges by different types of provider for some services, and confirms comparisons by users of different types of facility.

A study by Msamanga et al. (1996) conducted in two regions of Tanzania to assess equity in access to the three types of health facilities (public, private and voluntary) examined, among other things, average amounts of money spent on selected types of treatment per visit and per admission, based on information from users. The results show that, for example, average amounts of money spent on the treatment of malaria per visit were Tsh 1045, 1241 and 1333 for public, voluntary and

Table 8.4   *Average amount of money spent, and the range, on some*
              acute and chronic diseases per visit and per admission by
              health facility type (Tsh)

Diseases	Public	Voluntary	Private
(a) *Per visit*			
Malaria	1042 (50–5000)*	1241 (350–3500)	1333 (1000–2000)
Hypertension	1533 (0–5000)	870 (250–1300)	1333 (700–2500)
Diabetes	730 (0–4000)	880 (500–1600)	1266 (800–1500)
(b) *Per admission*			
Malaria	1565 (300–1000)	3572 (1500–10 000)	4500 (100–10 000)
Hypertension	1393 (0–4900)	5200 (1500–15 000)	5525 (1100–10 000)
Diabetes	730 (0–5000)	5750 (1100–12 000)	1750 (1500–2000)

* Range of spending.
Source: Msamanga et al. (1996, p. 66).

private health facilities respectively. As expected, the highest average is in the private health facilities, but the differences are small, and furthermore the range of charges is very large. Table 8.4 sets out selected results from this study.

Data on average amounts spent on the treatment of malaria per visit as shown in the study by Msamanga et al. (1996) are similar to mean and median payments for chloroquine injections in the Dar es Salaam study. In the latter study, the mean for religious facilities was Tsh 1269 (median 1500), while the mean for the for-profit private health facilities was Tsh 1195 (median 1200). While religious facilities' charges were quite strongly concentrated above Tsh 1000, there were quite a lot of cheap injections available in the business sector, raising concerns about quality. The data from Msamanga et al. give charges per visit, and therefore may have included costs other than treatment, for example a consultation/registration fee.

The most striking differences between the sectors in Table 8.4 are for in-patient admissions. The lack of distributions and further detail of the data do not allow even tentative conclusions about price setting, but the closeness of average payments for some standard treatments is at least consistent with some price competition between facilities. The difference in payments for admissions supports a widespread view that people do pay higher charges in these facilities either because they have no other option or because of a well-founded view that quality is better in non-government in-patient facilities. Increased competition between the public and private sectors in health care provision can be viewed as an outcome of, among other things, underfunding of public sector health care, particularly in developing countries. To the extent that these data support this view, this suggests a need to think through the role of public facilities and public sector charging where competition has emerged.

4. THE ROLE OF USER FEES IN A LIBERALIZED ENVIRONMENT

The above analysis shows that Tanzanian government health facilities are now operating, in some urban localities only, in a context of private sector competition and diversity of charging policies in both non-governmental sectors. Policies on charging for government facilities must take this context into account. In particular, developing an effective charging policy for government facilities implies a prior decision about the role of public provision in a mixed system – a debate that is still continuing.

Impact of User Fees on Services and Access

One of the objectives underlying the introduction of user fees was to alleviate the shortage of drugs and essential medical supplies in public health facilities. Although the amounts collected have helped in alleviating this problem, these amounts have not been adequate and there has been a tendency for user fees to replace government resources instead of adding to them. Table 8.5 shows the sums collected for two recent years.

The data in Table 8.5 show rising total user fees collected in the public health care system between 1993/94 and 1994/95. While this appears to be a good start, it is much less than the projected collection of Tsh 6.8 billion annually (DANIDA, 1995).

In a report evaluating the implementation and impact of user fees, Mmbuji et al. (1996) found mixed views. Out of 356 patients who were

Table 8.5   Summary of users fees collected, 1993/94 and 1994/95 (in Tsh)

Hospital level	1993/94	1994/95
District hospitals	–	105 336 303
Regional hospitals	250 660 192	301 545 411
Consultant hospitals	164 888 798	193 990 957
Total	415 548 990	600 872 671

Source: Ilomo (1995).

asked whether the availability of drugs had improved or not after the introduction of user fees, 35 per cent felt that drugs were more available while 28 per cent felt there was no improvement; 41 per cent of the patients had no comment. In the study by Msamanga et al. (1996), drug availability was the number one reason given by respondents for choosing voluntary and private hospitals (80 per cent and 83 per cent respectively). This is in contrast to public hospitals, where only 7 per cent indicated drug availability as a reason for choice. More than 50 per cent of the respondents who attended public health facilities indicated dissatisfaction with the quality of care primarily because prescribed drugs were not available.

Another concern regarding the impact of user fees had been the ineffective waiver system. The user fee system was intended to include exemptions for those unable to pay, to improve equity in access to health services. A study which explored the possibility of introducing user fees in Tanzania (Abel-Smith and Rawal, 1992) noted that the inadequate supply of drugs and food in hospitals meant that patients incurred substantial costs when using the 'free' services in addition to travel costs. The study subsequently recommended that modest user fees with exemptions for the poor would be more equitable than the existing situation, assuming the revenue gained would be used to ensure an adequate supply of drugs and essential medical supplies. In the study by Msamanga et al. (1996), only a tiny percentage of those who requested to be exempted got the exemption; 5 per cent and 4 per cent of patients in public and voluntary facilities respectively were refused treatment because they could not pay.

Ineffectiveness of the exemption system has an adverse impact on the poor and vulnerable, who are unable to pay for basic social services such as health care. Studies have shown that the poor and vulnerable groups have been more adversely affected by cost sharing than the well-to-do. Mwabu et al. (1995) found that attendance at public clinics in a

district in Kenya dropped by 50 per cent when user fees were introduced. When the fee system was suspended, attendance rose by 41 per
cent in seven months. In Ghana, hospital fees were shown by Anyimawi
(1989) to reduce attendance. In other countries, for example Zaire,
vulnerable groups such as women and children were found to be
adversely affected by user fees as manifested through, for example,
increased maternal mortality rate (MMR). A study by Walraven (1996)
found that after introduction of user fees in one rural hospital the
number of out patient department (OPD) visits and that of elective
operations dropped by about 70 per cent and the number of deliveries
and admissions dropped by 30 per cent in the first three months.

The 1993/94 Human Resources Development Survey in Tanzania
(World Bank and URT, 1994) indicated that while at hospital level
more people in the richest quintile group of the population visited
government hospitals relative to the poorest quintile group (20 per cent
vs 15 per cent), more people in the latter group visited government
dispensaries and health centres (55 per cent vs 26 per cent). Also, only
6 per cent of the poorest quintile group utilized private health centres
and dispensaries for outpatient services compared to 24 per cent of the
richest quintile. A high level of government dispensary and health
centre utilization by the poorest quintile could be a reflection of the
fact that user fees have not been introduced at these two levels yet,
and of the fact that government dispensaries and health centres are the
most readily available type of health facilities in the rural areas where
the majority of the poor live. According to the Tanzania poverty profile
(World Bank, 1993b) which utilized 1991 data, 51 per cent of the
population had incomes below an absolute poverty line, and about 85
per cent of these were living in rural areas.

Context-specific and Policy-led User Fees

The importance of user fees in providing partial funding of government
health facilities notwithstanding, the above analysis indicates that user
fees need to be instituted on a context-specific basis, depending on the
socioeconomic status of the area and the existence of other types of
providers in the area. Where there is wide provision of private health
care with a high level of competition, then a decision on the role of
government facilities in the health care system needs to precede a
charging decision.

If government facilities are to act as safety nets for those who have no
ability to pay, then in areas such as Dar es Salaam, with a proliferation of
non-governmental dispensaries, two conditions are necessary. Those

unable to pay the fees in the private sector must be able to reach a public sector alternative, which may not always be possible at present. And the fees set in the public health care sector must be lower than the private sector fees and/or offer an exemption system for the completely indigent. There are obvious policy problems here: good-quality cheaper public provision could undercut decent non-governmental provision while leaving dangerously cheap inappropriate private provision to operate – a set of outcomes which may be the opposite of those intended. It may be better for government facilities to charge the 'going rate', but with effective exemptions if criteria for those can be locally established. At present, as just shown, the effectiveness of user fees in government-owned health facilities in terms of providing a safety net to those with no ability to pay seems to be minimal.

In areas where there is limited private health care provision, modest user fees could be set for those with the ability to pay, but again this has to be implemented together with a transparent and effective exemption system to ensure access to those with no ability to pay. The objective of user fees in these areas would remain that of generating funds to supplement the limited government resources, and not competition with largely non-existent private providers. User fees should vary by area, as should exemption schemes, to take account of sharp local differences in ability to pay and sources of destitution. If the principle of equity is to be upheld, effective mechanisms must be put in place for identifying those with no ability to pay, as well as effective strategies for implementation and management of the exemption system. Such strategies should include use of local committees in identifying the truly indigent. At present, the only way for the poor to be able to get service is if that service is of such poor quality that all those who can afford to pay will pay for better-quality care.

The discussion so far has not considered the implications of liberalization for fee setting at the different levels of the system. Liberalization, and the patchy development of private provision, has generated considerable debate in Tanzania about what could be effective forms of collaboration among different providers in attempting to ensure quality and equitable access to services. The areas where there is price competition, and those where there is little market development, need again to be distinguished.

Price competition in health care provision implies that health care must be perceived as one system, even though it seems to be a system displaying considerable segmentation. If the government's objective, as regulator, is that the system should provide quality and, at least, increasingly equitable services to the population, then it needs to focus on identifying what could be more effective forms of cooperation or collaboration between the different types of health care providers so as to ensure that health care goals are attained.

Analysis in this chapter has shown that although there is some element of price competition within the non-government health subsector, prices in this sector seem to be substantially higher than prices in government facilities. This, plus a rather ineffective exemption system in government hospitals under the user fees system, raises an issue as to whether the increase in private provision of health care does result in more government spending on the poor. The World Bank (1996) argued that liberalization and the development of a private sector allowed and encouraged the better-off to move to private facilities, leaving the government facilities to be used by the poor. Such an argument assumes that charges in government facilities would be relatively lower than in other facilities and that the exemption system will be effective in terms of ensuring that those who cannot pay are exempted and that the system is not abused by those who can. However, as shown earlier, this has not been the case. Existence of informal charging, ineffective implementation of the exemption system and costs incurred in travelling long distances to seek medical care and/or in paying for drugs which are not available in government health facilities raise concern as to whether the poor can afford even to seek medical care in government facilities. In addition, in Dar es Salaam in particular, almost all dispensaries are private and hospitals do charge.

Such concerns demand a thorough analysis of what type of health care market arrangements can work in the Tanzanian context in terms of providing quality but equitable health care. The market arrangements should ensure a system of collaboration which is compatible with the market, for example, cross-referrals, government support for free preventive services in the private facilities, training agreements and joint supervision. The appropriate forms of collaboration and charging in government facilities will certainly be region-specific, given the different levels of competition between rural and urban areas and among regions. Issues which should be addressed here include determining the role of different providers in different contexts. In areas where there is no competition, lower-level government facilities need to be sustained and developed. Where there is competition, and where there are few lower-level public facilities, then the integration of private facilities into an effective referral system is an acute problem.

Health care provision should be perceived as a service industry – and an 'infant' industry on the private sector side in Tanzania – with typical developing industrial patterns of varying quality and production systems, a changing market, and, in the Tanzanian case, low levels of industrial self-regulation. One policy approach for the government is to view this industry as – potentially – a public–private partnership whereby the three sectors could collaborate in the provision of health services, with a government objective of providing quality and equitable services. The question should then be how it is possible to improve complementarity and collaboration within the system. Mills (1997) proposes several comprehensive market strategies which include giving private providers the opportunity to bid to provide services in the underserved low-income rural areas and entering into contracts with private providers in urban areas to provide different types of care. Success of such a system would, however, depend on the system of incentives in place. For example, there is a need for incentives for private providers, whose objectives include profit making, to move to rural areas.

It would also be appropriate to consider alternative forms of health care financing which could be more equitable and at the same time ensure quality health care. With increased private sector participation in health care provision and cost sharing in the public sector, coupled with an ineffective exemption system, what is required is a system of health care financing which will be more effective in terms of ensuring quality and equity. One such alternative is the insurance schemes which involve risk sharing, thus making it possible, for example, for the better-off to subsidize the poor and the healthy to subsidize the sick (Bennett et al., 1994). Such a scheme, although likely to face risk of abuse, guarantees steady income to providers which is likely to translate into improved quality of health care. In Tanzania plans are currently under way to introduce a national health social insurance scheme.

Other schemes include community health insurance schemes supported by the World Bank and currently being piloted in five districts of mainland Tanzania, and employer-based insurance schemes such as the one covering a group of informal sector workers in Dar es Salaam. In the latter case, the scheme works by individuals paying some premium to their umbrella organization which entitles them to primary care at selected private health facilities and secondary care at government health facilities. While the potential benefits of such schemes may be recognized, the challenge is how to ensure their effective and efficient management.

5. CONCLUSION

This chapter has examined charges for health care in a liberalized environment in Tanzania. The objective has been to try to draw out implications for policy on public sector charging and user fees in a quite competitive though infant health care market made up of public, private and voluntary providers. Analysis has shown existence of competition, particularly at lower facility levels. Some market segmentation has also been indicated, with a few facilities charging relatively higher prices. The benefits of apparently lower charges in government facilities seem to be undermined by anecdotal evidence of informal charging and other extra-treatment costs in the public sector, and by an ineffective exemption system. Such a situation raises concern about equity of access to this basic service.

The chapter has thus suggested ways in which the emerging health care market can best function to ensure equity without compromising quality. An effective means-testing system to identify the truly indigent, and collaboration among providers in the three subsectors, are seen as prerequisites to achieving health care goals in a liberalized environment. Context-specific collaboration among the subsectors has been proposed to ensure effectiveness and efficiency in the provision of services. As the health care market grows, its success in the provision of quality and equitable services may to a large extent depend on the type of public–private partnership forged in both provision and regulation of the services in the health care market. The issue of public sector charging remains important in determining the outcomes of health care goals and further research in this area is needed to identify determinants of differences in charging and their implications for policy.

NOTES

1. Details in this paragraph and background information on the health care system are drawn from current research on health care in Tanzania funded by the UK Department of International Development (DFID), whose support is gratefully acknowledged. The views expressed in the chapter are those of the author alone, and do not represent official policies or practices of the DFID. The author thanks Marc Wuyts for assistance with interpretation and presentation of data.
2. Information from the continuing research referred to in note 1.
3. Mean consultation fee in the business facilities was Tsh 663 (standard deviation 940), the mean fee in the religious facilities was Tsh 312 (standard deviation 131); the difference between the means is significant at the .01 significance level.
4. The mean fee in the hospital and clinic category was more than three times the mean dispensary consultation fee (Tsh 1354 as against Tsh 397); the difference between the means is statistically significant at the .01 level.

5. The mean for the hospitals group is Tsh 440 as compared to Tsh 289 for dispensaries (standard deviations 40 and 24 respectively).
6. Standard deviations 708 and 212 respectively.

REFERENCES

Abel-Smith, B. and Rawal, P. (1992), *Health Sector Financing Study for the Government of Tanzania. Report on the Potential for Cost Sharing*, Ministry of Health (MOH)/ODA, Dar es Salaam.

Anyimawi, C. (1989), 'The social cost of the International Monetary Fund's adjustment programs for poverty: the case of health care development in Ghana,' *International Journal of Health Services*, **19** (3), 329–41.

Asiimwe, D. et al. (1997), 'The private sector activities of public sector health workers in Uganda', in Bennett, S., McPake, B. and Mills, A. (eds), *Private Sector Health Providers in Developing Countries: Serving the Public Interest?*, London: Zed Books.

Bennett, S., Dakpallah, G., Garner, P., Gilson, L., Nittarayamphong, S., Zurita, B. and Mujinja, P. (1994), 'Carrot and stick: state mechanisms to influence private provider behaviour', *Health Policy and Planning*, **9** (1).

Danida (1995), *Health Sector Tanzania: Strategy for Danish Development Cooperation Programme*, Discussion Paper, Dar es Salaam.

Economic and Social Research Foundation (ESRF) (1997), *Tanzania Civil Service Reform and the Budget Framework*, a consultancy report submitted to the Civil Service Reform Programme, Dar es Salaam.

Gilson, L. (1997), 'The lessons of user fees experience in Africa', *Health Policy and Planning*, **12** (4), 273–85.

Ilomo, P.A. (1995), 'Report on the implementation of cost sharing policy for health services 1993/95', paper presented at the meeting for Regional Health Officers, 25 March 1995, Dar es Salaam.

Mann, J.M. and Tarantola, D. (1996), *AIDS in the World*, Oxford: Oxford University Press.

Mills, A. (1997), 'Improving the capacity of public sector health services in developing countries: bureaucratization vs. market approaches', in Colclough, C. (ed.), *Marketizing Education and Health in Developing Countries: Miracle or Mirage?*, Oxford: Clarendon Press.

Mmbuji, P.K.L., Ilomo, P.A. and Nswila, A.L. (1996), *Implementation of Health Services User Fees in Tanzania: An Evaluation of Progress and Potential Impact*, Ministry of Health, Dar es Salaam.

MOH (1994), *Cost Sharing Operations Manual*, Dar es Salaam.

MOH (1995), *National Aids Control Programme Review Report*, Dar es Salaam.

Msamanga, G.I., Urasa, D.P. and Mujinja, P.G. (1996), *Equity of Access to Public, Private Not-for-Profit and Private for-Profit Health Facilities in Two Regions of Tanzania*, Final Research Paper submitted to UNICEF, New York.

Mujinja, P. and Mabala, R. (1992), *Charging for Health Services in Non-Government Health Facilities in Tanzania*, Bamako Initiative Management Unit, UNICEF, New York.

Munishi, G.K., Yazbeck, A. and Lioneth, D. (1995), 'Private sector delivery in health care in Tanzania', *Major Applied Research Paper*, No. 14, Health Financing and Sustainability Project, Dar es Salaam.

Mwabu, G.S. Mwnzia, J. and Liambila, W. (1995), 'User charges in government health facilities: effects on attendance and revenue', *Health Policy and Planning*, **10** (2), 164–70.

Ravicz, M.T., Tobin, M. and Follmer, A. (1996), *Tanzania Social Sector Expenditure Review: 1990–1996*, Dar es Salaam.

Tibandebage, P., Semboja, H., Mujinja, P. and Ngonyani, H. (forthcoming), *Private Sector Development: The Case of Private Health Facilities*, Dar es Salaam: Economic and Social Research Foundation (ESRF).

URT (1991), *Amendment Act No. 26 of 1991: An Act to Amend the Private Hospitals Legislation Act of 1977*, Dar es Salaam.

URT (1992), *National Social Economic Profile of Tanzania*, Bureau of Statistics, Dar es Salaam.

URT (1995a), *Health Statistics Abstract*, Ministry of Health, Dar es Salaam.

URT (1995b), *Social Sector Strategy*, prepared by Consultative Group Meeting, Dar es Salaam.

URT (1996a), *Health Statistics Abstract*, Ministry of Health, Dar es Salaam.

URT (1996b), *Dar es Salaam Regional Statistical Abstract*, Planning Commission, Dar es Salaam.

URT (1997), *Guidelines for the Preparation of the Fifth Rolling Plan and Forward Budget for the Period 1997/98–1999/2000*, Planning Commission and Ministry of Finance.

Walraven, G. (1996), 'Willingness to pay for district hospital services in rural Tanzania', *Health Policy and Planning*, **11** (4), 428–37.

Wangwe, S.M., Semboja, H.H. and Tibandebage, P. (1998), *Transitional Economic Policy and Policy Options in Tanzania*, Dar es Salaam: Mkuki na Nyota Publications.

World Bank (1993a), *World Development Report*, Washington, DC: The World Bank.

World Bank (1993b), *Tanzania: A Poverty Profile*, Washington, DC: The World Bank.

World Bank (1994), *Tanzania: Role of the Government: Public Expenditure Review*, Report No. T2601-TA, Washington, DC: The World Bank.

World Bank (1995), *Tanzania Social Sector Review*, Report No. 14039-TA, Washington, DC: The World Bank.

World Bank (1996), *Health Policy in Eastern Africa: A Structural Approach to Resource Allocation. Vol. 1*, Draft Report No. 14040, AFR, Washington, DC: The World Bank.

World Bank and URT Planning Commission (1994), *Tanzania Human Resources Development Survey 1993/94*, Washington, DC: The World Bank.

9. The water industry in England and Wales: the problems of public interest regulation[1]

Richard Schofield and Jean Shaoul

1. INTRODUCTION

Privatization was the cornerstone of the British government's attempts to roll back the state in the 1980s. It is a policy that has been emulated throughout the world. The Conservative government justified its privatization programme on the grounds that it would improve industrial performance by subjecting the nationalized industries to the discipline of the market and yield benefits, via greater efficiency, to the industry, customers and the nation (Department of Industry, 1982; Moore, 1983 and 1985; Department of Transport, 1984; Department of the Environment, 1986; Department of Energy, 1988).

In the particular case of the water industry, the government claimed that the private sector would provide the finance for the huge investment programme required by the European Union (EU) for coastal water clean-up, urban waste water treatment and the restoration of drinking water quality. Indeed the ability of the capital markets to provide what the public sector could not has been the chief justification for privatizations world-wide.

But within a few years of privatization, the privatized water and sewerage industry in England and Wales was rarely out of the news. Press and media comment initially focused on financial concerns about the high level of water prices, excessive director remuneration, large dividend payouts and failed diversifications. More recently the press has focused on the industry's physical performance: the crumbling infrastructure, pollution, river abstractions, hosepipe bans, leakages and the adequacy and safety of the water supply. In March 1998, the press reported that the water companies had lowered water pressures, as a way of reducing leakages, instead of replacing the leaking joints. This had jeopardized firefighters' ability to put out serious fires.

Public opinion was particularly outraged when the public water supply system to West Yorkshire failed during the exceptionally dry summer of 1995 and supplies were only maintained by means of a mass road tankering operation lasting several months at a cost of £50 million. The problem of adequacy of the water supply is now being used as the justification for introducing water metering. But such service breakdowns are not confined to the privatized water industry or Britain, as the failure of the privatized electricity supply to Auckland, New Zealand, for several weeks in March–April 1998 has testified.

Others have analysed the engineering and managerial problems that lay behind the failure in the water supply to West Yorkshire (OFWAT, 1996a; Uff, 1996). But there was little serious discussion about how such problems could have arisen when the government had put in place a regulatory system designed to protect the public from a potentially rapacious monopoly. After all, the government had stated:

> Privatisation should lead to improved standards, greater efficiency, and a better allocation of resources within the water industry. *Provided that the customers are fully protected* – and Section 4 of this White Paper sets out how the Government intends to do this – the water industry, their customers and the nation as a whole should all benefit. (Department of Environment, 1986, p. 13, emphasis added)

The government devised a system of quality, environmental and economic regulation to ensure consumer protection. The role of the economic regulatory agency, the Office of Water Services (OFWAT), was to protect the customer from monopoly pricing while at the same time guaranteeing the financial viability of the industry. The latter duty was imposed since the essential nature of the goods and services which the industry produced meant the water businesses could not be allowed to fall prey to the ultimate sanction of the market: bankruptcy (although provisions were made in the legislation to cope with such an eventuality). Essentially, regulation to protect the consumer was two-dimensional: first, 'price capping', which would limit prices and provide managers with the pressure and incentives to deliver greater efficiency, quality, reduced costs and effective investment; and second, a system of monitoring to ensure certain minimum standards of service delivery.

We have assessed elsewhere the financial and social outcomes of privatizing the utilities in general (Froud et al., 1996) and water in particular (Shaoul, 1997). Our primary concern here is to explain the problems of the British regulatory regime which lay behind the failure of the public water supply in West Yorkshire in order to draw some general conclusions. We therefore evaluate the effectiveness of public interest regulation by examining the experience of the privatized water industry, described more fully elsewhere (Schofield and Shaoul, 1996, 1997).

This chapter explains the background to the water industry, its structure and regulation. It then briefly examines the extent to which the industry is able to finance its activities. The next section assesses the publicly available information about its physical performance: the levels of service, targets, quality measures and other indicators of performance, and the actions taken by the regulator. The final section then addresses two crucial questions: whether the regulator has sufficient powers to protect the public so as to ensure, maintain and improve the supply of essential services; and whether and how these powers are used. In this way we examine the regulatory framework as set out by the government; the way it has actually operated and changed over time; whether it protects the public; and finally the extent to which it is indeed possible to regulate the industry in the public interest.

2. THE BACKGROUND TO THE PRIVATIZED WATER INDUSTRY

The Structure of the Water Industry

The origins of the publicly owned water industry lie in the last century and in the fact that the private sector could not be relied upon to provide 'wholesome' water or sewerage services in a way commensurate with public health and safety. It was precisely for this reason that the water industry in nearly every country in the world has been in public ownership. Various Public Health Acts (1848 and 1875) empowered public authorities to supply 'wholesome' water to any part of the country not covered by private companies. By 1913, the municipal authorities provided 80 per cent of the water supplied.

In 1973 the municipally owned industry was restructured on the basis of geographic rather than political or administrative boundaries and ten water and sewerage authorities were created, based in and serving ten regions in England and Wales. These ten publicly owned water authorities were reconstituted in 1989 as private companies owning the infrastructure network and assets of the industry. They were then floated on the Stock Exchange as ten companies whose main subsidiary supplied water and sewerage services. This was in contrast to other countries, such as France, where the private companies do not own but manage the assets on behalf of the government (Winpenny, 1994). The water industry comprises these ten companies and the former privately owned statutory water-only companies, reduced in number via takeovers and mergers from 29 to 19, of which nearly all were owned by four companies by April 1996.

Here, however, we are concerned only with the ten water and sewerage companies, since these were the subject of the claims about improved performance under private ownership. For the sake of brevity, we refer to them as the water companies. Each of the water companies is organized as a group or parent company with a number of subsidiaries, one of which is the core or regulated water and sewerage business. Our analysis relates to the core businesses, which constitute about 90 per cent of the activities of the parent companies.

The core businesses essentially have three major activities: water supply, treatment and distribution; sewerage collection; and sewage treatment. They take their water supply from some combination of reservoirs, bore holes, aquifers and river abstractions, treat it at water treatment works and distribute it with the aid of pumping stations via an underground network to domestic, industrial and commercial consumers. There is no national or even very comprehensive regional grid. They collect and convey the 'domestic' sewage from household and industrial properties, trade and industrial effluent and surface waters via the underground sewerage system. They then pump the sewerage to sewage treatment works where up to three levels of treatment may be provided before the waste is disposed of. In some cases waste is dumped directly into the sea via long outfalls without even preliminary treatment.

While privatization was being considered in the 1980s, the financial implications of EU legislation on improved water quality and waste water treatment became apparent. It was estimated that more than £28 billion of capital expenditure would be required to compensate for years of neglect and underinvestment resulting from successive governments' macroeconomic policy of reducing public sector capital expenditure, and the need to restore service provision to that required by public health and environmental standards. This estimate was later revised upwards (OFWAT, 1990a) and additional investment programmes have since been required (OFWAT, 1993a, 1994b). The European obligations, without price rises, would have made the privatization unattractive in the City. It was essential therefore that the government resolve the question of regulation, in particular economic regulation.

The Forms of Regulation

The regulatory functions were split three ways: environmental, drinking water quality and economic. The Environment Agency (EA), formerly the National Rivers Authority (NRA), is responsible for the overall management and resource planning of the water environment, environmental regulation and the implementation of the EU directives. The Drinking Water Inspectorate (DWI) sets the standards for and monitors the quality of the drinking water. These regulators, to a large extent, determine the expenditure on urban waste water management, coastal waters clean-up, drinking water quality, and so on. Finally, the Office of Water Services (OFWAT) is responsible for the economic regulation of the companies and sets the upper limit on the prices, known as the 'price cap', that the companies may charge their customers.

Thus the economic regulator operates within a wider regulatory regime and the interrelationship is important. If any of the quality regulators change their standards, this imposes costs on the companies, which may then apply to OFWAT for an adjustment to their price cap. OFWAT has no direct role in assessing the financial implications of and deciding on environmental policies. Price capping is only applied to the core activities of the companies despite the fact that the parent company typically has a number of other subsidiaries, some of which sell the bulk of their output to the core business.

It is important to make a few points about water charges. The price that domestic consumers pay for water is based not on volume, but on a form of property valuation which provided the basis for local taxes in an earlier period. This system was inherited from the days when the water industry was run by the local authorities. This meant that water charges, subsumed within local taxes, were invisible until the run-up to privatization. Charges are set for the year and collected in advance. Before privatization, the poorest households received welfare payments or tax rebates which largely covered their water charges. But this system, which ensured that everyone had access to water services, came to an end around the time of privatization. Non-payment of water charges, therefore, under the private regime, leads to disconnection with the consequent implications for squalor and public health. The Labour government has therefore introduced legislation to outlaw disconnections.

The government, in its capacity as the regulator of a publicly owned utility, set the price cap at about 5 per cent above the rate of inflation, as measured by the Retail Price Index (RPI) in 1989 before privatization. The ability of the government and later the regulator to raise prices is of course predicated on the fact that Britain is a relatively high-income country. The price cap set for each company was based first upon the average efficiency of the industry, and second on the company's investment programme. Such 'yardstick competition' was intended to give incentives to the businesses to improve efficiency and earn extra profits over and beyond that implied by the price-capping formula. The price cap, once fixed, was to stand for five or ten years. The regulator would not claw back the extra profits during the five-year period but would pass on the long-term benefits of improved efficiency to the consumer via the price-capping formula for the next period (OFWAT, 1992a).

As part of its responsibility for protecting the public, OFWAT was also charged with ensuring that the companies comply with conditions set out in their licence of appointment to provide water and sewerage services; that the supply and quality of services are maintained; and that the interests of customers are protected. This necessarily includes monitoring levels of service to customers: risk of water shortage, low water pressure, unplanned interruptions to water supply due to burst mains, flooding from sewers, actual restrictions of water usage, responses to complaints and enquiries, and other measures. Achievement of satisfactory targets would be taken into account when setting the companies' price caps. Failure to achieve such targets would result in financial penalties via lower prices at the next price review.

While service standards were conceived as being part of 'fully protecting the customer', this should not obscure the fact that (i) the regulator's primary duty was to ensure the financial viability of the companies and that consumers' interests came second; and (ii) that price restraint was to be the primary mechanism for protecting the public. Protection was conceived as an economic question and operationalized by means of a system of financial carrots and sticks.

3. FINANCIAL ANALYSIS OF THE PRIVATIZED WATER INDUSTRY

Our examination of the financial evidence shows that the water industry is one of the most cash-generative industries in the country. It is therefore, in principle at least, more able than most to maintain and enhance the infrastructure. But the claims of the new owners for dividends and dividend growth resulted in a conflict over the surplus which was resolved in favour of the shareholders at the expense of the water and sewerage network and (future) consumers. This invalidates the central assumption of the regulatory approach – that if the companies had the money, they would spend it on maintaining and enhancing the water and sewerage businesses.

Our analysis is based on the published accounts of the regulated subsidiaries of the ten water and sewerage companies and is described more fully elsewhere (Shaoul, 1997). Although privatization took place in December 1989, information is presented for several years before privatization in order to lend a historical perspective to the analysis.

As Table 9.1 shows, sales revenues rose rapidly in the years after privatization. But the total weighted average volumes of both water delivered and sewage collected declined (OFWAT, 1995d), largely as a result of the changing composition of industry and level of industrial demand, and is not expected to rise significantly (OFWAT, 1994c). The increase in revenue was therefore the result of the price formula rather than any increase in the volume of business. The water companies' revenues were thus cushioned by the prices set by the government in its capacity as regulator in 1989.

As a primary industry, the water industry spends little on bought-in goods and services as a percentage of revenues – 29 per cent in 1995 – since most of its raw materials, except energy, are free. Since it is a capital-intensive industry, labour costs are also low at 19 per cent of revenues in 1995. And the surplus is correspondingly high. The proportion of the sales revenues available for distribution (52 per cent), as well as the industry's absolute size, makes it unique and in principle at

Table 9.1   Revenues and cost structure of the water industry

	Sales (£m)	Purchase/ sales	Labour/ sales	Surplus/ sales
1985	2249	0.32	0.23	0.44
1986	2467	0.29	0.21	0.50
1987	2742	0.28	0.20	0.52
1988	2932	0.24	0.22	0.55
1989	3172	0.26	0.21	0.53
1990	3326	0.33	0.20	0.47
1991	3698	0.31	0.19	0.49
1992	4196	0.30	0.19	0.51
1993	4539	0.29	0.19	0.53
1994	4859	0.27	0.18	0.55
1995	5155	0.28	0.18	0.54
Average		0.29	0.18	0.54

Source: Annual reports and accounts (various) of ten water and sewerage businesses.

Table 9.2   Cash flow statement for ten water and sewerage businesses

(£m)	1990	1991	1992	1993	1994	1995	Total
Cash from activity	1626	1907	2084	2310	2655	2924	13 507
Returns							
Net interest	–344	126	6	–79	–184	–199	–674
Dividends to plcs	–2651	–615	–793	–1253	–786	–762	–6862
Interest leases	–7	0	0	–24	–1	11	–21
Total returns	–3003	–490	–787	–1356	–971	–951	–7557
Tax	0	–1	4	–10	–7	–7	–20
Investment activities							
Fixed assets	–1365	–1731	–2287	–2229	–2014	–1733	–11 360
Subsidiaries	–15	–2	0	–220	–15	–2	–195
Renewals	–267	–270	–331	–330	–271	–266	–1736
Disposals	34	48	38	41	69	44	273
Total	–1582	–1955	–2580	–2739	–2201	–1957	–13 016
Net cash	–2960	–537	–1279	–1795	–525	9	–7086
Financing							
Loans/leases	–216	1027	978	857	566	–11	3172
Share issue	4203	90	0	600	0	0	4892
Total	3987	1117	978	1457	566	–11	8095
Net cash	1028	581	–311	–338	41	–2	1009

Note: Fixed asset expenditure is shown net of government grants.

Sources: Annual reports and accounts (various) of ten water and sewerage businesses; OFWAT reports on companies' performance.

least more able than other industries to satisfy the numerous and conflicting demands on its distribution: the requirements for dividends and future growth, interest, tax and capital expenditure for maintaining and improving services.

Table 9.2 shows how the surplus cash (after paying external costs and labour) was spent. The companies paid little in the way of tax, despite a tax rate of 35 per cent, as a result of the investment programme and the £7.7 billion capital allowances set at the time of privatization (NAO, 1992). The debt write-off in 1989 meant that the companies had almost no debt to service, although this has been increasing for reasons that will become apparent. More than half of the cash surplus for the six-year period went in the form of dividends to the parent companies. The parent companies paid out about 30 per cent of this to the shareholders, 18 per cent on acquiring other companies to secure future earnings growth, and recycled the rest back to the core businesses in the form of interest-bearing debt to finance the investment programme (OFWAT,

1994e). These loans to the core businesses provided the parent companies with an additional source of revenue while at the same time constituting a further claim on the surplus of the core businesses.

Expenditure on Capital Investment

However, the largest single claim on the surplus was the capital expenditure programme (expenditure on fixed assets) required by the EU for coastal water clean-up, urban waste water treatment and the restoration of drinking water quality. Investment between April 1989 and March 1995 totalled £11.36 billion or 85 per cent of the cash surplus. Unlike most major capital expenditure programmes, the level of investment even at the height of the investment programme turned out to be less than expected, due to a decline in real terms in construction costs (NEDC, 1992). OFWAT reported that capital expenditure was '15% below the level assumed in 1989' (OFWAT, 1992e, p. 4) While OFWAT did not draw attention to this underspending or compare actual and expected expenditure for each year since privatization, it did recognize that it had occurred (OFWAT, 1994b).

The ten water and sewerage companies spent 5 per cent more than expected on water services, 7 per cent less than expected on sewerage services and 2 per cent less than expected overall (OFWAT, 1995a). No explanation was offered as to why this might be, nor indeed evidence that any or all the companies had actually implemented all the projects as specified in their 1989 plans and the privatization prospectus (Schroders, 1989). But to cite just two examples, Yorkshire Water received government help to reduce its costs by £50 million on sewage treatment works: the Department of the Environment declared that the coastal waters began within three miles of Hull. This meant that Yorkshire Water could dump untreated sewage straight into the estuary which had now been defined as coastal waters which were not subject to the same stringent regulations as an estuary. In the event, the local authority obtained a reversal of this via a judicial review. A few months after the 1994 price review, which set prices on the basis of the investment programme, Thames Water announced that it would be making big 'efficiency savings' on its investment programme. It is therefore difficult to avoid the conclusion that inflated investment programmes were submitted to the regulator in order to justify high prices.

Expenditure on Infrastructure Maintenance

In addition to the expenditure on improving the system, there is the cost of maintaining the infrastructure: the renewal of the underground network sewers and water mains. Renewal covers repairs to burst mains, leaks, sewers, and so on, that is, to both the water and the sewerage systems. This is because the water industry has a vast and ageing underground network of infrastructure assets: mains, sewers, impounding and pumped raw water storage reservoirs, dams and sea outfalls, which have a long life and must be maintained indefinitely.

By 1995, the companies had spent £1.7 billion on renewals. But the adequacy of this expenditure for future service provision needs to be considered in relation to the size of the system as a whole. The author of a Treasury report, who is also coincidentally the economic regulator of the water industry, argued that current cost accounting measures economic performance best, ensures capital maintenance and is particularly important in industries where there are no competitive markets for their products (Byatt, 1985). We therefore base the following assessment of capital maintenance requirements on current cost accounting measures.

The underground network represents 75 per cent of the industry's assets and is worth about £110 billion at current replacement cost (OFWAT, 1995e). The assets have a life expectancy of about 60–100 years, implying an annual renewals programme of about 1–2 per cent of their replacement value, or 6–12 per cent over the six-year period or higher if the infrastructure was in a poor state. But far from spending 10–12 per cent, the companies actually spent 1.5 per cent. Irrespective of the age and condition of the network, this does not indicate a very extensive renewals programme. In the context of a decaying and ageing network, this is a very low spend. They spent less on the sewerage system (£680 million) than on the water system (£1146 million), both in absolute terms and in relation to the size of the two systems: 0.8 per cent and 3 per cent respectively (OFWAT, 1995a). Furthermore, they spent less than budgeted, as measured by the 'provision for renewals' charge in the accounts, every year. As a result of postponing the maintenance programme, the companies built up a cash reserve of about £285 million to be spent on renewals at some future date when its value will have been eroded by inflation (Table 9.3). So not only was their expenditure low and declining; it was less than planned. While the industry argues that the assets have a life of not 60–100 years but 300 years, such a long life does assume that, like a car, the individual parts are replaced and maintained.

Table 9.3   Expenditure on infrastructure renewals

Financial year ending March 31	Amount spent on renewals (£m)	Provision for renewals (£m)	Amount spent on additional fixed assets (net of grants) (£m)
1988		217	385
1989		224	736
1990	267	329	1274
1991	270	367	1808
1992	331	364	2369
1993	330	338	2344
1994	271	340	2147
1995	266	283	1988
Total 1990–95	1736	2021	11 930

Source: Annual reports and accounts (various years).

Thus by any objective financial maintenance criteria, the renewals programme set at privatization was low and this raises questions about the ability to deliver services in the future. Yet in the 1994 periodic review, the regulator rejected higher levels of expenditure on maintenance on the grounds that such levels had maintained services to consumers in the past: 'This review of historical data indicates that there has not been a *general* decline of serviceability in recent years' (OFWAT, 1994b, p. 37, emphasis added). This was despite universal acknowledgement that maintenance levels under public ownership had been inadequate since the 1970s and government claims that privatization would enable the crumbling infrastructure to be replaced and renovated! One year after accepting five-year plans which included expenditure on renewals, the regulator reported that four companies had reduced their renewals charge, but did not raise any objections. One can only assume that he concurred with this 'saving'. It should also be noted that the programme of infrastructure renewals was determined by past patterns of expenditure, not the objective physical or even financial requirements of the system. The regulator admitted that there had been some decline in serviceability, meaning that he approved of the running down of the underground network.

However, the surplus created by the industry was more than the total expenditure on investment and infrastructure renewals. This gives the lie to the chief justification for privatization: that the capital markets would provide the finance which the public sector could not. But it also means that the companies could not only have covered their investment expenditure entirely from revenues, but could also have spent more on renewing the infrastructure, if they had not had to satisfy the demands imposed by private ownership for dividends and future dividend growth. As it was, the combination of dividends and investment exceeded the available cash. This negative cash flow could only be offset by increased short- and long-term debt, thereby mortgaging the future.

Although investment provided the justification for higher prices, the regulator did not insist that dividends were paid only *after* satisfying the requirements of the investment programme. But the high level of dividends paid to the parent companies poses a further problem. The water companies will have difficulty maintaining dividends at anything like that level in the future, given the essentially static demand (OFWAT, 1994c), the already low level of costs and the requirements of the Stock Market for increasing dividends, assumed at privatization to increase at 2 per cent per year (Littlechild, 1986).

The regulator did recognize that the price formula set by the government had front-loaded the revenue stream and warned the companies against paying out too much in dividends (OFWAT, 1991b, 1992e). But the companies were able to ignore the warnings with impunity and provide the shareholders with an above average return on their original investment. While the regulator reported this, he did not draw any attention to or conclusions from it (OFWAT, 1994b). Thus in practice he took no steps to ensure that the companies spent the money as planned or agreed with the regulator, or to ringfence or protect the finances of the water subsidiaries from the predatory parent companies.

4. ENFORCING SERVICE STANDARDS

While the financial analysis shows an underspend, it does not necessarily follow that the physical output has been or will be affected. We therefore examine the levels of service provision in order to assess the extent to which the services and the system as a whole are being maintained and improved; OFWAT is monitoring and enforcing the levels of service; and the levels of service relate to the regulatory regime in general and the price-capping system in particular – in other words, how the regulatory regime worked in practice to ensure levels of performance higher than in 1989–90. The regulator set his own criterion for the frequency of hosepipe bans, which are imposed to conserve the domestic water supply: 'hosepipe bans, on average, once every ten years' (OFWAT, 1995c, p. 40).

But the status of these levels of service indicators, and targets, is far from clear. While at least one of the companies has argued that there are obligations flowing from the statutory duties imposed on the companies (MMC, 1995), the regulator has variously interpreted them to be free-standing indicators of performance; criteria of satisfactory performance to be used as the basis for rewards or penalties during the 1994 price review (OFWAT, 1994b); and indices which determine how much extra maintenance expenditure needs to be allowed for in the price review (MMC, 1995). The notion of a target implies an improvement, yet in the price review the regulator said that improvements must be achieved without higher price limits (OFWAT, 1994b). Similarly, the regulator's own criterion of the adequacy of the water supply, hosepipe bans once in ten years, was not used to judge a company's performance.

The ambiguity in the status of the indicators is reflected in the way the annual reports present, interpret and discuss the data, reported annually since April 1990 (OFWAT, 1990b, 1991c, 1992f, 1993b, 1994d, 1995c). They contain a mix of aggregated and individual company data which are not consistent in their format from year to year. This makes historical comparisons of the companies' performance impossible without recourse to the previous reports. After 1992, the reports no longer presented the companies' targets alongside their performance. Not surprisingly, therefore, there was no evaluation of the companies' performance in relation to their targets, the regulator's criterion of the adequacy of the water supply or any analysis of or explanation for the results. But perhaps most surprisingly of all, the regulator focused on industry performance instead of company performance. He largely interpreted the data to mean that the industry's performance was improving.

By way of contrast, we show the levels of service and targets relating to physical performance (DG1–5) for each company in Tables 9.4–9.8 for the post-privatization period. These tables show that well before the drought of 1995, when the regulator finally took action, some companies were not maintaining or achieving target levels of performance. To cite but one example in some detail, for several years Yorkshire Water underperformed relative to other companies, its own targets and previous levels of performance, particularly in relation to the adequacy of the water supply (Table 9.5) and unplanned interruptions to the water supply due to emergency repair work (Table 9.7). Furthermore, when the number of people estimated to be at risk of inadequate water supply (Table 9.4) was compared with the location of actual water restrictions in summer 1994 (before the drought), and indeed other years, there was little correspondence between actual and expected

Table 9.4   *Percentage of population at risk of inadequate water resources (DG1)*

Company	Pop.	Population below reference level						
		Actual (%)						Target (%)
		1989–90	1990–91	1991–92	1992–93	1993–94	1994–95	1994–95
Anglian	3839	0	0	0	0	6	6	0
Northumbrian	1172	0	0	0	0			0
North West	6800	1	0	0	0			0
Severn Trent	6851	41	41	41	2	<1	6	0
Southern	2125	0	0	36	16	5	5	0
South West	1462	3	7	8	20	<1	<1	0
Thames	7269	76	76	75	76	75	75	75
Welsh	2740	5	7	5	2	<1	<1	1
Wessex	1117	2	0	0	0			0
Yorkshire	4398	0	0	0	0			0
Customers at risk (000s)			12 672	10 198	6355	6080	6401	

Source: OFWAT, *Levels of Service Reports* (various years).

restrictions. Yorkshire Water had not predicted that its customers would be at risk of restrictions even though it had imposed hosepipe bans in four out of the previous six years (Table 9.5). But if these very crude figures show that Yorkshire Water was short of water before the drought, then it must have been 'tea room gossip' in the industry. Nevertheless the regulator took no action. This at very least calls into question the accuracy of the measure used to assess adequacy of the water supply. As a result of the public outcry in 1995, OFWAT announced that a full review of water resources would be carried out.

When interpreting the performance data, the regulator repeatedly referred to the poor and varying data measurement methodologies and seemed to imply that it was therefore difficult to place much reliance on the data so obtained for inter- or even intra-company performance. But he did not insist on a complete review of the entire system and a standard measurement and reporting methodology for regulatory purposes as he did for the accounting information. Yet unlike the other utility regulators, OFWAT did insist upon a standard method of reporting accounting information (OFWAT, 1991a, 1992b, 1992c, 1992d, 1994a). Despite the limited reliability of the data, some of which is acknowledged in the 1994–95 report, OFWAT summarized the findings as follows: 'although there are occasional fluctuations in levels of per-

Table 9.5　*Percentage of population subject to water restrictions, hosepipe bans (DG4)*

Company	Population affected by hosepipe bans (%)						
	1989–90	1990–91	1991–92	1992–93	1993–94	1994–95	Target, 1994–95
Anglian	0	15	27	0	0		0
Northumbrian	0	0	0	0	0		0
North West	0	0	0	0	0		0
Severn Trent	66	0	0	0	0	*	0
Southern	66	55	28	28	0		N/A
South West	97	43	0	2	0		7
Thames	78	100	0	0	0		0
Welsh	0	0	0	0	0	*	0
Wessex	0	0	0	0	0		0
Yorkshire	100	100	0	12	0	*	0

Notes:
N/A　Not available.
*　Hosepipe bans.

Source:　OFWAT, *Levels of Service Reports* (various years). 1993–94 and 1994–95 data not published on company basis in this way.

Table 9.6   Percentage of population at risk of low pressure of water
             mains (DG2)

Company	Population below reference level (%)						
	1989–90	1990–91	1991–92	1992–93	1993–94	1994–95	Target, 1994–95
Anglian	3.0	2.4	1.79	1.65	1.34	1.15	1.7
Northumbrian	1.0	0.7	1.23	1.31	1.03	0.59	N/A
North West	1.1	1.1	0.98	0.77	0.65	0.72	0.2
Severn Trent	N/A	0.6	0.79	0.62	0.48	0.58	0.3
Southern	0.2	0.1	0.12	0.13	0.12	0.11	0.1
South West	0.8	0.9	0.85	0.92	0.89	0.74	0.6
Thames	6.6	0.6	0.60	0.24	0.15	0.18	N/A
Welsh	0.3	0.3	0.57	0.70	0.39	0.14	0.4
Wessex	0.5	0.5	0.49	0.43	0.35	0.32	0.5
Yorkshire	3.4	3.0	2.97	2.87	2.24	0.81	1.7

N/A   Not available.

Source: OFWAT, *Levels of Service Reports* (various years).

Table 9.7   Percentage of population with unplanned interruptions to
             the water supply (DG3)

Company	Population below reference level (%)						
	1989–90	1990–91	1991–92	1992–93	1993–94	1994–95	Target, 1994–95
Anglian	0.1	0.1	0.09	0.25	0.79	0.11	0.1
Northumbrian	0.2	0.1	0.09	0.01	0.18	0.09	0.1
North West	0.8	0.6	0.22	0.64	0.11	0.12	0.6
Severn Trent	1.0	0.0	0.03	0.03	0.29	0.20	0.0
Southern	0.2	0.0	0.02	0.02	0.05	0.08	0.0
South West	0.1	0.9	0.25	0.24	0.07	0.82	0.1
Thames	6.5	0.33	0.24	0.20	0.33	0.32	N/A
Welsh	0.7	1.3	0.50	0.33	0.17	0.13	N/A
Wessex	0.0	0.0	0.01	0.00	0.17	0.03	N/A
Yorkshire	0.4	0.6	0.15	0.71	1.54	1.07	0.3

N/A   Not available.

Source: OFWAT, *Levels of Service Reports* (various years).

Table 9.8   Flooding from sewers – population at risk (DG5)

Company	Population at risk of flooding from sewers – below reference level (%)						
	1989–90	1990–91	1991–92	1992–93	1993–94	1994–95	Target, 1994–95
Anglian	0.14	0.14	0.13	0.11	0.10	0.07	0.11
Northumbrian	0.01	0.01	0.01	0.01	0.01	0.01	0.01
North West	0.06	0.06	0.09	0.08	0.07	0.11	0.01
Severn Trent	0.06	0.06	0.05	0.05	0.05	0.05	0.03
Southern	0.04	0.04	0.05	0.04	0.04	0.04	0.02
South West	0.08	0.08	0.07	0.07	0.09	0.08	0.05
Thames	0.18	0.18	0.16	0.18	0.16	0.18	N/A
Welsh	0.11	0.11	0.07	0.07	0.05	0.05	N/A
Wessex	0.14	0.14	0.12	0.09	0.09	0.08	0.11
Yorkshire	0.07	0.13	0.11	0.09	0.05	0.04	0.05

N/A   Not available.

Source: OFWAT, *Levels of Service Reports* (various years).

formance, the overall trend has been one of steady improvement' (OFWAT, 1995c, p. 4).

More importantly, OFWAT did not appear to have taken any action in relation to the underperforming companies before 1995. When reporting on the levels of service for 1994–95, the regulator did explain he had written to those companies whose performance was particularly poor (OFWAT, 1995c). But this was only after public concern over some of the companies' performances began to emerge.

To conclude, these results show that levels of service provision are poorly defined and very limited in scope; there is no common reporting methodology; and parts of the system are under stress in different ways for a number of the companies. Not only is the status of these indicators unclear, but the relationship between these measures of performance and the price-setting process is also unclear. It does not seem that the regulator demands compliance until the public becomes concerned, even though some companies were underperforming.

Quality Indicators

The issue of quality in relation to water is complex and multi-dimensional. It encompasses a large number of parameters relating to drinking water quality and a similarly large but different set of parameters relating to river, estuary and bathing water quality.

Furthermore, the issue here is not simply the extent to which quality has improved but the degree to which the economic regulator has ensured that the billions of pounds made available to the companies via price rises were used to meet the required standards as specified in the investment plans and the prospectus issued at privatization (Schroders, 1989). This in turn implies that the regulator presents information relating to compliance with the quality standards by each company on an annual basis, analyses and interprets the data and relates them to the past and projected investment programme.

Only in the case of drinking water quality is there any consistent annual reporting on *company* performance (Drinking Water Inspectorate, 1995), and even this is not unproblematic. The reliability and validity of the sampling, measurement and reporting procedures is unclear. Neither is it apparent how the criteria have been determined or the nature and extent of the risk that such levels present to the public. Furthermore, while the current standards of drinking water quality encompass chemical, mineral, pesticide and coliform composition, they exclude lead and more detailed microbiological measures, for example, cryptosporidium. Yet the latter are increasingly the subject of public health concerns as a result of outbreaks of water-borne illnesses and possible EU directives.

In general the data show an improvement for the *industry* as a whole with the exception of one measure (PAHs), where there has been a significant deterioration (WSA, 1995, Table 3.13). Remedial action requires the removal and replacement of the defective pipes which have given rise to this problem with pipes of a different material. As yet, no historical analysis has been carried out for the individual companies. There is no consistent historical reporting of *company* performance published either by the Environment Agency or OFWAT relating to pollution, compliance with discharge consents, river and bathing water quality compliance, and so on, although some of this material can be obtained on request to the regional environment agencies. The Environment Agency and its predecessor, the National Rivers Authority, does produce some of this information in their annual reports, but on a regional basis which therefore includes several water companies. The evidence as published in a summary form does show an overall improvement for the industry as a whole (NRA, 1995, WSA, 1995).

But the absence of such publicly available information on a company basis means that it impossible to monitor company performance; know how rigorously the regulator is monitoring company performance; determine how these measures are being evaluated in relation to the investment programme; and assess accountability of the regulatory processes (Shaoul, 1998). The regulator has, however, announced that he does in future intend to measure investment by outputs (OFWAT, 1995a), but this only begs the question about the reliability and validity of the quality data.

System Performance Measures

Very little information is publicly available about the system and the network performance, for example the number of burst mains, sewer collapses, complaints about water discolouration, and so on, and the amount of actual maintenance carried out, which would enable an evaluation to be made of whether in fact the companies were maintaining the water and sewerage system. The only evidence is of an indirect nature – the length of water mains and critical sewers renewed or replaced and the amount of water lost due to leakages. While OFWAT reports some of this information in its annual reports on the companies' financial performance and capital investment, it presents no analysis or interpretation.

Using data from OFWAT and the Water Services Association (WSA, 1995), it was possible to estimate the extent of the renewal of the underground network and this is presented in Table 9.9. It should be noted that because of the way the data are reported, the extent of maintenance is overestimated. First, companies are required to report on rehabilitation in kilometre lengths even if the amount carried out is very small. Second, if several repairs are carried out on the same stretch, each is reported separately. A total of 4 per cent and 4.6 per cent of the water mains have been relined and renewed respectively. Less than 1 per cent of the critical sewers have been renovated and replaced. Five per cent of the communications pipes have been replaced. There was considerable variation between the companies. There had been far less work done on the sewerage system than on the water network. Thames and Yorkshire Water had carried out almost no sewerage system maintenance. Based upon investment levels in the last five years, it would take more than one century and five centuries to renew or replace the water mains and critical sewers respectively.

While OFWAT did not dispute the facts, its own interpretation was rather different. OFWAT recognized that it would take more than a century to replace the water mains, but claimed that good progress was being made in renovating the old stock. Since 14 per cent of the old stock (more than 60 years old) had been replaced and a further 14 per cent had been renovated in five years, it would take about 33 years to replace all the stock currently older than 60 years. But this makes no

Table 9.9 *Percentage of maintenance activity on underground assets, 1990–91 to 1994–95*

	Water mains relined (% km)	Water mains renewed (% km)	Communications pipes replaced (%)	Critical sewers renovated (% km)	Critical sewers replaced (% km)
Anglian	0.4	5.7	7.0	0.2	0.5
Northumbrian	7.0	5.4	7.0	3.7	0.5
North West	0.4	5.8	9.0	1.2	1.3
Severn Trent	13.0	5.8	9.0	0.8	2.2
Southern	1.0	1.0	3.0	0.4	0.3
South West	6.0	1.3	3.0	1.8	0.8
Thames	1.0	0.5	1.0	0.7	0.3
Welsh	2.0	3.7	7.0	0.4	1.4
Wessex	1.9	2.7	4.0	1.3	0.5
Yorkshire	2.9	2.6	3.0	0.4	0.0
Total	3.7	3.9	6.0	0.8	0.8

Source: OFWAT (1995a), WSA (1995).

allowance for the ageing of the rest of the stock. 'Taken together with the renewals programme, this implies a significant catching up on maintenance of older assets' (OFWAT, 1995a, p. 46).

Most of the work took place immediately after privatization. Thus the rate is actually declining. Yet OFWAT reported: '*One interpretation is that urgent renewals and renovation activity on critical sewers has been completed, and the emphasis of maintenance expenditure is returning to renovation rather than renewal*' (OFWAT, 1995a, p. 46, emphasis added). The fact that no other interpretation was offered must indicate some cynicism about the situation.

The only other information available about the state of the water distribution system is the amount of leakages (OFWAT, 1996d). This is frequently reported in relation to the total distribution input. But such losses are misleading because the higher the losses, the more the input, so the percentage is adjusted accordingly. Hence the absolute amount of losses as well as the percentage of total losses for each company is presented in Table 9.10. One third of the total distribution input was lost in 1995, yet the target for 1995 was 26 per cent. Thames Water's losses increased by 50 per cent in absolute terms but from 28 per cent to 39 per cent, 11 percentage points, in relation to the distribution input. Leakages increased for seven companies. Furthermore, three companies had actually set targets which were equal to or higher than the amount of losses in 1992–93.

Note that the targets were set by the companies and were not imposed externally, as it was considered that the companies were in the best position because of their knowledge of their own system to make realistic estimates of leakage control. The targets were voluntary and not mandatory. Two companies (Thames and Yorkshire) set new targets in 1993–94 which were even less demanding than their original strategic business plans (SBP), which provided the basis for the prices to consumers. The SBP leakage control targets were equivalent on a national basis to 25 per cent in 1992–93, 24 per cent in 1994–95 and 19 per cent in 2014–15. The regulator considered this to be a 'significant' reduction. Although only three companies had achieved their 1990 targets for 1994–95, this passed with little comment until the drought of 1995.

Some companies argued at the time of the 1994 price review that additional expenditure needed to be allowed for increased leakage control activity. This was rejected, since 'the levels of capital maintenance expenditure allowed for are sufficient to *maintain* current leakage levels' (OFWAT, 1994b, p. 43, emphasis added). This suggests that at the time the regulator was not unduly concerned about the rising levels

Table 9.10   Total distribution losses for each company

	Total losses (ml/day) and as % of distribution input in 1992–93	Total losses (ml/day) and as % of distribution input in 1994–95	1997–98 total losses target (ml/day) and as % of 1994–95 distribution input
Anglian	207	231	211
	(19%)	(20%)	(18%)
Northumbrian	94	101	101
	(22%)	(24%)	(24%)
North West	936	877	705
	(38%)	(37%)	(30%)
Severn Trent	563	665	410
	(28%)	(30%)	(19%)
Southern	159	133	100
	(25%)	(21%)	(16%)
South West	156	145	110
	(32%)	(31%)	(23%)
Thames	726	1117	740
	(28%)	(39%)	(26%)
Welsh	376	390	354
	(36%)	(38%)	(35%)
Wessex	135	140	124
	(33%)	(33%)	(29%)
Yorkshire	488	536	476
	(34%)	(37%)	(33%)
All ten	3840	4335	3331
companies	(31%)	(33%)	(26%)

Source: OFWAT (1996d).

of leakages and viewed the issue in terms of maintaining levels rather than reducing them.

OFWAT publishes no other system performance measurements. It was only after the adverse criticisms of the industry in 1995 that OFWAT, despite collecting information on an annual basis, started to publish the 'non-confidential' data (OFWAT, 1996c). OFWAT does not require the companies to provide an ageing analysis of its assets, the length of defective pipes, and so on. Yet none of this information, vital for estimating the financial expenditure required to maintain the system, is confidential since the companies operate as regional monopolies. The absence of such information makes it difficult to know whether the expenditure plans are appropriate and the regulator is ensuring that services are being maintained and improved. Indeed the independent inquiry into the failure of Yorkshire Water's water supply in West

Yorkshire made the point that Yorkshire Water's plans had been reviewed by OFWAT and its reporters (consulting civil engineers) in 1994, and neither OFWAT nor the Environment Agency had drawn attention to the deficiencies in the system (Uff, 1996).

To conclude, the failure of the public water supply in West Yorkshire within six years of privatization should not have come as a surprise to any observer of the industry, let alone the regulator. Furthermore, it was not simply an aberration or due to some rogue company or freak weather conditions, but was systemic. However, it is unfortunately likely, on the basis of this evidence, to be only the first significant failure to deliver water and sewerage services. This in turn means that the government's plans to protect the customer turned out to be ineffective either because the regulator had been given insufficient powers of enforcement or because he had failed to use them.

5.   THE HORNS OF THE REGULATORY DILEMMA

We examine next the regulator's powers and the extent to which he used them to determine whether the failures in service delivery stem from the regulator's lack of power or his will to act. Our analysis shows that although the regulator has sufficient powers of enforcement, it is in practice impossible, under private ownership, to use them without increasing prices to a politically unacceptable level. All the ambiguities and contradictions in setting and monitoring standards and relating performance to prices stem from this central dilemma. Thus the lack of will to act flows inexorably from the financial relationships of the industry.

Under the Water Industry Act 1991 (WIA) the regulator must enforce the various statutory duties of the water companies, the most important of which are the duties to maintain an efficient and economical system of water supply and sewerage services. This means monitoring the water companies' compliance through the levels of service indicators, for example low hosepipe bans, the unplanned interruptions to the water supply, and so on, and the quality and system performance measures.

The regulator has three potential ways of enforcing performance standards: via the price-capping mechanism, the licence conditions and/or statutory regulation. His choice depends upon how he views the performance measures, which is, as we have shown, far from clear. In the 1994 interim price review, the regulator evidently did not demand compliance since he did not penalize companies for failing to achieve their performance targets. More recently the regulator has been forced, largely as a result of public pressure, to address the issue of levels of service more directly. Even then he preferred persuasion and licence renegotiation. In 1996, he persuaded some of the water companies to raise some of their target levels of performance (OFWAT, 1996b).

Later still, the regulator indicated that he was prepared to take account of such failures in the price-setting process: 'If companies fail to meet these [leakage] targets in 1997–8 I will take action, for example by recommending mandatory targets to the Secretary of State. I will also take account of such failures at the next price review' (OFWAT, 1996d, p. 2). Since then he has made leakage targets, but not other performance targets, statutory. This allows him to take direct enforcement action and/or use the price-cap mechanism to penalize the companies if they fall below target. But this was a last resort. Before this, the regulator did not define any statutory standards.

Let us now take Yorkshire Water's poor performance before the drought in 1995 as an example. In the regulator's opinion, the performance was not bad enough to constitute a contravention of the company's duties, although the public might disagree. But this then raises a difficult question. How far below these target/monitoring levels does performance have to fall before contravening the general statutory duties? If all the standards were statutory regulations, the regulator would have a duty to enforce them. But in that case the companies could apply for a price increase, because the regulator must take into account their statutory duties when setting prices. The regulator had previously warned against statutory maximum levels of leakage for this very reason (OFWAT, 1995b). Even when standards are mandatory, and he has set prices on that basis, the regulator cannot enforce the targets if by doing so this would override his duty as laid down in the Water Industry Act 1991: 'to ensure that undertakers' functions are properly carried out and that undertakers are able to finance their functions'. The regulator has so far tried to avoid the use of statutory standards of performance; this makes it impossible to determine whether or not Yorkshire Water's performance was inadequate.

If compliance with only one performance measure, such as leakage targets, is made mandatory, while the other measures remain voluntary and incomplete in scope, then there are incentives for the companies to 'play the system'. For example, the companies can achieve a reduction in their leakage targets by reducing the water pressure, since compliance with the latter target is not mandatory. Moreover, the agreed indicator of water pressure measures risk, not performance. Thus compliance with one target is at the expense of another. Furthermore, if the target for leakages is set in percentage rather than absolute terms, little may be achieved in practice, as the example of Thames Water, cited earlier, showed.

While the public might think that Yorkshire Water's performance constituted a contravention of its statutory duties and the regulator was therefore in breach of his duties to protect the public by failing to seek an enforcement order, a member of the public has no right of redress against the regulator. Furthermore, despite the fact that the public believes that the regulator is there to protect them, his primary statutory duty is to ensure that the companies can finance their activities. The Labour Government's Green Paper on utility regulation proposes to make consumer protection the primary duty, to placate public opinion. But this duty is still subject to the proviso: 'The duty should also make explicit the need to ensure that the regulated companies are able to finance the carrying out of their functions' (Department of Trade and Industry, 1998, p. 15, para. 3.79). Since under private ownership the functions include dividends, changing the primary statutory duty in this way ensures that the basic conflict between finance and levels of service remains the same. As yet, the claims of both the government for tax and the providers of finance capital for interest are small. As these increase, which they must, the conflicts between the claimants will multiply.

6.   CONCLUSION

We set out to examine whether, in the light of the experiences of the privatized water industry in England and Wales, it is indeed possible to regulate it in the public interest. We found that:

- Privatization increases the claims on the financial surplus of the industry because the new owners have different objectives from those of the state.
- Because the owners have first claim on the surplus, this becomes a problem when the surplus is inadequate to meet other claims.
- Under conditions where demand is static and costs are already low, investment and maintenance must be squeezed.
- The regulatory system appears to build in safeguards in terms of physical indicators of quality and performance to protect consumers.
- But they are impossible to enforce, not so much because of a poor regulatory system as the lack of regulatory will.

- The regulator's apparent unwillingness to enforce service standards and protect consumers stems from his duty to ensure the financial viability of the industry which includes the requirement for dividends and dividend growth.

The source of the problems experienced by the public was not regulation *per se*, but an insufficient surplus, relative to the amount of capital invested in the industry, to meet the additional claims of the new owners for dividends and dividend growth. Without these claims, the industry could not only finance itself but also operate in the public interest. In this industry, the surplus can only be significantly increased by the regulator allowing prices to rise. But this in turn would generate the political uproar that regulation was supposed to prevent.

The government's claims that all would benefit ignored the conflicting claims of the numerous stakeholders and the particular circumstances of the water industry. In these circumstances it was and is impossible to reconcile all the claims and protect the public. Regulation allowed a resolution of these claims by ensuring that the priority was given to shareholders. Thus privatization was at the expense of the public both as consumers, present and future, and taxpayers, past, present and future. Under the guise of consumer protection, regulation legitimized the redistribution of wealth to the new owners.

Since the regulator's primary duty is to ensure the financial viability of the companies, which includes dividend payments, tax obligations in a few years' time, an increasing burden of debt, investment programmes to improve the environment and water quality which are subject to external regulation, and maintenance of a crumbling infrastructure which cannot be indefinitely postponed, it follows that the regulator will continue to allow prices to rise or require the companies to increase their debt levels. Thus the cost will be borne by the customer. In that case privatization plus economic regulation means that the water companies are a *de facto* nationalized industry operating in the interests of shareholders rather than consumers and the workforce. While the Conservative government's declared objective was to 'roll back the state', the end result is a different kind of state: not one which considers the public interest but quite explicitly privileges the few. Public services provided by the state have been replaced by commodity production for private profit.

This analysis suggests that the success of privatization in general depends upon the size of the surplus and its ability to grow to meet the demands of all the claimants. At best, cost cutting or delaying investment provides only a short respite. Even an industry as profitable as the water industry is incapable of generating sufficient profits to satisfy all the claims on it. Privatization and its consequences have increased the social, economic and political conflicts which were to some extent at least assuaged under public ownership by reducing the number of stakeholders with claims on the surplus. The struggle between the industry and the public is set to intensify. All the ambiguities and contradictions in the regulatory process stem from the impossibility of reconciling all the claims on the surplus, making it virtually impossible to regulate the water industry in the public interest. It is an outcome far removed from the promises of privatization.

NOTE

1.   Acknowledgement: this chapter is based on our article 'Regulating the water industry: by any standards?', *Utilities Law Review*, vol. 8, no. 2, 1997, pp. 56–70. We are grateful to the editor for permission to use this material.

REFERENCES

Byatt, I.C.R. (1985), *Accounting for Economic Costs and Changing Prices*, vols I and II, Treasury, London: HMSO.
Department of Energy (1988), *Privatising Electricity: The Government's Proposals for the Privatisation of the Electricity Supply Industry in England and Wales*, Cmnd 322, London: HMSO.
Department of the Environment (1986), *Privatisation of the Water Authorities in England and Wales*, Cmnd 9734, London: HMSO.
Department of Industry (1982), *The Future of Telecommunications in Britain*, Cmnd 8610, London: HMSO.
Department of Trade and Industry (1998), *A Fair Deal for Consumers: Modernising the Framework for Utility Regulation*, Green Paper, CM 3898, London: The Stationery Office.
Department of Transport (1984), *Buses and Deregulation*, Cmnd 9300, London: HMSO.
Drinking Water Inspectorate (1995), *Drinking Water Quality: Report by the Chief Water Quality Inspector*, Department of the Environment, London: HMSO.
Froud, J., Haslam, C., Johal, S., Shaoul, J. and Williams, K. (1996), 'Stakeholder Economy?', *Capital and Class*, **60**, Autumn, 119–34.
Littlechild, S. (1986), *Economic Regulation of Privatised Water Authorities*, Department of the Environment, London: HMSO.
Monopoly and Mergers Commission (MMC) (1995), *South West Water Services Ltd: a Report on the Determination of Adjustment Factors and Infrastructure Charges for South West Water Ltd*, London: HMSO.
Moore, J. (1983), 'Why Privatise?', speech given to the annual conference of City of London stockbrokers Fielding, Newson Smith at Plaisterers' Hall,

London Wall on 1 November, HM Treasury Press Release 190/83. Reprinted in Kay, J., Mayer, C. and Thompson, D. (eds), *Privatisation and Regulation: The UK Experience*, Oxford: Clarendon Press, 1986.

Moore, J. (1985), 'The Success of Privatisation', speech made at opening of Hoare Govett Ltd's new City dealing rooms on 17 July, HM Treasury Press Release 107/85. Reprinted in part in Kay, J., Mayer, C. and Thompson, D. (eds), *Privatisation and Regulation: The UK Experience*, Oxford: Clarendon Press, 1986.

National Audit Office (1992), *Sale of the Water Authorities in England and Wales*, London: HMSO.

National Economic Development Council (1992), *The United Kingdom Water Industry*, London: NEDC.

National Rivers Authority (1995), *The State of the Water Environment: Six Year Trends Report*, Bristol: National Rivers Authority.

OFWAT (1990a), *Annual Report 1990*, Birmingham.

OFWAT (1990b), *Levels of Service Report for the Water Industry of England and Wales 1989–90*, Birmingham.

OFWAT (1991a), *RAG 2.01, Classification for Infrastructure Expenditure*, Birmingham.

OFWAT (1991b), *Profits and Dividends* (MD55), Birmingham.

OFWAT (1991c), *Levels of Service Report for the Water Industry of England and Wales 1990–91*, Birmingham.

OFWAT (1992a), 'Issues involved in regulation of privatised water utilities', speech by Alan Booker, Deputy Director General, OFWAT, to the Institute for International Research, Malaysia, at the Financing Water Utilities Symposium, Birmingham.

OFWAT (1992b), *RAG 1.02, Guideline for Accounting for Current Costs*, Birmingham.

OFWAT (1992c), *RAG 3.03, Guideline for the Contents of Regulatory Accounts*, Birmingham.

OFWAT (1992d), *RAG 4.01, Guideline for the Analysis of Operating Costs and Assets*, Birmingham.

OFWAT (1992e), *1991–92 Report on Capital Investment and Financial Performance of the Water Companies in England and Wales*, Birmingham.

OFWAT (1992f), *Levels of Service Report for the Water Industry of England and Wales 1991–92*, Birmingham.

OFWAT (1993a), *1992–93 Report on the Capital Investment and Financial Performance of the Water Companies in England and Wales*, Birmingham.

OFWAT (1993b), *Levels of Service Report for the Water Industry of England and Wales 1992–93*, Birmingham.

OFWAT (1994a), *RAG 5.01, Transfer Pricing in the Water Industry*, Birmingham.

OFWAT (1994b), *Future Charges for Water and Sewerage Services*, Birmingham.

OFWAT (1994c), *Future Levels of Demand and Supply for Water*, Occasional Paper 1, Birmingham.

OFWAT (1994d), *Levels of Service Report for the Water Industry of England and Wales 1993–94*, Birmingham.

OFWAT (1994e), *1993–94 Report on the Financial Performance and Capital Investment of the Water Companies in England and Wales*, Birmingham.

OFWAT (1995a), *1994–95 Report on the Financial Performance and Capital Investment of the Water Companies in England and Wales*, Birmingham.
OFWAT (1995b), 'Mandatory leakage targets will mean higher customer bills says OFWAT', News Release, Birmingham, 31 October 1995.
OFWAT (1995c), *1994–95 Report on the Levels of Service of the Water Companies in England and Wales*, Birmingham.
OFWAT (1995d), *1994–95 Report on the Cost of Water Delivered and Sewage Collected*, Birmingham.
OFWAT (1995e), *Report on Company Performance in 1994–95*, Birmingham.
OFWAT (1996a), *Report on Water Company Service Failures during the Freeze/ Thaw of December 1995 to January 1996*, Birmingham.
OFWAT (1996b), *Report on the Conclusions From OFWAT's Enquiry into the Performance of Yorkshire Water Services Ltd*, Birmingham.
OFWAT (1996c), *Format for the July Return, Regulatory Accounts and Information from Quality Regulators from 1996*, Birmingham.
OFWAT (1996d), *Leakage of Water in England and Wales*, Birmingham.
Schofield, R. and Shaoul, J. (1996), *Regulating the Water Industry: Swimming Against the Tide or Going Through the Motions?*, Public Interest Report, Department of Accounting and Finance, University of Manchester.
Schofield, R. and Shaoul, J. (1997), 'Regulating the Water: Industry By Any Standards?', *Utilities Law Review*, **8** (2), March–April, 56–70.
Schroders (1989), *Prospectus: The Water Share Offers*, offers for sale by Schroders on behalf of the Secretary of State for the Environment and the Secretary of State for Wales, Schroders, London.
Shaoul, J. (1997), 'A critical financial analysis of the performance of privatised industries: the case of the UK water industry', *Critical Perspectives on Accounting*, **8**, 479–505.
Shaoul, J. (1998), *Water Clean Up and Transparency: the Accountability of the Regulatory Processes*, Public Interest Report, Department of Accounting and Finance, University of Manchester.
Uff, J. (1996), *Water Supply in Yorkshire*, Report of the Independent Commission of Inquiry, London: Tourcrete Ltd.
Water Services Association (1995), *Waterfacts 95*, D. Burnell (ed.), London: Water Services Association.
Winpenny, J. (1994), *Managing Water as an Economic Resource*, London: Routledge.

10. Management control, ownership and development: illustrations from a privatized Bangladeshi enterprise

Shahzad Uddin and Trevor Hopper

1. INTRODUCTION

Many developing countries have embarked on programmes of privatization, often at the behest of external agencies (Hemming and Mansoor, 1988; Cook, 1986), or in imitation of reforms in developed economies (Hood, 1991). Development economists and policy makers advocating privatization claim that ownership changes will increase efficiency via the importation of superior management controls mainly of an accounting nature. However, this is highly questionable. Accounting controls are not neutral, objective systems that unequivocally flow from rational choice or environmental determinants. They are shaped by other controls over production and labour, managerial choices and associated conflicts. Accounting controls complement, interact with, and are substitutable by, other controls, for example internal labour markets. As the case study research of a recently privatized Bangladeshi firm reported below reveals, actual controls after privatization may bear little resemblance to policy expectations derived from economics, often of a neo-classical bent. This chapter will relate how management controls may become more repressive and be associated with reduced external regulation upon privatization, with adverse consequences for labour, economic performance, distributional issues and broader development goals.

2. THE POLITICS OF THE BANGLADESHI ECONOMY AND PRIVATIZATION

Bangladesh was liberated on 16 December 1971 and it undertook a significant readjustment of its industrial sector. The new government, led by Sheikh Mujibur Rahman, was politically committed to socialism and their election manifesto announced their intention to nationalize heavy industries. The government faced an industrial ownership vacuum, as fleeing West Pakistanis abandoned their substantial share of industrial and commercial enterprises. In response, the Awami League government included all abandoned property within their broader programme of state ownership of industry, agricultural self-sufficiency, import substitution and industrialization through state intervention and central planning.

This interventionist approach to development resulted in serious macroeconomic difficulties. The cost of capital, subsidies and major investment in an unprofitable public sector led to large budget deficits (Ghafur, 1976; Ahmad, 1976b). Public enterprises were responsible for over 25 per cent of gross domestic capital formation and their inefficiency had a direct impact on public investment (World Bank, 1993). Their losses swallowed up 30 per cent of annual project aid disbursements, diverting resources from other high-priority activities. Not surprisingly, this strengthened the hand of adversaries of the public sector.

A military coup overthrew the Sheikh Mujib government and killed Mujib in August 1975. Three months later, through another coup, General Ziaur Rahman came to power. He assumed full power in 1977 and his government initiated liberal economic policies. Some Bengali-owned enterprises were returned to their owners, which limited the scope of state intervention, but these reforms were neither well organized nor policy-oriented. In 1982, General Ershad came to power, overthrowing the Bangladesh Nationalist Party (BNP) government. In 1982 there was a turning point in post-independence economic policy towards encouraging the private sector and readjusting the public sector. In 1986, the industrial policy of 1982 was reformulated to squeeze the state's scope for intervention, and many public sector enterprises were put into a holding company as joint stock companies. These subsidiary companies tried to sell shares as part of what was termed the '51–49 Plan' by the government, who retained 51 per cent of total shares to maintain government control (Humphrey, 1990).

In 1991, following a long mass movement, the BNP were re-elected to power. They formulated the Industrial Policy '91, advocating private sector development consistent with previous industrial policies. They liberalized foreign trade, relaxed exchange controls and restructured import tariffs. After the 1996 elections the Awami League formed a government but they remained committed to previous privatization policies (*The Daily Star* (Bangladesh), 14 June 1996), believing that public enterprises in Bangladesh were inefficient and underutilized. World Bank reports (1993, 1995, 1996, 1996a, 1996b) were influential in shaping political opinion. The 1995 report justified privatization thus: fiscal considerations; improvement of poor efficiency, productivity, costs and services of state-owned enterprises (SOE); and the political problems of public sector reform. Some of these reasons had little firm empirical basis, as the report conceded.

By 1995, following World Bank and IMF recommendations for structural adjustment, including ownership changes, 125 large and medium industries had been privatized, leaving 225 enterprises in the public sector. The privatization efforts had not run smoothly (World Bank, 1995). In October 1991, 40 public manufacturing enterprises operating under the Ministry of Industries were selected for privatization. However, by the end of 1992, only four had been sold (World Bank, 1993). At the 1993 Aid Group Meeting, the government promised to accelerate privatization by completing divestiture of at least 50 per cent of the 40 industrial units earmarked earlier, but again it fell short of target. For example, by 1995 only three of the 20 textile mills had been privatized (World Bank, 1996). The 1996 government promised donor agencies to speed up privatization (*The Bangladesh Observer*, 1 January 1997). However, a recent World Bank report claimed that tenders had been offered for only 24 units, seven of which had been referred to the cabinet for approval (Reuter, 4 March 1997). The results of the denationalization programme in each sector had not met expectations.

The performance of public enterprises in Bangladesh is contentious. Ahmad (1976a) argued that it is fashionable to talk of public sector inefficiencies and to laud private sector efficiencies, uncritically accepting profit as the yardstick. Despite their worsening position, public sector enterprises did create an industrial base in Bangladesh in important socioeconomic areas covering infrastructure, basic manufacture, and large and essential trade, in addition to assuming the management of abandoned industrial and commercial units (Alamgir, 1978). Moreover, public sector performance was seriously constrained by government decisions, managerial failures, political interference and misconceived price policies (Ghafur, 1976; Sobhan and Ahmad, 1980; Sobhan, 1991; Uddin and Siddique, 1995).

Studies of the post-privatization performance of firms in Bangladesh are few and inconclusive. Lorch (1990) and Sobhan (1991) evaluated post-privatization performance through cross-sectional comparisons of privatized and public sector enterprises. Sobhan (1991) presented statistics for divested small, medium and large units, noting that:

> The BOI (Board of Investments) has 497 disinvested enterprises registered with it. Of these units, the BOI managed early in 1991 to survey for the first time 290 or 58 per cent of the registered units. Of these surveyed units, only 137 or 47 per cent were found to be in operation. 75 or 26 per cent of the units had ceased production. Another 78 or 27 per cent of the disinvested units had been abandoned altogether and were using the premises for other purposes than for running an industry. Whilst this is not reported, the impression of the BOI field surveys was that of the 137 units in operation, many were not in good shape. (p. 148)

The inconsistent results of privatization in developing countries make the dangers of blanket prescriptions of privatization apparent (Wortzel and Wortzel, 1989; Cook and Minogue, 1990). Moreover, privatization may not improve public finances by generating capital revenue through the sale of assets. Adam et al. (1992) note that such sales result in the public and private sectors adjusting their relative liquidity positions, leaving their respective net worth and budgets relatively unaltered.

3.   THE ECONOMICS OF OWNERSHIP AND DEVELOPMENT

Privatization policies in developing countries are a response to public sector problems but they also reflect ideological pressures emanating from non-governmental agencies such as the IMF and the World Bank. These agencies have been increasingly influenced by liberal economists emphasizing markets and private ownership. However, the nature and scale of the problem of public sector performance in developing countries is as contentious elsewhere as in Bangladesh. Some studies allege that public sector enterprises in developing countries fail to generate significant contributions to GDP and are less profitable than the private sector (World Bank, 1981, 1983; IMF, 1986; Ayub and Hegstad, 1986; Killick, 1983; Kim, 1981; Funkhouser and McAvoy, 1979). Others contend that the public sector cannot be evaluated by private sector criteria because governments require them to pursue non-commercial objectives (Prager, 1992; Cook and Kirkpatrick, 1988, 1995). Moreover, some researchers claim that public enterprises are more efficient than private ones (Milward, 1988; Wortzel and Wortzel, 1989).

Internal politics and external pressures can influence privatization policies in developing countries (Adam et al., 1992; Hemming and Mansoor, 1988; Cook, 1986; Ramanadhan, 1989). Some governments have based their industrial policies on Western ideologies, especially Thatcherism and Reaganism, to legitimize undemocratic actions. For example, the vulnerable Ershad government in Bangladesh facing political outcry against their rule solicited Western support by following their policy recommendations for industrial restructuring. Given that donor agencies such as the World Bank and the IMF are prime sources of external aid and tend to make loan facilities conditional upon privatization (whether public enterprises are loss-making or not), it is unsurprising that such policies ensue.

Theoretically, privatization is often advocated on the basis of productive and allocative efficiency gains. Productive efficiency stems from microeconomic theories of property rights and agency within contractual relationships (Adam et al., 1992), whereas allocative efficiency covers the macroeconomic effects of privatization upon public finances, capital markets and private sector investments (Cook and Kirkpatrick, 1995).

Production efficiency theorists claim that low production costs stem from management controls and incentives that reinforce productivity targets. Neo-classical economists of this hue argue that high productive efficiency is impossible in public enterprises because of political interference, leading to poorly motivated, badly paid and inadequately monitored managers. In addition, given the economic centrality of public sector activities, their labour unions tend to be powerful actors locally and nationally. These factors combine to reduce the productive efficiency of public production (Hemming and Mansoor, 1988). It is argued that under private ownership managerial efficiency is better related to business performance as its narrower objectives make it easier to devise efficiency-enhancing incentive contracts. This is underpinned theoretically by agency theory and property rights theory.

Property rights theory expounds that managers minimize costs if their rewards are directly related to economic performance (Furubotn and Pejovich, 1972). It is argued that private owners induce more efficient managers through managerial controls and incentives that maximize profits and thence the value of property rights. There is a missing link between ownership and management control in the public sector as no one has an incentive to do this: perceived costs will outweigh benefits since the latter do not accrue to individuals (Hanke, 1986). In contrast, if private sector owners do not produce efficient management controls or buy and sell assets to compete effectively they will suffer market failure or a takeover. Because public assets are not individually owned they lack transferability characteristics (Hanke, 1986, p. 16) and are buffered from competitive forces.

The claim that the creation of property rights is a necessary condition for effective control over management has been criticized. Adam et al. (1992) argue that depictions of the public sector as a homogeneous social welfare maximizer and the private sector as a pure profit maximizer are naïve or analytical simplifications. In reality, neither sector conforms to these stereotypes, and carrying such assumptions through to practical applications like privatization obscures rather than clarifies links between ownership and efficiency (Adam et al., 1992). Such theorizing may be relevant for classical small firms but in the modern large limited liability corporation the property rights of owners are diluted. This reduces owners' control over managers: the latter have considerable discretionary power to further their own interests (Commander and Killick, 1988; Adam et al., 1992).

The basic tenet of agency theory is that agents act self-interestedly; therefore principals must structure incentives to make them act in congruence with their aims. This is rendered more complex by information asymmetries. It is argued that principal–agent relationships in the private sector are simple compared to the public sector, as shareholders have access to information to monitor management and sanction its actions accordingly (Adam et al., 1992). In an efficient capital market, failure to perform to potential leads to low share values, making the company liable to hostile takeover bids. This threat creates a self-regulating incentive scheme (Jensen and Meckling, 1976) which is absent in the public sector. Moreover, performance-related pay systems, central to agency theory, are more difficult to implement and devise in public sector organizations than in private sector ones (Rees, 1985).

Critics argue that this contains assumptions of dubious empirical validity. In practice, access to complete information rarely prevails; information processing is highly complex; and conflicts within organizations create transmission barriers. Perfectly competitive markets are unlikely to occur in developing countries where poorly organized capital markets prevail. Moreover, relationships and motivations are more complex than agency theory envisages and possibly beyond its scope to model them because, for example, trust is ignored (Armstrong, 1991; Neu, 1991). Links between a manager's efforts and outputs in terms of profitability are frequently more difficult to identify and measure than is alluded to.

Public enterprises are often created to improve income distribution and resource allocation within an economy through investment in modern technology. However, technological efficiency may be a necessary but not sufficient condition for efficient resource allocation (Rees, 1984). Neo-classical economists claim that public enterprises cannot match levels of allocative efficiency achieved under market competition, as the pursuit of personal goals by politicians, managers and workers within state enterprises diverts performance into other channels. Competition enhanced by private ownership is seen as essential for allocative efficiency as it reveals information crucial to efficient input usage (Adam et al., 1992). Without these market references principals cannot determine the correct amount and performance of management or the appropriate rewards. For example, a profit fall could be due to lower demand or managerial inefficiency: in a market profit and price information from competitors enables principals to analyse and react to such situations whereas weakened competition produces weaker signals of input–output links important to internal efficiency. This enables management of public enterprises to enjoy a tranquil life under monopoly (Adam et al., 1992). Privatization advocates see public financing, allocative efficiency and privatization as intertwined. Privatization is claimed to reduce net budgetary transfers, eliminate contingent external debt liabilities and reduce the adverse effects of deficit financing.

Critics counter that allocative efficiency is possible with public enterprises, as competition is a result of market structure and state policy, not ownership. Moreover, deregulation, liberalization and the establishment of market competition are not essential or sufficient conditions for privatization programmes, though they may be linked to its success (Jackson and Palmer, 1988). In addition, the fiscal effects of privatization are misconceived, especially the role of privatization in reducing budget deficits by eliminating financial subsidies and uneconomic activities (Adam et al., 1992). Subsidies stem from budget policy rather than the enterprises executing it (Ramaswamy, 1988): they could continue after privatization, for example price support to farmers. Also, when privatization reduces budget support for loss-making enterprises, ascertaining liquidity needs is difficult: governments must examine each case individually and tailor remedial measures according to circumstances (Ramaswamy, 1988).

4. PRIVATIZATION, DEVELOPMENT, ACCOUNTING AND MANAGEMENT CONTROL

Advocates of privatization consistently presume that ensuing superior management controls will induce better performance (Vickers and Yarrow, 1988). Empirical research on this claim in less developed countries is sparse and inconclusive (Cook and Kirkpatrick, 1995). Potts (1995) examined denationalization and production efficiency in Tanzania, finding improved, effective and innovative management after privatization in two states but in others a decline of organizational effectiveness. Weiss (1995) found no significant evidence that public enterprises had inferior performance to private ones. The closest development economists have come to studying privatization and accounting controls is Karatas's (1995) comparative evaluation of pre- and post-privatization enterprise performance based on financial measures such as turnover, profit margins and productivity. He found it difficult to demonstrate that privatization had any impact on performance.

Despite desired outcomes being contingent upon management control practices in their underlying theories of privatization, development economists display little interest in empirically studying their intricacies. Some accounting researchers have studied controls under different ownerships (Jones, 1985, 1992; Espeland and Hirsch, 1990; Wright et al., 1993; Ogden, 1993). Espeland and Hirsch (1990) claim that accounting played an important legitimatory role in justifying ownership changes. Wright et al. (1993) found that a privatization through management buyout had several positive impacts, including the introduction of more appropriate financial control systems, employment contracts and negotiating machinery, and the release of investment constraints on subsidiaries. Ogden's work (1993, 1994) is the most comprehensive accounting study of privatization and control. Through a Foucauldian analysis of economic governance he shows how customers and markets were constructed in newly privatized UK water companies, that is, markets were created through accounting rather than being omnipresent. After privatization, accounting helped transform political objectives into apparently organizational performance matters. Wickramasinghe (1996) is one of the few accounting studies to have addressed privatization issues outside of developed countries. He traces how accounting controls in a public and recently privatized Sri Lankan corporation changed in response to cultures, colonization and post-colonial politics. He argues that economic rationality emphasizing incentives for motivation was insufficient for explaining changes in control given the importance of traditional beliefs about authority and the nature of political struggles.

There have been several accounting studies of controls in Bangladeshi public enterprises (Hoque and Hopper, 1994, 1997; Alam, 1990, 1997; Murshed, 1989). These found technically sound, detailed and bureaucratic accounting systems operating within a system of centralized state planning which were largely irrelevant for managerial purposes as they bore little resemblance to operational realities. Control was dominated by political factors, especially politicians acting in cahoots with trade union leaders. Accounting appeared to be directed at legitimating state activities to external aid agencies by demonstrating the existence of financial accountability and rational economic planning. Not surprisingly, there was widespread managerial dissatisfaction with controls, which was reflected in poor enterprise performance.

Despite accounting controls being central to their privatization proposals, development economists pay little attention to their design, implementation problems, or whether their expectations ever materialize. Accounting research addresses such issues, but almost exclusively in developed countries; management accounting in developing economies remains unexplored, under-researched and untheorized. Bangladesh, like many other developing countries, has had severe public sector inefficiencies, leading to large budget deficits, and it has embarked on a privatization programme to improve management controls. Control problems within the public sector and the costs and benefits of private ownership are widely discussed at all levels of Bangladeshi society (see Ghafur, 1976; Ahmad, 1976a). Yet there is little research examining the substance of these debates and policies at an organizational level. This study addresses this research lacunae through an intensive case study of a single manufacturing firm to ascertain (a) How did control systems change following privatization? (the empirical question) and (b) What were their ramifications for organizational performance, participants, public policy and economic development? (the policy questions).

5. PC CHEMICAL COMPANY

The study was carried out in a large, recently privatized, manufacturing organization in Bangladesh, anonymized hereafter as 'PC', which makes soaps and cosmetics. Table 10.1 shows ownership and control changes in PC over time. PC started operations in 1959, becoming profitable immediately. It faced little domestic competition, being protected from

Table 10.1   Changes in ownership and control of PC

Period	Ownership	Control
1959–71	Private	Private
1972–88	Government	Public corporation
1988–93	Government plus private	Dual control but predominantly government
1993–present	Private	Private/family

multinationals by the then Pakistan government. PC rapidly expanded and it increased its product range and production volume. After the 1971 War of Independence, its owners fled because of their Pakistani origins and the new government nationalized the company as abandoned property on 26 March 1972, placing it within a newly formed public sector corporation anonymized here as 'Y'. In 1988 PC was reformed and registered as a joint stock company under the Companies Act (1913) under the government's 51–49 plan whereby 49 per cent of shares were sold privately (34 per cent to the public and 15 per cent to employees), with the remainder held by government agencies whose representatives remained predominant on the board. In 1993, PC was fully privatized: the government's shares were sold to one person. The firm became family-controlled, the owner becoming managing director and the two other senior management posts being held by younger brothers.

Research Methods

The complexity of the issues and the importance of political factors in Bangladeshi enterprises led to the researchers' decision to conduct an intensive case study within a political-economy approach (Burchell et al., 1980; Neimark and Tinker, 1986; Hopper et al., 1986, 1987; Hopwood and Miller, 1994). Theoretically, the research was based upon Burawoy's theorization of how management controls manufacture employee consent. This traces how internal labour markets, the internal state (collective bargaining) and gaming behaviour combine to shape management controls ranging from coercive to consensual systems. The researchers added accounting information systems as a key factor. The aim was to study the micro-processes of changes after privatization, how controls changed, their effects on behaviour and performance, and broader implications for development policy. Details of the theoretical approach, research methods and the case study results are reported elsewhere (Uddin, 1997; Uddin and Hopper, 1997). This chapter concentrates on the impact of ownership and control changes upon enterprise performance and development policy aims.

The research collected data from interviews, participation observation, and relevant documentation over seven months (from February to September 1995). Semi-structured interviews were conducted with managers; accounting staff; supervisors; local trade union leaders; past managers of PC; civil servants from the Ministries of Industries, Planning and Labour and the Privatization Board; Bangladesh Bank officials; a World Bank official; and national trade union leaders. Interviews with PC employees covered the control strategy of the organization; organizational structures; work loads; budgets; performance measures; incentive systems; trade union activities; marketing strategies; production processes; and attitudes to the control systems and work environment of PC. Different issues were covered with government bureaucrats and World Bank and Bangladesh Bank officials. For government officials, the topics included the privatization process, the influence of external fund agencies, and government regulatory constraints on privatized organizations. The interviews with the World Bank and Bangladesh Bank officials covered their involvement in privatization, liberalization and redundancy programmes; and the impact of these on the Bangladesh economy. Discussions with the national trade union leaders covered their capacity to influence organizational activities; resistance to privatization; redundancy programmes; and the impact of the state and external funding agencies upon trade union activities. In total 55 interviews were held, ranging from one to two hours.

To obtain a good experiential understanding of the behaviour of managers and workers on the shop floor, one of the researchers worked in the soap plant (the main production department of PC) as a casual labourer for one month. In addition, documents, reports and manuals were collected from government offices, the World Bank, libraries, trade unions and PC covering industrial laws, orders and regulations of the government, and reports by external agencies, PC (published and unpublished) and newspapers. This information helped validate the qualitative data from the interviews and participant observations and provided important quantitative data.

6.   CONTROL DURING PUBLIC OWNERSHIP

Upon nationalization PC became an arm of a government committed to state ownership and centrally planned development as the first step of socialism. New control systems, paragons of rational bureaucracy for central planning and accountability, were established through legislation and Presidential Orders. The Nationalization Order made PC accountable to the public through its parent ministry and the Ministries of Finance and Planning. PC became a unit within a public sector corporation (Y) which shaped PC's controls through directives often based on government instructions to the ministries. The Enterprise Board of PC (its top authority) was responsible for implementing the directives of Y, who in turn had to deal with ministries and parliament. PC had nine functional departments: Administration, Accounts and Finance, Material Planning and Control, Purchase, Welfare, Marketing, Quality Control, Production and Engineering. These departments were subject to tight control from corresponding functional departments in Y, they had long chains of command, and virtually no functional area was free from legal laws and provisions (Ronson, 1984; Uddin and Siddique, 1995).

Many of the dysfunctions of bureaucracy, such as rule-bound behaviour and slow, remote, decision making, abounded within PC. One past manager of PC commented:

> If we needed anything urgently, we did not get it because of three layers of command – from PC to Y and Y to the ministerial bodies. Therefore, feedback was always late.

Cumbersome procedures and a lack of delegated discretion frustrated PC's managers. For example, the purchasing department had no final authority to buy raw materials except in small quantities. Placing an order instigated an investigation from the material planning department prior to its despatch to Y. The considerable influence of Y over PC was exercised slowly and in terms of maintaining compliance with government directives rather than commercial criteria. One past purchasing manager remarked:

> We had no authority for purchasing except recommendations. We were very careful and made sure that all government rules and regulations were scrupulously followed.

A senior official explained:

Actually we always tried to prevent ourselves from causing any discrepancies by strictly following government rules and regulations. Frankly, we never used our own judgement for the betterment of the enterprise.

PC's purchasing department had a long chain of command and its managers had little to do but write out requirements. One official commented:

Due to these layers and the centralisation of decision making, the required raw materials in terms of quantity and quality often mismatched the production schedule. Sometimes stock carried huge raw materials involving high costs and sometimes production was interrupted due to materials shortages.

The marketing policy of PC was also in the hands of Y. All units, including PC, had to sell their products through selected distributors or Y's depot. PC had little scope to change marketing strategy. For example, the central marketing and publications department of Y was responsible for the advertisements of each unit's products – PC's products could not even be advertised locally without central office approval. A Y marketing official remarked:

These are to protect the potential discrepancies of units. Since Y is a large corporate body, a chain of command is needed to do things properly.

In contrast, a PC manager commented:

These rules were unnecessary because they prevented our normal courses of action.

The centre's marketing rules prohibited PC delivering to distributors; consequently PC had no direct contact with customers, which made it difficult to be responsive to their needs. When managers tried to change systems they received little cooperation from Y, whose major concern was to prevent undue influence from local managers and trade union leaders. PC's lack of control over marketing operations divorced it from market realities.

Personnel was another area essential to management control where PC could not intervene. Government directives gave enterprise units little power to hire, fire, promote, demote, reward or punish anyone. PC effectively had no power to control employees without approval from Y. A manager from PC remarked:

We had nothing to do with labour indiscipline. Production managers handled this situation very carefully since they had no power to fire anybody. It was also aggravated by the strong presence of trade union leaders on the shop floor.

The centralized bureaucratic systems, embracing detailed internal labour markets and elaborate collective bargaining systems, had been established to ensure impartial employee relations but they had become politicized. For instance, trade union leaders interfered with managerial promotions and appointments, exploiting their political connections with ministers. Central interventions into personnel affairs created problems for production managers. One commented:

> Since we were never able to recruit our personnel, there was overemployment in some positions and underemployment in others.

The centralized systems reduced accountability as managers could use them as excuses for poor performance. Despite their original worthy intentions, bureaucratic controls had become commercially dysfunctional whilst ceasing to maintain impartial arm's-length governance within rational central state planning.

Financial Controls

After nationalization, accounting at PC came under strict, formal scrutiny at various government levels. The preparation, approval and despatch of accounts to the sponsoring ministry and the Ministries of Finance and Planning followed rigid rules and regulations. The Nationalization Order of 1972 stipulated that each public sector enterprise must submit annual accounts to the government. Each public sector corporation had to follow the accounting and auditing provisions for Bangladesh industrial enterprises. In addition, the Comptroller and Auditor General fulfilled an important audit role through the Office of the Director of Commercial Audit. Their reports on the annual accounts formed the basis of the review of public enterprises by the Public Accounts Committee of parliament (Hoque, 1993). PC also had to file accounting reports upon request for other government agencies and ministries. This resulted in a large accounting department at PC which was invariably busy.

The preparation of budgets was a legal requirement in PC following nationalization. Each public sector unit had to submit budgets to government agencies via Y for approval, particularly by the Ministries of Finance and Planning. However, the budgets were an ineffective control system at PC: their preparation was rule-bound, highly procedural, voluminous and had to pass through many managerial layers. Each department prepared budgets for the accounts department but they were perceived as an exercise in central control; consequently they were manipulated. Managers based budgets on previous year's figures and Y's directives, with little regard to operational realities. Sometimes the accountants used approximations because relevant data were unavailable. Variations from targets were supposed to be monitored within PC and at Y with a view to implementing corrective action, but such reviews rarely took place. Nevertheless, government and Y officials invariably sought higher production to demonstrate their efficiency to parliament and the populace. Y instituted a bonus system for managers and workers that rewarded production above target. Thus the prime budget consideration became production for rewards rather than sales or profit. This resulted in unauthorized collusion between production managers and the shop floor to achieve the physical targets set by Y: accounting and budgets became irrelevant in PC's day-to-day controls. They became a ceremonial ritual whereby managers made them compatible with official regulations and rules to satisfy higher officialdom whilst maintaining a semblance of day-to-day control of operations through unofficial, informal and, occasionally, unethical deals with trade union leaders.

State Involvement in Industrial Relations

State interventions into the industrial relations of PC, via Y, politicized management controls. Since labour policies in the individual company or corporation could have important repercussions elsewhere in the economy, many industrial relations issues were resolved centrally by the state. PC was no exception to this rule. Y had an employee relations division which dealt with the labour matters of its constituent enterprises. At the enterprise level there was a labour officer responsible for the general welfare of workers, implementing Y's directives and referring industrial disputes upwards, but PC had no powers to solve industrial disputes. Trade union leaders submitted their charter of demands for increased wages and other benefits to Y's employee relations department which forwarded them, with their comments, to the Ministry of Industries. Trade unions were organized along party political lines, and sometimes different trade union federations submitted different demands. These were dealt with by the minister of the corporation concerned and political leaders and, in most instances, political considerations were the prime motivation in the settlement of disputes (Uddin, 1997).

Although PC had no authority to deal with labour issues, PC's managers could not ignore them. As one production manager commented:

> Control of production gets out of the control of managers if labour problems arise, since the government has sole authority to solve the issues instead of us.

A past manager of PC said:

> Y had to take actions according to the government's demands. Furthering their political interests was very common for them.

PC's management did not negotiate with local collective bargaining agents since they had representation centrally. Government and management alike were not interested in dealing with unions at the plant level, due to political sensitivities. As one senior official at Y argued:

> Government or politicians do not want to promote any unmanageable situations by involving a large number of people; rather, they like to confine these matters to a few.

PC's centralized industrial relations led to politicized decisions. A past manager said:

> When an industrial dispute arises we immediately let Y know, so that they can inform the minister concerned. It was also seen that the decision of the minister always went the way of serving the best political interests of the ruling party.

The interventions of the state, paradoxically through bureaucratic rules devised to reinforce legal–rational norms, produced unsanctioned politicized controls locally. The centralized and politicized industrial relations led PC's managers to perceive their labour force as uncontrolled and uncontrollable; for example, the local trade unions controlled machine speeds. The weak powers of managers induced them to strike unofficial deals with trade unions and workers locally: concessions on overtime, manning and breaks were conceded to maintain production, worker cooperation and effort.

The Effect of National Politics

Managers' control problems following the power of trade unions after nationalization were compounded by direct interventions by the governing political party into matters normally within the remit of management, for example, the appointment of employees, and financing and pricing decisions. Political ends normally outweighed commercial considerations. A Y official remarked:

> We had to listen to what the government said. Usually they furthered their political interest.

The Nationalization Order of 1972, which granted the minister concerned powers to exercise government authority over corporations and enterprises, proved inadequate for effective commercial control (Sobhan and Ahmad, 1980). The Corporation Board was 'to supervise, coordinate and direct the enterprises under it' (Government of Bangladesh, 1972). The ministry concerned appointed the Corporation Board who in turn appointed Enterprise Board members. The Enterprise Board's authority was closely controlled by Y's management powers. The lack of any formal procedures for appointing chairmen and members of the Enterprise and Corporation Boards led to the minister becoming very powerful (Alam, 1982). The sponsoring ministry became the source of all appointments, including those in PC, giving the ministers concerned enormous powers to control everyday activities in enterprises.

The politicization of appointments became part of the organizational culture of PC from its inception as a nationalized enterprise. For example, after independence Awami League ministers and MPs appointed most of the workers desperately needed in all public sector enterprises, including PC. The workforce of PC increased over the years due to ministerial interventions despite countervailing factory requirements. A senior manager remarked:

> We did not have any control over the appointments of workers or employees. The minister or the MP or trade union leaders recommended these. Sometimes the opposition party leaders' recommendations had to be maintained to preserve the balance within the organization.

There were frequent changes in the top management of PC due to political interventions. The culture of change meant top officials had poor knowledge of enterprise matters, which inhibited their exercise of close control. A past manager commented:

> Top management did not want to be over-involved with the enterprise to avoid problems. They just followed Y's instructions.

A past MD remarked:

The top officials sought better production targets or at least the same production target as the year before, under their regime. They ignored the cost of production or the market situation. They liked to show their performance to the minister and Y by planning excess production.

Middle management at PC took advantage of this situation. They legitimized their behaviour by preparing ambitious production targets and, if they failed to achieve them by the year end, they attributed this to problems outside their control such as labour unrest or machinery breakdowns. Top executive officers could not ascertain the real reasons due to their temporary nature and their lack of knowledge and commitment to the enterprise.

Shop-floor appointees of politicians worked as political workers. In each government epoch, new additional workers were appointed to work for the governing party's trade union. It was difficult for foremen or supervisors to give them orders or for production managers to control them, especially as they often had insufficient tasks to allocate. A production manager recalled:

> Some workers did not have to work because they were leaders/political workers or we were unable to allocate tasks to them. Other workers wanted to have the same opportunity [not to work]. Balancing this situation was really problematic.

These problems were never reflected in budget allocations because those who fixed budget targets were divorced from such problems. Thus production managers endeavoured to achieve targets through unsanctioned covert activities such as allowing overtime to workers, which also helped them maintain working relationships with trade union leaders and their members.

External politics affected marketing during the public sector period. PC was production-oriented, and consequently marketing and distribution were neglected. The production budget drove the sales budget but the former failed to reflect the reality of the enterprise. Many past managers complained:

> During budget preparations, sales forecasts had never been regarded as important. Sales variances were neglected or overlooked by the top officials.

One manager, when answering a question about changes in marketing strategies, stated:

> Nobody wanted to change these systems. For top marketing officials, it would

involve much work and responsibilities. For politicians, it would squeeze their hands to intervene and cause adverse reactions to their political ends.

PC had to market and sell its products through a centrally determined list of distributors. The sales force was expected to check that distributors' actions were consistent with the company's Code of Conduct. This merely revealed how politicians exploited marketing for their own ends. A past manager commented:

> Politicians tended to be the major force in the selection of distributors. Distributors always had good connections with ministers or trade union leaders. These connections helped them to earn undue extra profit from the distributors, in excess of their commissions.

Many managers complained that distributors set product prices in excess of those fixed, which was prohibited by the Code of Conduct, but, owing to the distributors' political connections, this was overlooked. It was alleged that some marketing managers were also involved. A production manager remarked:

> We had to balance all matters. Since trade union leaders and ministers were happy with it, we could not deal with this.

Production managers' incentives were not related to sales performance, nor were they driven by organizational goals set exclusively by top bureaucrats and politicians. Managers realized that decisions over marketing, pricing, staffing, financing and procurement were taken externally, on political rather than commercial criteria, and managers employed their own strategies to cope with the situation. They realized that rule-bound behaviour increased their ability to rationalize performance failures. Budgets had been established to create an accountable organization but they became insignificant documents for the efficient functioning of production with no impact on control processes: the incentives to bloat targets were great and the sanctions for failure were slight. In the face of complex local political factors involving industrial relations, managers endeavoured to cope through indulgent deals with rival trade unions and their shop-floor members.

Performance of PC during the Public Sector Period

Management control systems were not effective: as the critics of public ownership argue, managerial incentives were lacking, market responsiveness was poor and political interference was rife. Technically sound control systems were maintained but their subservience to political ends rendered them ineffective for either bureaucratic or commercial ends. Nevertheless, and probably despite its control systems, PC was commercially successful, unlike most of the Bangladeshi public sector.

PC's production from 1979–80 to 1987–88 was good compared to similar business enterprises in Bangladesh (Bangladesh Bureau of Statistics, 1993). Capacity utilization ranged from 105 per cent to 51 per cent with an average of 70 per cent. As a production manager commented:

> Although we had some problems in terms of industrial relations and politics, we had reasonable productivity.

Wastage of capacity was not always due to internal organizational problems such as industrial relations disputes or machine breakdowns; external factors such as raw materials shortages, external politics and electricity failures also played a role.

Up to 1988–89, PC increased sales and never incurred a loss. For example, sales in 1985–86 and 1987–88 were 467 and 519 million taka, and profits Tk 31 and 7 million[1] respectively. The period 1985–86 saw PC's highest return on capital employed (ROCE) of 29.2 per cent and 1987–88 the lowest, at 2.3 per cent. In the last eight years of public ownership PC's ROCE averaged 12.4 per cent. Value-added analysis revealed that from 1983 to 1988 PC generated Tk 896 million (total), an annual average of Tk 179 million. The government received an average of Tk 57 million per year from 1982 to 1988, whereas workers were paid an average of Tk 40 million. PC was a profitable concern under state capitalism, with many of the benefits flowing to government. Nevertheless, PC became earmarked for privatization.

7. CONTROL DURING PARTIAL PRIVATIZATION

PC was registered as a public limited company in 1988 and became a member of the Dhaka Stock Exchange. PC offered 34 per cent of its shares to the public and 15 per cent to the workers. PC's control problems were the main justification for the government's policies. However, why PC was placed on the privatization list, given its profitability, was a source of speculation and debate. A past manager remarked:

> The government chose this company for two reasons. First, PC was not a loss-making company and therefore the public would be interested in buying

its shares. Second, it helped the government to rationalize their actions to fulfil the conditions of loans provided by the World Bank and the Western aid agencies.

However, rather than promoting superior management control systems based upon private sector practices, partial privatization merely worsened the situation.

The Effects of Divided Control

PC became governed by a board of directors comprising nine members: five from Y Corporation (government representatives); three from the general shareholders' group; and one from the employees' group. Divisions amongst the directors inflamed organizational conflicts. A manager remarked:

> The inclusion of private directors made the authority relationship more complex and uncertain.

Another stated:

> There was a messy situation under the dual authority which occurred after partial privatization. We had to manage both sides to implement any decisions.

Control problems, including their politicization and ceremonial rule-bound bureaucracy, remained, as partial privatization retained the final authority of Y, which enabled ministers and government officials to continue to intervene in PC. But private participation brought new pressures upon managers due to the interventions of private directors. A past manager remarked:

> The conflicts between the two sides of directors on the board did not allow the enterprise to run smoothly.

The conflicts resulted in frequent changes of PC's top executive. A past MD of PC commented:

> No top officials were interested in this post because PC's performance had fallen dramatically, owing to various conflicts within the organization. On the other hand, the MD was accountable not only to bureaucrats or ministries but also to the private directors as the representatives of the general shareholders – which was really an uncomfortable position.

The middle management of PC became frustrated and uncertain about the future and a significant number left for positions elsewhere in Y, leaving a managerial deficiency in PC. Productivity and production plummeted and workers became even more difficult to control. The internal management conflicts and the dearth of suitable managers led PC into making major financial losses. The changed ownership failed to transform controls: it merely made their weaknesses more acute.

Changes in Accounting and Budgeting Systems

After partial privatization, PC's financial accounting system became regulated by the Company Act of 1913 which maintained the rules and regulations of the Dhaka Stock Exchange Commission. In addition to accounting reports, auditing played a new role as the Company Act stipulated that an auditor must be appointed by the shareholders. However, as Y was the majority shareholder, it could determine the choice of auditors. Thus state bureaucrats remained influential in company affairs despite PC being constituted as a private company. Accounting officials at PC now had to comply with both Y's directives and the Company Act, which proved difficult. Nevertheless, managers reported that the external reporting systems were strictly maintained according to the regulations of the Company Act.

The status, form and operation of budgetary control systems remained much as before, though the reporting became more complex. One past accountant of PC now located in Y commented:

> Before partial privatization, we had to send reports to the board of directors for approval. After these changes we had to give reports to private directors as well. Consequently we had to wait for a long time to get them approved. It was really frustrating.

A production manager remarked:

> Budgetary processes became more complicated after the inclusion of private directors. In those periods, we had to start the budgetary year without budgets, because of the delay.

The budgetary control systems still had to follow the regulations of Y and gain their approval. Many managers claimed that the preparation of budgets, production managers' attitudes towards budgets, and the role played by Y changed little following privatization; consequently the role of accounting and budgets in shop-floor controls remained ineffective. One accountant remarked with a laugh:

> Accounting and budgeting systems were only changed in terms of the number of reports. We had to make several reports to government as well as to private directors, which only increased our workloads.

The problems of bureaucratic and politicized controls persisted in PC – the ownership change merely gave rise to additional managerial problems.

Changes in Trade Union Politics

The managerial conflicts added fuel to the fire of trade union politics, especially as private directors sought occasional alliances with trade unions. An official remarked:

> The new private directors had a good relationship with trade union leaders, as they tried to dominate over the Y officials.

This reinforced the influence of trade union leaders over shop-floor controls. Both government and opposition parties continued to use their trade unions for political ends. For example, the government trade unions at PC induced the state to increase rewards despite the worsening organizational performance. A past manager commented:

> After partial privatization trade unions became more aggressive and powerful. No workers were laid off, rather the labour costs were increased owing to the excessive overtime.

The government's stated intention of converting PC into a fully privatized company exacerbated aggressive trade union agitation; for example the union arranged a series of demonstrations and lock-outs to bolster their demands that PC be reconverted to a public unit. A trade union leader revealed:

> We knew the next step would be full privatization. We wanted to keep pressure on the government to get it back. Workers gave full support to us because they were also afraid of losing their jobs.

The disputes seriously affected PC's productivity. A manager commented:

> Workers and trade unions were very much involved in demonstrations and they were also less motivated to work since they were uncertain about their jobs. Under these circumstances making them produce and controlling them was hard for us.

The resistance increased and became more volatile when the local grievances merged with broader political movements to overthrow the military rule of Ershad. Even the government trade unions had to bow to the strong reactions of their members and appear to support this resistance. Subsequently the true intentions of various parties to the disputes have become a matter of contention. A manager commented:

> It was an intentional move of the policy makers and directors (potential buyers) because this situation created the necessary grounds for complete privatization.

Performance during Partial Privatization and Preparations for Full Privatization

The control problems of PC during partial privatization severely affected performance. The annual reports show a marked decrease in production, for example soap production dropped from 10545 metric tonnes (MT) in 1988–89 to 2793 MT in 1992–93. Overall capacity utilization dropped from 53 per cent in 1988–89 to 14 per cent in 1992–93: the average capacity utilization over the whole period was only 25 per cent. The Tk 7.5 million surplus in 1988–89 dropped to a Tk 60.4 million loss in 1992–93. Over the five years of partial privatization PC accumulated an overall loss of Tk 173 million. In real terms the government share of value added decreased though the workers' share remained broadly intact.

Full privatization came to be seen as the solution for the failure of partial privatization. A government official justified the government's decision thus:

> The government and Y could not bear these losses which were affecting other units of Y and the government. Therefore, we had to take the decision of selling the government's shares to the public.

Preparations for full privatization commenced at the beginning of 1993. Legally, the Accounts Division of Y was responsible for valuing its holding of 51 per cent of PC's shares. However, the market price of the ordinary shares[2] issued in 1988 had decreased to below par, due to PC's low productivity and profitability. Y decided to invite tenders to buy all their shares in PC as one unit rather than floating individual shares. An accountant at Y remarked:

> The share price of PC at the market had an adverse impact in attracting

investors to buy the Y portion. However, we expected a significant number of tenders for buying these shares.

The trade unions of PC tried to prevent the tendering by workers surrounding Y's offices for a long period. A past trade union leader recalled:

> We had two objectives. One was to prevent external investors from submitting their applications and the other was to submit our own bid, using the consolidated Provident and Gratuity funds owned by the workers ... It was our survival point, because we knew that private owners would make workers redundant at the beginning of their takeover. We took this decision for all workers. The elected trade union groups had also voiced their concern about this.

The elected trade union submitted tenders on behalf of the workers. They offered a low price, assuming that they would not face any competition. However, on the final day of the tender period it was disclosed that another, higher, bid had been submitted. One worker commented:

> We had sufficient money in our Provident Funds to defeat the present owners' bid. These leaders betrayed us.

Many workers and other trade union leaders complained:

> It was sabotage. Elected trade union leaders [the government's labour wing] allowed the present owners to submit their tender because they were bribed.

It is difficult to verify these allegations. Nevertheless, conflicts between the trade unions enabled the present owners to purchase PC cheaply and take over its management in August 1993.

8.   CONTROL UNDER FULL PRIVATIZATION

The new owner and his two brothers became directors and dominated PC almost immediately, making major changes to controls. They assumed control of operations by dismissing the leaders of all but one trade union faction. In addition nearly 75 per cent of the permanent workforce was made redundant and replaced by cheaper (and fewer) casual workers. Middle management was reconstituted as a mix of existing managers (Y officials hired by PC for a period) and new managers with private sector experience. New personalized physical controls were introduced over management. The role of accounting changed:

budgets and external reports passed from public view into the control of the family. However, cost-saving preoccupations permeated management through instructions from the family, reinforced by fears of dismissal.

The Emergence of Family Management

The new management quickly reduced the managerial chain of command, which resulted in fewer managers in all departments except marketing, which grew substantially, and included the recruitment of a new sales force. The role of marketing was to increase sales and provide reliable sales forecasts for production plans. The marketing director (one of the owners) commented:

> The marketing department was the most neglected part of PC during previous periods. Production almost ignored marketing trends. As a result, sales have decreased in a newly competitive market. We have made many investments in this department in terms of advertisements, the restructuring of marketing strategy and a trained sales force.

New marketing managers with long experience in multinational companies replaced Y officials who previously had been responsible only for distribution (not marketing!). The importation of experts brought a distinctive marketing culture. A past marketing manager commented:

> We were busy with administrative work to control the huge layers of management. Eventually, we had no power to do anything new in the department. Under the new management, on the contrary, new managers, although they are not given power, they are given special tasks. They can give new ideas to directors to implement and they are also given high salaries.

The owner-managers (directors) saw marketing as important antenna for family control. The marketing department gathered sales forecasts from the field which became the basis of production budgets. The preparation of budgets changed substantially after full privatization. A budget was prepared annually by a budget committee of eight members: one apiece from the departments of Accounting, Production, Administration, Marketing and Purchasing, plus the three brother directors. Delegated financial budgets ceased: financial information became a preserve of the inner sanctums of the family who exerted control downwards through imposed physical targets and exhortations to reduce costs, mainly by taking out labour.

Budgetary controls became centralized rather than delegated, physical rather than financial, and focused on markets rather than on production as previously. A production manager explained it thus:

> Initially we make a production plan on the basis of yearly and monthly budgets as fixed at the beginning of the year and at the beginning of the month. Then we revise the targets as new information comes through. In this case the ED [owner] plays the vital role.

The annual budget, expressed in physical terms, was reviewed monthly and often weekly, in the light of market data from informal and formal sources. Physical targets and product lines were reshuffled continually by the owner (ED). Following telephone calls he would informally arrange at short notice a meeting with marketing and production managers to revise targets or make product line changes. Production managers exerted little influence: they were there merely to execute ED's commands.

However, sales recovered little from the depths of the partial privatization period. Marketing officials blamed the centralized and arbitrary control systems dominated by the family. A top marketing official complained:

> I worked in a multinational company. There I enjoyed a considerable amount of authority to discharge my duties. Here it is not possible. Some of the ideas which I wanted to implement at PC were not appreciated and encouraged by the Marketing Director. I am one hundred per cent sure that if my plan is introduced, sales will go up. Of course, he [the Marketing Director] is not a professional, he won't understand the problems.

The employment of new senior marketing managers from the private sector and newly graduated marketing students resulted in clashes with retained Y officials. The new recruits, perceiving themselves as more dynamic, complained:

> Y officials don't know anything about the new environment. They have grown up in a bureaucratic environment so they always cause the decisions to be delayed.

By contrast, Y officials commented:

> We are experienced managers. We know the ins and outs of this organization but these new managers are alien. We know exactly what we need to do. These alien managers always cause problems.

The intra-departmental conflicts were complemented by conflicts within production, but their operational impact was slight, given the owner-managers' centralized authority.

Organizational changes extended to the production department which the owning family perceived as too politicized. Foremen and supervisors were made accountable to production managers who, in turn, reported to ED. Their performance was evaluated by the achievement of physical budget targets. Production managers had to report any deviations to ED, who wanted to see reasonable cause. Although feedback systems were improved in terms of accuracy and speed, they were essentially *ad hoc* with arbitrary imposed targets. The budgets disciplined managers not because they were accepted and internalized, or because they were reinforced by economic rewards, but because of power relationships. The owners were the final authority on recruitment, punishments, promotions, dismissals and all other company matters including budget targets and performance appraisal. Managers knew from the cull of managers following privatization that failure to meet expectations meant dismissal. A production manager remarked:

> We have no choice but to produce. We have got a very tight schedule for production since the production budget is even reshuffled daily due to the market situation. This is possible now because we don't have any labour problems.

Production managers conveyed this pressure onwards to first-line managers who now had more responsibility for realizing production targets. New reporting systems were introduced for foremen and supervisors. Each day they submitted log books to the Deputy Chief Chemist (DCC) which contained shift information such as production volumes, machine working hours, stoppages and their causes, wastage, and the number of casual workers employed. In addition, the ED and other senior managers such as the DCC frequently made unannounced visits to the shop floor to oversee operations. Supervisors were almost always temporary casual employees: occasionally during such visits, ED would grant one a permanent position. This remote prospect, coupled with the sanction of instant dismissal for failure, created an industrious, if cowed, first-line management.

Similar changes were enacted in other functional departments, such as Procurement, Material Planning, Stores and Quality Control. All came under the direct supervision of ED; all had their chain of command reduced; all except for the marketing department had fewer employees than before. The new owners retained some technical and experienced officials from Y and appointed new managers to junior managerial positions. The ED argued:

> It is easy to control. I don't have to oversee the long chain. All the heads of departments keep in touch with me every day. Therefore, decisions are not delayed at all.

Centralized, personal control over each department was pervasive. A head of department commented:

> We don't have to give final decisions. We merely give advice. ED gives us decisions which we must follow.

Almost all managers at PC recognized that the decision making was centralized. Some complained about its adverse motivational effects but, as one manager commented:

> The present system of control is, in one sense, good for us, because we don't have to think about the consequences of decisions.

The changes increased the workloads of managers. One commented:

> We have too much work because of insufficient employees in the department. On almost every day of the week we have to do work after office hours (9.00 a.m. to 5.00 p.m.). Sometimes I have to do other jobs because of the lack of employees.

Another remarked:

> Owing to huge workloads I am unable to give enough time to my family. It is really frustrating but I can do nothing about it. You know the job market is almost dead though I am looking for another job.

In several senses the change of ownership shifted controls in the direction predicted by advocates of privatization. The owners instituted tighter individualized performance measures perceived as congruent with their goals, though they were reinforced by fears of unemployment rather than performance-based rewards. Management was reduced in number and cost, alongside increased work intensification. Managerial resources were devoted to marketing in an effort to be more market-responsive. However, there was little sign of private sector managerial technologies involving delegated budgeting or systematic performance evaluation. Indeed, many of the technically rational (though politically corrupt) formal control systems were abandoned and replaced by direct, somewhat coercive schemes based on the authority and whims of the owning family.

Changes to Industrial Relations and the Internal State

Before full privatization industrial relations were governed by a recognized internal state embracing collective bargaining and internal labour markets. However, like the management controls, these purportedly rational–legal bureaucracies had become politicized, with decision powers residing with trade unions and party politicians. After privatization, industrial relations in PC became governed by the Industrial Relations Ordinance (1969) which detailed institutionalized procedures for controlling workers. Their inadequate provisions were exploited to the full by the new owners.

The Ordinance accepts management's prerogative to pursue a hire and fire policy at will. A senior manager confided:

> Any employee of the company can be sacked without prior notice if the board is satisfied that he or she went against the interests of the company.

The power this gave the present management of PC over its workforce was reinforced by the Ordinance's lack of provision for labour contracting and casual workers' trade union rights. Moreover, the Government of Bangladesh declared that, 'If labourers are not directly employed in any organisation, they will not be eligible to join the trade union of that particular organisation' (1986, p. 16). The appointment of casual workers had started in 1980, before privatization. The trade union federations had lobbied for provisions for casual workers, such as rights to join a trade union or reasonable payment. However, the government maintained its policy of non-involvement in such matters within the private sector, declaring in a directive:

> The government, hereby, declares that the use of contract labourers should be restricted in the public sector but the enterprises in the private sector and multinational holdings can use contract labourers according to their convenience and the responsibility for defining the rights of those labourers shall rest with the enterprise which employs them. (Government of Bangladesh, 1986, p. 4)

These announcements and provisions encouraged PC's owners to adopt a casualization strategy to control labour and to reduce labour costs. PC's new management took advantage of this to break the power of trade unions.

The trade unions resisted privatization by locking the factory and preventing the new owners from entering their offices for one month. Somehow, the owner-managers managed to make an agreement with the trade union faction responsible for the workers' failed purchase bid. After long negotiations the lock-out was withdrawn. One worker commented:

> We were stubborn about our steps. But some trade union leaders came up with new proposals such as no redundancies will be made and no financial incentives will be cut off.

The promises never materialized. The new owners immediately made 75 per cent of the workforce redundant, including the other trade union leaders. They also withdrew bonuses and contributions to the Provident and Workmen Participation Funds. The remaining shop-floor trade union leadership was managed by excusing them from work and giving them lump-sum payments, according to workers' reports. The power of the trade union is now limited. It retains little shop-floor power or allegiance and whilst it maintains formal collective bargaining with ED, it is unable to wreak concessions. A trade union leader admitted:

> We now have limited power because of job insecurity. Workers are not interested in taking part in any demonstrations although we have been trying to get the financial benefits back for workers.

Thus the owners were able to replace permanent unionized workers with cheap casual workers (about half the cost of permanent workers) unable to join trade unions. Casual workers had no legal rights to minimum wages policies or welfare provisions such as medical, clothing and leave allowances until they became deemed permanent by working for 90 days continuously. Shop managers managed this carefully, having informal arrangements with contractors about whom to fire and when – as instructed by ED. A past manager commented:

> The growing number of casual workers has been really effective in reducing labour militancy within the organization.

The existence of the unregulated casual labour force was an overt threat to the job security of the remaining permanent workers for, as a manager pointed out:

> Labour contracting may be considered as an additional advantage. If someone has to be discharged from his job, it does not pose any threat for

> his replacement; we can replace him within a few hours from the contract labourers.

Now production managers had full control of operations. One commented:

> Now we are not too worried about the production targets. We can use workers in whatever ways we want. Before privatization, this was not possible at all since trade union leaders and workers had a strong influence over production targets and operations ... Presently we don't have to face any serious problems on the part of the workers. The deviations in the production budgets are mainly due to raw material shortages or machinery breakdowns.

The creation of dual labour markets, one casual and another permanent, wrought internal divisions amongst workers, thereby weakening any potential resistance. The remaining permanent workers were cowed by their potential job insecurity whereas casual workers were subject to harsh coercive management tempered by the dream of permanent status. The vestiges of the internal labour market remained, but whereas it was previously the province of political favour, it was now at the whim of family.

Accounting Changes

PC maintained the external reporting system used previously but internal systems changed greatly upon full privatization. Computerized systems for recording information speeded up the supply of internal information. However, the researchers could not find any professional cost accountant or associated system dedicated to providing cost information to managers. The managing and executive directors kept all financial information, which was processed according to their instructions. Other managers outside of the family had little idea of the company's performance since they were not privy to financial information. Accounting information was now used more for decisions regarding pricing and product line evaluations by the three directors. Nevertheless, since privatization, cost reduction has become central to managers. This has tended to mean taking out labour through redundancies, labour casualization, work intensification and cuts to benefits and allowances. Measurement was by arbitrary assessments of financial implications, reinforced by physical measures as delegated cost systems ceased under the present regime.

PC's accounting systems became the province of the owning family. An accountant of PC reported:

We have to send daily reports regarding cash and other transactions to the owner-managers of the company. The Executive Director and Managing Director actually receive these daily reports in order to have a clear understanding about the financial condition of the company.

As another accountant remarked:

We record those bills or memos which are signed by the MD or ED. All departmental expenditures and incomes have to be signed by these two directors. Otherwise we refer the bills back.

The financial records were apparently kept in two forms. A senior accountant remarked:

We have two systems for accounting information. One is informal which is a restricted area only usable with the permission of the ED. The other system is external reporting which is for other shareholders, the bank, the tax authority and the Stock Exchange.

External reports have not been published since 1994 for no discernible valid reason. As a company listed on the Dhaka Stock Exchange, PC has to submit audited annual accounting reports to the Stock Exchange office, but somehow it managed to delay publication for general shareholders. Thus the substantial body of minority shareholders or external bodies such as employees, creditors, financial institutions and government agencies are inhibited from monitoring performance. Since the present owner-managers own the bulk of the shares they use this unlawful advantage[3] (Company Law 1994, Section 81–1&2). For instance, the present management did not publish the 1993–94 annual reports until 1995.

Several respondents expressed their doubts about the accuracy of annual reports since their preparation was not transparent to either managers or minor shareholders. As an accountant admitted:

We have to maintain many informal systems. You know, business is competitive. You can't maintain all of them in a straightforward way.

PC's accounting reports were prepared somewhat secretively as far as tax was concerned. Excise duty and income tax matters were dealt with informally by the official concerned. It was alleged that sometimes the headings of transactions were changed to avoid tax, for example increasing the number of tax-exempted items. One manager admitted that:

> We don't have to worry about these matters since the ED has a good
> relationship with the government officials concerned.

Auditing appeared relatively light compared to common practice elsewhere. One individual commented:

> Some informal transactions are kept in the 'I owe you fund account' for
> irregular payments to trade union leaders and bribery of government and
> tax officials. These transactions usually appear under other headings in the
> annual reports.

Normally companies wish to show flawless reports to shareholders,
creditors and Stock Exchange officials to preserve their reputation and
to ensure their survival. As advocates of privatization point out, a
driving force for efficiency is the fear of takeover, should performance
become perceived as below potential. But this assumes access to relevant information and a relatively strong capital market. This was not
apparent in this instance. The external reporting problems raise
important issues of equity, failures of regulatory control and enforcement, and potential market failures within the privatization process.

The Economics of Privatization and Development

The most recently available annual reports (1993–94) show that PC
remains unprofitable, although there are doubts about their veracity.
Sales increased slightly to Tk 292.43 million but the company incurred
a loss of Tk 38.76 million – less than the three previous years of partial
privatization though still the fourth worst on record. Capacity utilization
remained low at 18 per cent. The distribution of value added to government remained at the low levels of the partially privatized years.
However, labour's amount and share of value added fell: over the five
years of full privatization it averaged Tk 49.7 million – in 1993–94 it
dropped to Tk 37.6 million.

The economic development literature advances privatization on the
basis of property rights, agency theory and public finance rationalization
claims (Adam et al., 1992). Property rights theory assumes a simple
relationship between private ownership and good incentives and controls. In contrast, observations at PC suggest an inverse relationship
between private ownership and individualized economic incentives.
Indeed, individualized incentive schemes regulated by the internal state
receded in the face of punitive sanctions emphasizing production to
avoid losing one's job. Controls changed and they may have reinforced
owners' profit objectives more effectively but this rested mainly on

coercion rather than consent. With the exception of marketing and computing, private ownership brought few more modern and compassionate managerial technologies. Rather, the private owners instituted *ad hoc* and arbitrary controls over employees, abandoning technically sound but ineffective systems rather than reforming them. Some development researchers argue that property rights theory has limitations in large organizations with diluted ownership and hence lessened control over managers (Commander and Killick, 1988; Adam et al., 1992). The observations in PC extend these arguments further, suggesting that even where owners have direct access to controls, property rights predictions may not materialize. For instance, in PC the rise of family domination produced non-transparent accounting systems and harsh and arbitrary controls based on coercion, rather than individualized incentive schemes marrying the interests of workers and owners.

The principal–agent relationship is a complex one in PC. In one sense, some principals became agents of the firm since the family, with a majority shareholding, captured control and became the top managers. This makes the principal–agent relationship difficult to model dynamically: minor shareholders (almost 30 per cent) became powerless given their inability to secure sound statutory information. Western managerial literature tends to ignore the effects of family ownership upon internal organization and external accountability, assuming professionalized management and a degree of separation of ownership and control. However, in many countries – especially Asian and developing ones – families dominate ownership and management with very different results (Ansari and Bell, 1991). Given family control in corporations working within weak and poorly regulated capital markets, the market signalling and takeover threats central to economists' advocacy of privatization become irrelevant for control purposes.

The public finance theorists' claim that budget support to loss-making public sector enterprises will cease following privatization, thereby releasing funds to other more desirable projects, is not supported in this study. PC was not a loss-making company during the public sector period (debatably, this may have been assisted by protection no longer sustainable under subsequent open market policies). Indeed, government policies induced by external aid agencies in the partial privatization period caused PC's profitability, productivity and liquidity to deteriorate markedly. Since partial privatization PC has contributed less to GDP and state coffers: it has contracted significantly in terms of sales and employment; and it is difficult to argue that it has set new standards of enterprise management that might have beneficial spin-offs to other sectors of Bangladeshi society. There was little evidence of the benefits of privatization trickling down to labour: full privatization had a deleterious effect on distributional issues, produced harsher controls, and diminished workers' rights to representation and workplace protection. The reservations of political economists critical of the public finance case for privatization in developing countries are supported in the case of PC (Wortzel and Wortzel, 1989; Cook and Minogue, 1990).

The vision of privatization bringing transparent accountability, enlightened and effective management, and increased returns to the state appear unrealistic in a developing country with weak capital markets. The privatization process and subsequent regulatory regime pursued by the Bangladesh state bears closer resemblance to 'Crony Capitalism' (Hemming and Mansoor, 1988) than the self-equilibrating market processes of textbooks.

9.   CONCLUSION

We wish to conclude by reflecting as accountants upon the research above. The issue is not one of heroes and villians or golden ages *vis-à-vis* ones of darkness. For example, the controlling family's alternatives to managing as they did may have been constrained by socioeconomic and political circumstances and the norms of conducting business within Bangladeshi society. Nor do we wish to idealize the public ownership period: public sector inefficiency in Bangladesh was a source of rising budget deficits and poor economic growth, hindering efforts to emerge from poverty, high unemployment and inequality (Sen, 1980). The World Bank and the IMF have a history of trying to eradicate these problems in Bangladesh to little avail, partly due to political problems. As accountants we have no panacea for curing these almost intractable issues. Our point is that neither do currently fashionable neo-classical economists, advocating privatization policies based more on shibboleths than circumstances.

Economic theorists formulating workable development polices tend to neglect the importance of formulating controls according to specific circumstances and needs. Too often markets, controls, ownership and regulation are assumed to exist in a homogeneous fashion. It is hoped that the experiences at PC illustrate the folly of this and the need for tailored, localized policies. For example, there was an array of non-public sector forms of ownership possible upon privatization, ranging from employee, family, diffuse and (possibly) institutional. Each would have different effects upon efficiency, controls and the achievement of broader development goals. In PC, the 'choice' of family ownership produced unanticipated and unsought effects including a loss of employment rights, greater income inequalities, and reduced state revenue. This was compounded by the markets which predominate in Bangladesh – weak, small, concentrated and susceptible to insider dealing – very different from models of strong markets in richer Western countries. For example, in PC minority shareholders have few effective powers given weak capital markets, the lack of information on accountability and control, and the difficulties of enforcing their rights. Thus they are unable to play their role within cycles of control assumed by economists advocating privatization. Also, the powerlessness of unorganized unskilled labour in unfettered labour markets renders them susceptible to coercive and exploitative conditions of employment, as in PC. If humane democratic development policies are to emerge from privatization, then greater scrutiny of types of ownership, conditions of sale, employee and customer rights and socioeconomic contexts are needed. Above all, supporting regulatory mechanisms cannot be assumed either to exist or to be enforced, or to emerge as a corollary of privatization. The case of PC is worrying in that transparency and accountability (admittedly problematical under public ownership), essential for oiling market processes and for protecting other stakeholders, declined so markedly. In retrospect, the neglect of devising, imposing and enforcing regulatory safeguards when privatizing PC makes it difficult to see how and why broader development aims and stakeholder rights will ensue, even if the enterprise is commercially restored. The suspicion is that such factors are swept aside due to mistaken beliefs about properties of abstract models holding in reality. Ownership, competition and regulation are complex intertwined issues that need examining holistically on a case-by-case basis rather than rushed through on a standard model liable to corruption and insider dealing – the elimination of which is purported to be an original purpose of the exercise.

NOTES

1. Tk 40 approximately equals. US$1.
2. When PC first issued the shares to the general public they were oversubscribed, owing to the previous good reputation of PC.
3. Shareholders can take the company to court as per section 81–2 (Company Law 1994). However, since they are scattered they do not bother about the general meeting or publication of accounts.

REFERENCES

Adam, C., Cavendish, W. and Mistry, P.S. (1992), *Adjusting Privatization–Case Studies from Developing Countries*, London: Currey.

Ahmad, M. (1976a), 'Whither public enterprise?', *Bangladesh Journal of Political Economy*, Bangladesh Economic Association, **2** (1), 3–12.

Ahmad, M. (1976b), 'The historical perspective of public sector enterprises in Bangladesh', *The Journal of Management Business and Economics*, Dhaka: Institute of Business Administration, **2** (3), 252–94.

Alam, A.M.Q. (1982), 'Administrative problems of public enterprises in Bangladesh', *Administrative Science Review*, Dhaka: National Institute of Public Administration, **XII** (2), 77–100.

Alam, M. (1990), 'The budgetary process in uncertain contexts: a study of public sector corporations in Bangladesh', unpublished Ph.D. thesis, London School of Economics.

Alam, M. (1997), 'Budgeting process in uncertain contexts: a study of state-owned enterprises in Bangladesh', *Management Accounting Research*, **8** (1), 147–68.

Alamgir, M.K. (1978), 'Public enterprises and the financial system in Bangladesh', *Bangladesh Journal of Political Economy*, Bangladesh Economic Association, **8** (1), 4–12.

Ansari, S.L. and Bell, J. (1991), 'Symbolism, collectivism, and rationality in organizational control', *Accounting, Auditing and Accountability Journal*, **4** (2), 4–27.

Armstrong, P. (1991), 'Contradictions and social dynamics in the capitalist agency relationships', *Accounting, Organizations and Society*, **6** (1), 1–25.

Ayub, M. and Hegstad, S. (1986), 'Public industrial enterprises: determinants of performance', *World Bank Industry and Finance Series*, Washington, DC, No. 17.

Bangladesh Bureau of Statistics (1993), *Statistical Yearbook of Bangladesh*, Dhaka, Bangladesh: Statistical Division, Ministry of Planning.

Burchell, S.C., Clubb, C., Hopwood, A., Hughes, J. and Nahapiet, J. (1980), 'The role of accounting in organizations and society', *Accounting, Organizations and Society*, **5** (1), 5–28.

Commander, S. and Killick, T. (1988), 'Privatisation in developing countries: a survey of the issues', in Cook, P. and Kirkpatrick, C. (eds), *Privatisation in Less Developed Countries*, New York: Harvester Wheatsheaf, pp. 91–124.

Cook, P. (1986), 'Liberalisation in the context of industrial development in less developed countries', *Manchester Discussion Paper in Development Studies*, No. 8602, University of Manchester.

Cook, P. and Kirkpatrick, C. (1988), 'Privatisation in less developed countries', in Cook, P. and Kirkpatrick, C. (eds) (1988), *Privatisation in Less Developed Countries*, New York: Harvester Wheatsheaf, pp. 3–31.

Cook, P. and Kirkpatrick, C. (1995), *Privatisation Policy and Performance: International Perspectives*, New York: Harvester Wheatsheaf.

Cook, P. and Minogue, M. (1990), 'Waiting for privatization in developing countries: towards the integration of the economic and non-economic', *Public Administration and Development*, **10** (4), pp. 389–403.

Espeland, W.N. and Hirsch, P.M. (1990), 'Ownership changes, accounting practices, and the redefinition of the corporation', *Accounting, Organizations and Society*, **5** (1/2), 77–96.

Funkhouser, R. and McAvoy, P.W. (1979), 'A simple observation on comparative prices in public and private enterprise', *Journal of Public Economics*, **11** (1), 353–68.

Furubotn, E.G. and Pejovich, S. (1972), 'Property rights and economic theory: a survey of recent literature', *Journal of Economic Literature*, **10** (4), 1134–62.

Ghafur, A. (1976), 'On the nationalised industrial sector controversy', *Political Economy*, Journal of Bangladesh Economic Association, **2** (1), 5–10.

Government of Bangladesh (1972), President's Order No. 27. The Bangladesh Industrial Enterprises (Nationalisation Order), *The Bangladesh Gazette Extraordinary*, Ministry of Law and Parliamentary Affairs, Government of Bangladesh, 26 March.

Government of Bangladesh (1976), *Guidelines on the Relationship Between Government and Autonomous Bodies/Corporations and the Autonomous/Corporation and Enterprises Under Them*, Cabinet Secretariat, Cabinet Division, May.

Government of Bangladesh (1986), *Contract Labourers*, Dhaka, Bangladesh.

Hanke, S.H. (1986), 'The privatisation option: an analysis', *Economic Impact*, **3** (55), 14–20.

Hemming, R. and Mansoor, A.M. (1988), *Privatisation and Public Enterprises*, Washington, DC: IMF Occasional Paper, No. 56.

Hood, C. (1991), 'A public management for all seasons', *Public Administration*, **69**, Spring, 3–19.

Hopper, T., Cooper, D., Lowe, T., Capps, T. and Mouritsen, J. (1986), 'Management control and worker resistance in the NCB: financial control in the labour process', in Knights, D. and Willmott, H. (eds), *Managing the Labour Process*, pp. 109–41, Aldershot: Gower.

Hopper, T., Storey, J. and Willmot, H. (1987), 'Accounting for accounting: towards the development of a dialectical view', *Accounting, Organizations and Society*, **12** (5), 437–56.

Hopwood, A.G. and Miller, P. (eds) (1994), *Accounting as Social and Institutional Practice*, Cambridge: Cambridge University Press.

Hoque, A.K.M.Z. (1993), 'Management Control in the Jute Industry of Bangladesh', unpublished Ph.D. thesis, University of Manchester.

Hoque, A.K.M.Z. and Hopper, T.M. (1994), 'Rationality, accounting and politics. a case study of management control in a Bangladeshi jute mill', *Management Accounting Research*, **5** (1), 5–30.

Hoque, A.K.M.Z. and Hopper, T.M. (1997), 'Political and industrial relations turbulence, competition and budgeting in the nationalised jute mills of Bangladesh', *Accounting and Business Research*, **27** (2), 125–43.

Humphrey, C.L. (1990), *Privatisation in Bangladesh – Economic Transition in a Poor Country*, Boulder, CO and Oxford: Westview Press.

IMF (1986), *Fund Supported Programmes, Fiscal Policy and Income Distribution*, Washington, DC: Occasional Paper, No. 46.

Jackson, P.M. and Palmer, A.J. (1988), 'The economics of internal organization: the efficiency of parastatals in less developed countries', in Cook, P. and Kirkpatrick, C. (eds), *Privatization in Less Developed Countries*, New York: Harvester Wheatsheaf, pp. 159–70.

Jensen, M.C. and Meckling, W.H. (1976), 'Theory of the firm: managerial behaviour, agency cost and ownership structure', *Journal of Financial Economics*, **3**, August 1975–May 1976, 305–60.

Jones, C.S. (1985), 'An empirical study of the role of the management accounting systems following take-over or merger', *Accounting, Organizations and Society*, **10** (2), 177–200.

Jones, C.S. (1992), 'The attitudes of owner-managers towards accounting control systems following management buy-outs', *Accounting, Organizations and Society*, **17** (2), 151–68.

Karatas, C. (1995), 'Has privatisation improved profitability and performance of the public enterprises in Turkey?', in Cook, P. and Kirkpatrick, C. (eds), *Privatisation Policy and Performance: International Perspectives*, New York: Harvester Wheatsheaf, pp. 244–62.

Killick, T. (1983), 'The role of public sector in the industrialisation of African developing countries', *Industry and Development* (UNIDO), **7**, 47–76.

Kim, K. (1981), 'Enterprise performance in the public and private sectors: Tanzanian experience, 1970–75', *Journal of Developing Areas*, **5** (3), 471–84.

Milward, R. (1988), 'Measured sources of inefficiencies in the performance of private and public sector enterprises in less developed countries', in Cook, P. and Kirkpatrick, C. (eds), *Privatisation in Less Developed Countries*, New York: Harvester Wheatsheaf, pp. 143–57.

Milward, R., Parker, D., Rosenthal, I., Summer, M.L. and Topham, N. (1982), *Public Sector Economics*, London: Longman.

Murshed, A.J.M.H. (1989), 'The role of financial information in collective bargaining in a developing country: the case of Bangladesh', unpublished Ph.D. thesis, University of Manchester.

Neimark, M. and Tinker, T. (1986), 'The social construction of management control systems', *Accounting, Organizations and Society*, **11** (4/5), 369–95.

Neu, D. (1991), 'Trust, contracting and the prospectus process', *Accounting, Organizations and Society*, **16**, 243–56.

Ogden, S.G. (1993), 'The limitations of agency theory: the case of accounting-based profit sharing schemes', *Critical Perspectives on Accounting*, **4**, 179–206.

Ogden, S.G. (1994), 'Accounting for organisational performance: the construction of the customer in the privatised water industry', *Fourth Interdisciplinary Perspectives on Accounting Conference*, University of Manchester, July.

Potts, D. (1995), 'Nationalisation and denationalisation of state agriculture in Tanzania 1967–1990', in Cook, P. and Kirkpatrick, C. (eds), *Privatisation Policy and Performance: International Perspectives*, New York: Harvester Wheatsheaf, pp. 178–97.

Prager, J. (1992), 'Is privatisation a panacea for less developed countries? Market failure versus public sector failure', *Journal of Developing Areas*, **26**, April, 310–22.

Ramanadhan, V.V. (1989), *Privatisation in Developing Countries*, London: Routledge.

Ramaswamy, R.I. (1988), 'The privatisation argument', *Economic and Political Weekly*, 12 March.

Rees, R. (1984), *Public Enterprise Economics*, London: Weidenfeld and Nicolson.

Rees, R. (1985), 'The theory of principal and agents', *Bulletin of Economic Research*, **37** (1), 3–26.

Ronson, G. (1984), 'Financial accountability of public enterprises in Bangladesh', in Ramanadhan, V.V. (ed.), *Public Enterprises and the Developing World*, London: Croom Helm.

Sen, A.K. (1980), 'Levels of poverty: policy and change', *World Bank Staff Working Papers*, No. 401, July.

Sobhan, R. (1991), *The Decade of Stagnation, The State of the Bangladesh Economy in the Late 1980's*, Dhaka: University Press Limited.

Sobhan, R. and Ahmad, M. (1980), *Public Enterprise in an Intermediate Regime: A Study in the Political Economy of Bangladesh*, Dhaka: Bangladesh Institute of Development Studies.

Uddin, S.N. (1997), 'The role of management control systems in privatisation: a labour process analysis of a Bangladeshi case study', unpublished Ph.D. thesis, Manchester School of Accounting and Finance, University of Manchester.

Uddin, S.N. and Hopper, T.M. (1997), 'A Bangladeshi soap opera: privatisation, accounting, consent and control', *Fifth Interdisciplinary Perspectives on Accounting Conference Proceedings*, University of Manchester, June.

Uddin, S.N. and Siddique, A.B. (1995), 'Management control issues of public enterprises of Bangladesh – a critical review', *The Cost and Management*, Journal of the Institute of Cost and Management Accountants of Bangladesh, **XXIII** (9), July–August, 4–9.

Vickers, J. and Yarrow, G. (1988), *Privatisation: An Economic Analysis*, (eds), Cambridge, Mass: MIT Press.

Weiss, J. (1995), 'Mexico: comparative performance of state and private industrial corporations', in Cook, P. and Kirkpatrick, C. (eds), *Privatisation Policy and Performance: International Perspectives*, New York: Harvester Wheatsheaf, pp 213–24.

Wickramasinghe, D.P. (1996), Rationales of accounting controls and ownership change in a development context: a mode of production theory analysis of two Sri Lankan case studies', unpublished Ph.D. thesis, Manchester School of Accounting and Finance, University of Manchester.

World Bank (1981), *Accelerated Developments in Sub-Saharan Africa: An Agenda for Action*, Washington, DC: The World Bank.

World Bank (1983), *World Development Report*, Washington, DC: The World Bank.

World Bank (1993), *Bangladesh Implementing Structural Reform*, Report No. 11569-BD, 24 March, Washington, DC: The World Bank.

World Bank (1995), *Bangladesh: Privatisation and Adjustment*, Washington, DC: The World Bank.

World Bank (1996), *Bangladesh Government That Works: Reforming The Public Sector*, Dhaka: University Press Limited.

World Bank (1996a), *Annual Economic Update: Recent Economic Developments and Medium-Term Reform Agenda*, July, Washington, DC: The World Bank.

World Bank (1996b), *Bangladesh: An Agenda for Action*, World Bank South Asia Department I, Washington, DC: The World Bank.

Wortzel, H. and Wortzel, L.H. (1989), 'Privatization: not the only answer', *World Development*, **17** (5), 633–41.

Wright, M., Thompson, S. and Bobbie, K. (1993), 'Finance and control in a privatisation by management buy-out', *Journal of Management Studies*, **30** (1), 75–99.

Index